The
Pleasure
of
Their
Company

Prepared by the

BANK STREET COLLEGE
OF
EDUCATION

WILLIAM H. HOOKS
MANAGING EDITOR

BETTY D. BOEGEHOLD
SENIOR ASSOCIATE EDITOR

SEYMOUR V. REIT
ASSOCIATE EDITOR

A Frank E. Taylor Book

CHILTON BOOK COMPANY
RADNOR, PENNSYLVANIA

THE PLEASURE OF THEIR COMPANY

HOW TO HAVE MORE FUN WITH YOUR CHILDREN

Library of Congress Catalog Card No. 80-70382

Designed by William E. Lickfield
Manufactured in the United States of America

Cover photo by Ellen Galinsky

2 3 4 5 6 7 8 9 0   0 9 8 7 6 5 4 3 2 1

Contents

Part 2
PLAYTHINGS AND BOOKS

Part 3
LIVING WITH CHILDREN AND TELEVISION

Part 4
DAY BY DAY

Part 5

BIG EVENTS AND SPECIAL OCCASIONS

Part 6
SPECIAL RELATIONSHIPS

Preface

The pleasure of your children's company and their pleasure in your company is the theme of this book. We believe that adults and children can not only share pleasurable experiences but make these experiences a solid basis for the development of deep and lasting relationships. The ideas and suggestions in these pages are meant to help bridge generation and communication gaps and to lead to expanded trust and friendship.

Relationships we build will not eliminate all problems or provide instant harmony. Being human, we and our children will continue to make mistakes, get angry, forget what we've learned and in general lose our cool. But this book can make an important and comforting difference: we will be more aware of our actions, more alert to catch our mistakes, more ready to change and grow. We will have some guideposts to help us replace old patterns—quick reminders to help us reach our goal of pleasurable interchange.

Adult-child relationships are rarely ideal—any adult who spends time with children knows that reality has a way of falling short of expectations, leading in turn to disappointment, frustration, and guilt. The purpose of this book is to explore ways of making mutual interaction and commmunication *more enjoyable* for both adults and children. It deals not only with the special peak experiences, but also the ordinary events of daily living, and it offers a spectrum of possibilities. Whether you're a parent or grandparent, a step- or foster parent, an aunt, uncle, neighbor, friend, or professional caregiver, you'll find useful ideas and specific suggestions.

Do you yearn for a better relationship with your child?

Are you planning a long car trip, and worrying about how to keep the kids amiable and reasonably quiet?

Is there a dictator in your house with rabbit ears and a twenty-one-inch glass eye that hypnotizes your youngsters?

Do you dread long stretches of bad weather that keep the kids trapped indoors?

Do you long for more practical knowledge of the stages of childhood?

Are you faced with a birthday party or other festivity, and unsure how to arrange it?

Do you hope to find more satisfactory ways to communicate?

For these and dozens of similar situations, we think you'll find help in these pages—not all the answers and no rigid "musts" and "must nots," but concepts and options to spark your own ideas and creativity.

The book is shaped in terms of human relationships. It was written by men and women with many relevant personal experiences to draw on, and with long years of work in child development, parenting, psychology, sociology, and writing for and about children. All the writers have tried to share their practical information with the reader.

THE PLEASURE OF THEIR COMPANY is, in essence, an informal conversation among a variety of parents, grandparents, and other caregivers who are dedicated to exploring the rich possibilities of shared enjoyment between adult and child. It is based on sixty years of work with children at the unique institution called Bank Street College, in New York City. Lucy Sprague Mitchell, its founder, wanted to explore new educational theories, to find out for herself how young children learn, and to observe and test her ideas in a humanistic setting. A doctor, a social worker, psychologists, and researchers joined this experiment to work together and share their firsthand observations. A nursery school was established by the College and staffed with teachers and students eager to apply these new insights. Thus from the beginning children were learning from adults and adults were learning from children.

Mrs. Mitchell and her colleagues believed that the community the children lived in was an extension of the classroom; that as children explore the world around them, expressing their reactions and ideas through art, stories, and dramatic play, they increase their understanding of the larger world; that their experiences are a springboard not only for developing academic skills and creativity, but for stimulating further exploration and experimentation. Soon the school expanded to include a division of graduate education for students; a school for children from three through thirteen; outreach programs to help other educators; a research unit; a bookstore; a publications division; a day-care unit; and a Family Center.

But the basic philosophy of Bank Street is still built on the original premise, the theory now described as the "developmental-interaction" approach. "Developmental" refers to the patterns discernible as children grow physically, mentally, emotionally, and socially. "Interaction" includes not only the child's relationship with his or her physical environment, and with other children and adults, but also the internal interactions between the intellect and the emotions.

This approach can be applied in home life just as well as in school life. For of all the child's teachers the first and most enduring ones are the parents. Bank Street's humanistic, holistic philosophy concretely supports parents and other caregivers by helping children explore and better understand their world; by sharing interests and ideas with children while allowing them to develop their own curiosity; and by establishing a value system as a framework for and a guide to children's growing independence.

The many and diverse areas of parenting discussed here are based on these guidelines for living pleasurably and constructively with our children:

> Planning ahead but being ready to accept unexpected changes.
> Trying to perceive through the eyes of our children as well as from our own viewpoint.
> Following the children's lead whenever possible.
> Sharing experiences, arts, and work with our children.
> Making time spent with them a daily priority.
> Being aware of and enjoying each stage of their development.

> Trying to remember the important factor in each inter-
> change and letting go of the unimportant.
> Setting appropriate limits for our children.
> Remembering that, for better or worse, we are their models
> of behavior.
> Letting them know and sticking to our own values.

Perhaps we can describe the goal for which Bank Street strives as appropriate to parents also, if we add the word "children" to Mrs. Mitchell's words, now inscribed on a plaque in the lobby of Bank Street College:

> We hope to imbue students (and children) with an experi-
> mental, critical, ardent approach to their work and to
> the social problems of the world. If we can do this, we
> are ready to leave the future to them.

We hope that reading this book will bring you pleasure and suggest new ways you can enhance the pleasure you get from your children's company.

RICHARD R. RUOPP
President
Bank Street College

Acknowledgments

Grateful acknowledgment is made to Frank E. Taylor for bringing us the germinal idea for this book; to Mary Heathcote for her discerning and perceptive editing of the manuscript; to the Bank Street faculty who supported us in the venture; and to Nancy Connors and Amina Alquhaar for the manuscript preparation.

Part 1

THE PREMISE
AND
THE PROMISE

The Changing Needs of Children

DOROTHY W. GROSS

The premise of this book is that grownups and children can have fun and achieve satisfaction together if their shared activities are based primarily on the developmental needs of children. Adults have the principal responsibility for shaping these shared experiences, because satisfying times together don't just happen without some planning and stage-setting. Adults are also responsible for remembering that children's needs change as they grow. Each developmental stage is marked by its own physical capacities and limitations, its own unique quality of thinking, its own range of emotions.

Children are not merely small versions of adults, but changing human beings with special maturing tasks to accomplish as they grow. The drive for this maturing process, the motivation for learning and growing, emerges out of a complex interaction between the child's own nature and his environment, especially the human environment, the people who affect his development.

The First Three Years

In the first three years of life, a number of basic processes lay the foundation for everything that happens in subsequent years.

Separateness

Early on, a baby learns that he is a separate person with his own identity. Three-month-old Christopher wonderingly discovers his toes (although it will be months before he realizes they are his). Six-month-old Jennifer resists being held too closely because she wants to reach for her bottle or a toy. Nine-month-old Simon spits out the new vegetable. Thirteen-month-old Lori joyously runs away down the street. Eighteen-month-old Debby pushes her father's hand away if he tries to keep her from grabbing his book. Two-year-old David shouts, "Mine!" when his toys are touched.

These children are drawing boundaries around their bodies, wills, tastes, movements, and possessions to establish a sense of autonomy. Without this contrast between self and environment, there is no social reality.

Attachment

At the same time, the baby develops a feeling of closeness to the people who do the major mothering. Long before Christopher discovers his toes, he differentiates his mother's face from all others. Simon may spit out the vegetable his mother feeds him, but she is clearly his favorite, as shown by his uneasiness when a stranger approaches him. Although Lori scampers gleefully away on her own initiative, if her parents wave bye-bye and leave, her mood dampens. Even the relatively independent two-year-old may not stay happily for long with just any baby sitter.

Attachment means deep caring, a bonding so powerful that it can encompass anger and disappointment as well as love. It is as necessary for healthy development as the sense of separateness. Without it there is no human tie, no motivation for growth. Separateness brings loneliness, but it also brings an exciting sense of all that stimulation out there in the world. Attachment limits freedom, but it ties us to each other in comfort and love.

Competence

In the second year of life, attachment and sense of identity are accompanied and highly colored by a drive to do, to explore, to be effective—the "competence" drive. It shows in incessant movement, interest in every ray of sun, absorption in every chair leg, fascination with every sound a spoon can possibly make on the side of a refrigerator, the endless efforts to make things work, the frustration with failure, the patient persistence, the shining glow of success. This hungry thrust for experience will lead to thought and language. The baby tests his or her senses against the world, absorbing and shaping the range of things that stimulate him, and creates ideas and thoughts out of that contact with the world. Later he learns to express, to symbolize those thoughts through imitation, play, language.

First there are sensory and motor experiences, doing and feeling. Abby tastes everything—fingers, a ball, a spoon, the edge of a book, the crib bar, a ring of keys. She handles everything, manipulating, rolling, throwing. She moves her body in space, crawling, walking, running. She watches and listens. She is a scientist of the senses, daily amassing data. Next come patterns of thought based on these experiences—images and ideas of the doing and feeling. Abby learns as she experiences: a puppy is different from a kitten; both a bottle and a cup hold milk; a ball rolls; keys open doors; if you push hard the kitchen cabinet shuts. She becomes a scientist of ideas, testing them daily.

Third is the representation and communication of those thought patterns—expressing and telling the images and ideas. Abby translates her ideas into make-believe as a way of trying them out and understanding them. She plays Mommy feeding the baby, a barking dog, a bus driver, deepening her understanding of nurturing, of anger and animal nature, of powerful work, through pretending. Most important, Abby learns language for her growing ideas and talks about them: "I'm taking the baby shopping to the supermarket"; "Puppies and cats are both animals"; "Where is far away?" Abby is a scientist of exploration and recording, daily sharing discoveries about the world.

Loving Play Partners

At this stage of life parents are the significant human environment. Differentiating between "me" and "not me" is done in the human context of being cared for by a nurturing person who is increasingly seen as having an outline, an aroma, an identity of his or her own. This is vividly illustrated by the universal game of peek-a-boo. As the beloved face comes and goes, the world appears and disappears. Awareness of self becomes more poignantly real as awareness of the partner grows. In a beautiful paradox, as the parent is removed, he or she is reconnected through a feeling of attachment. The role of the parent of a baby or toddler is that of a loving play partner who is sensitive to the baby's cues and signals. With a parent who is reasonably responsive to his cues, a baby learns trust, because such response signals caring. Through touching, smiling, looking, talking, singing, tickling, holding, a parent makes his or her presence palpable, and therefore real.

Through matching one's behavior to the infant's temperament and preferences, a parent supports the child's unique personality and sets the stage for a harmonious relationship. Quiet murmuring to four-month-old Philip evokes burbles of pleasure, not the distress that active bouncing brings on. Seven-month-old Lisa enjoys bright colors and her father's early-morning tenor warbling. Ten-month-old Keith shrieks with delight when his mother crawls on the floor with him; the same game evokes tears in Bobby, also ten months old. The task is to look for the signs of what each unique baby enjoys.

Even the drive to explore and to go adventuring, insistent as it is in its own right, is nurtured by parental approval and encouragement for growth. Fourteen-month-old Danny lurches across the floor with the joy of a new walker, but watches for his parent's smile as he goes. "Look-a-Daddy!" calls Karen, who at seventeen months shares everything she finds in her explorations—twigs, stones, pencils, clips. The more a parent can share in the joy of discovery the more a toddler wants to discover. The more a parent enjoys his child's new skills, the more a toddler wants to develop them. The trick, of course, is to support and enjoy adventuring while providing protection from danger.

The Preschool Years, Three to Five

In the preschool years, when children begin to move further into the world, parents add to their earlier functions three new ones, those of interpreter, of partisan, of model.

Interpreter

At this stage a parent becomes a link to the world, not merely a protector from it. It is a somewhat more complex version of the earlier role of encouraging the toddler to try, to find pleasure in effort. Then, because the toddler's judgment was so ill developed, a parent appropriately carved out those areas of experience which were permitted, and tried to guard against early failure, danger, hurt, and disappointment.

In the preschool years a parent needs to substitute interpretation, explanation, thought, for mere protection. One can begin to explain the dangers of traffic to three-year-old Jesse, not merely remove him physically from the street. One can go beyond providing duplicates of a much-wanted toy for Billy and Joan and, instead, explain the rules of sharing. Understanding then becomes the child's protection. Very significant here is a parent's attitude toward the novel, the different: fear? puzzlement? excitement? reaching for? avoidance? Is the world a threat or an opportunity?

Being a link to the world implies not only openness to that world but also sensitivity to the child end of the link. The world's objective reality is at one end and the child's private fantasy life is at the other. A young child has his own ways of thinking and feeling which are not easily amenable to adult logic and are highly colored by his own personal needs. The parent needs to be a line both to reality and to the child's inner self, to explain and interpret the one while accepting and being sensitive to the other.

Four-year-old Susanna is very sad when her best friend moves across the country. She cannot really understand that Jill's father was transferred by his employer; she has a secret feeling that Jill left because of a fight they had over Susanna's toys. Susanna's parents can explain (perhaps many times) that Jill's father has to work in another place and that Jill and her mother have to go with him. They show Susanna pictures of California; they encourage "letter writing" and the exchange of photographs. On the other hand, they show Susanna that they understand how she feels. They encourage her to talk about Jill and to play "moving day." They do not expect quick and easy rational understanding. They function as mediators between reality and the private self, a bridge on which their child may walk to maturity.

Partisan

The partisan role is just that—a tendency to see your own child's point of view more quickly than anyone else's. Being on your child's side would have little meaning in the earliest years, because there was no consciousness of sides. Later on, a child will stand up for his or her own views, and will need his parents to be more objective. But in the preschool years children are still heavily self-centered and only just beginning to glimpse other points of view. They need to feel that their parents have a special understanding of their particular angle on the world, so they will not doubt their own developing judgments.

Three-year-old Susan wants to play by herself in the playground sandbox; she will find it supportive of her growing capacity to make choices if her mother doesn't insist that she always join the others. Four-year-old Elizabeth will wear nothing but her favorite purple skirt—to nursery school, to visit Grandma, to her best friend's birthday party. Can her mother understand and allow it (remembering when she herself would wear only blue jeans)? Five-year-old Matthew develops a passion for bugs—watching them, collecting them, talking about them. He gets into an argument with Mrs. Stevens, the next-door neighbor, when she expresses distaste for his passion. However Matthew's parents handle Mrs. Stevens' feelings and the social amenities, it is important that they demonstrate to Matthew an empathy for his concerns and pleasures.

What the preschool child needs is a sense that his irrationalities, his personal preferences, his growing individuality are, if not always allowed full play, at least understood and sympathized with.

Modeling

Three-, four-, and five-year-olds are champion imitators. They imitate parents' actions and facial expressions, ways of talking and laughing, styles of expressing feelings. They imitate, largely unconsciously, those aspects of adult behavior which the adults are usually least aware of, and which most reveal their underlying nature and preferences. They lay the foundation during these years for identification with their parents—their values, their emotional responses, their sexual identity.

Sexual identity is not the same as sex role. Sex role refers to the specific collection of behaviors and tasks which society connects with each sex, usually quite arbitrarily, like limiting kitchen activity to women or mechanical skill to men. Sexual identity refers to one's private sense of oneself as a man or a woman, in relation to one's body, one's interactions with other people, and one's personal goals in life. A child tends, to some extent, to identify with both parents because he or she is attached to both. In this way, he or she normally takes on both masculine and feminine characteristics, a necessary process for healthy development. The great majority of children, of course, identify most strongly with their same-sex parent, taking on important aspects of that parent's ways of being and living, doubts and conflicts, and judgments about the world and people.

The important thing for a child at this stage is a supportive atmosphere that encourages questioning and expressing confusions: "Can a boy be a mommy?" "When I grow up, I'm going to marry you." "Why does Daddy sleep in a different bed when you're mad at him?" Such strivings for understanding are a natural part of growing up, and a child needs parents who are willing to respond and to look at themselves with honesty.

The Middle Years, Six to Twelve

In the middle years of childhood, the parents' protective function translates into one of support and refuge, and the interpreting and modeling functions into standard setting.

The middle years of childhood are characterized by an expanded moving out into the world. This is expressed in developing friendships, interests, and abilities separate from those of parents and siblings; and in an internal change, a new kind of thinking and feeling.

New Friends and Interests

New friends, chosen by oneself, mean a lot; seven-year-olds Bonnie and Jean find a common interest in spiders and eight-year-old Tom admires Eric's athletic skill. New abilities and interests flower—reading, writing poetry, swimming, knitting.

Children in the middle years need friends of their own developmental stage. Peers can provide support, opinions on which to test and clarify judgments, and a bulwark against the hazard of overdependence on parents. They are the beginnings of the child's community.

Other adults—grandparents, teachers, friends—can provide rich opportunities for a middle-years child. They can help him or her to experience a new self through a wide range of activities: making and listening to music, reading and making up stories, looking at art works, growing things, cooking and construction, caring for animals, taking trips (all of which are discussed in later sections of this book).

These adults can help children see the world as fascinating, challenging, and receptive.

New Ways of Thinking

The middle-years child's thinking is no longer so dependent on the immediate, concrete environment, on the mere appearances of things or their appeal to the senses. When Johnny was a preschooler, he thought an airplane got smaller the further away from him it went. If the milk in his tall glass was poured into a squat pitcher, he thought it had become less. If he wished his friend would visit, and the friend appeared at the door, he was likely to think that the wish had brought the friend. In the middle years, increasingly, children can think about the laws of the physical world with a greater understanding of how they work and without reference to themselves.

Nine-year-old Debby earnestly tells her best friend, "I hate broccoli —but it's good!" She is struggling with the complex notion that there may be more than one way to view something and that one's own view of it does not necessarily define its nature. This newfound ability to think objectively has its implications for the interpersonal world as well. A child is no longer so dependent on parents for perceptions and interpretations and validation of judgment because he has identified with them. Nine-year-old Andy, tempted to take the shiny pocket-knife from his friend's locker, struggles with a sense of right and wrong that is now his and doesn't need his parents' presence to be activated. The child is freed of the need to turn to parents at every step. He can look to other adults and children for fresh stimulation and can value others' points of view.

Support and Refuge

When a child is creating a new identity, learning new skills, absorbing information, and finding his place in the world of peers, he is bound to make mistakes, to suffer disappointments and self-doubt. He needs a haven, a place to vent rage and confusion and misunderstanding, a source of reassurance that he is lovable and worthy.

Six-year-old Michael, who can't catch the ball; seven-year-old Jenny, who doesn't get chosen for the play; eight-year-old Sue, who is having trouble with reading; nine-year-old Roger, who keeps losing things—these children are struggling with the challenges of growing up. Parents whose demands are as stringent as those of the world outside provide no outlet for private licking of wounds and expressing of feelings. Time with middle-years children needs to be relaxed and easy and full of opportunities for fun and laughter.

Standard Setting.

Because middle-years children are increasingly aware of the objective world, they increasingly measure their parents against world standards. Because they are struggling to find places for themselves in the world, they need evidence that their parents have found stable and satisfactory places. Children tend to expect their parents to be virtuous, brave, honest, selfless—and find it difficult to discover that we are afraid, tired, not always honest, and often confused. Children can, however, accept adult imperfections if the adults show them that they do have standards and ideals and that they too are trying to live up to them. It is often difficult for adults to admit mistakes to their children, but if admission is combined with honest efforts to grow, it can provide a middle-years child with an important model of maturity. The child is then stimulated to share his own struggles with growing up, and the bond between parent and child becomes stronger.

Such a mutual relationship, with each child and parent giving what he or she can, according to his or her stage of development, may well serve as a model of all parenting.

Playing Together

EDNA K. SHAPIRO

The distinction between what is play and what is not play is an adult distinction. For children, play is what they do. In her book, *Play*, Catherine Garvey shows this in a dialogue between a mother and her six-year-old son:

> "Tom, I want to clean this room; go out and play."
> "What do you mean, 'go out and play'?"
> "You know what I mean."
> "No, I don't."
> "Well, just go out and do whatever you do when you're having too much fun to come in for dinner."
> "You mean toss the tennis ball against the garage? Finish painting my bike? Practice standing on my head? Tease Andy's sister? Check out the robin eggs?"*

Most children, whatever the structure of the family group they grow up in, take to playfulness naturally. They play alone, with siblings, with their peers, their pets, and with any grownups they can con into playing with them.

Infants play with their fingers and toes. Almost any kind of object can serve as a prop for play, almost any kind of activity can be an occasion for play. "Playing" is a kind of catchall concept that covers a lot of activities: trying out the properties of objects (banging two frying pans together), testing one's physical skill (balancing on a ledge), ex-

---

* Catherine Garvey, *Play* (Cambridge, Mass.: Harvard University Press, 1977), p. 2.

12

ploring and inventing (mixing noxious concoctions in the kitchen), taking on roles (playing house, train engineer, doctor), constructing small-scale environments (building with blocks), and more. There is play with no set rules or agreed-upon conventions as well as highly ritualized play—peek-a-boo, rhymes to accompany bouncing a ball or jumping rope. There are the conventions of games of chance and skill, both sedentary and active (Go Fish as well as soccer).

Play is universal. Animals play and people who study animal behavior have observed that mammals play more than other animals, and young mammals play more than mature mammals. Puppies and kittens, monkeys and lion cubs tumble and cavort. They tease and have mock fights. Dolphins and whales chase each other. The play of young animals with their age-mates not only gives them a chance to perfect physical skills but is also a critical part of learning to function effectively with their social group.

The most playful animal of all, and the one that has devised the most elaborate forms of play, is the human. Every culture has its games, and there are many common elements in the play of parent and child and among children in different parts of the world. Perhaps what keeps many adults in our society from being more playful is that play is so often opposed to work: play is seen as aimless, work as gainful; play as wasteful, work as productive. But play is a natural and essential part of life.

Why Play?

Why should a grown person play with children? Sometimes one has to. You cannot always get away with saying, "Go off and amuse yourself." Besides, most parents want to enjoy being with their children, and conversation between adults and young children has built-in limitations. Games are formalized ways of giving people things to do and talk about together. They can be especially useful when people do not have a shared repertoire of interests and activities.

A visiting aunt or grandfather who cannot know the everyday experiences of nephew or granddaughter can make contact more quickly by playing a game than by the usual "How is school?" conversation. The game is a shared experience that can be a preamble to other kinds of communication or may be enough in itself.

Everyone was once a child, and playing with children can be a way of getting in touch with parts of oneself that are often fenced off from everyday thoughts. Childish activities should not be labeled "escape." Playing with someone can indeed be an escape from the press of time, the tedium of chores; but at the same time it is a way of connecting with neglected aspects of oneself as well as with someone else. When that someone else is a child, it can be a special experience for both.

When playing with children adults are, to some extent at least, meeting children on their own ground rather than dictating what should be done and how. You are implicitly saying that the child's world is valuable. And if you can allow yourself to relax and "go with it," you can recapture some of that delightful intense absorption, the sense of suspension outside of the boundaries of time that are part of childhood's charm.

When you think of entertaining a child, you may naturally think of childhood activities that you have enjoyed yourself. But beware—the child you are talking to and playing with is not you. You may have loved a certain story, a game, or a card trick and produce it with relish only to find that it falls flat. Although many general statements can be made about children, one of the truest is that, like adults, they are not all the same. Psychologists and educators often talk and write about the "toddler," the "preschool child," the "nine-year-old," and so on. Of course there are certain similarities among nine-year-olds, and surely toddlers are more like each other than they are like nine-year-olds. But in general it is best to be a bit wary of general advice (even in high-class books like this one), and remember that not everything works for everyone.

And certainly not everything works for everyone all the time, because children change much more rapidly and dramatically than adults. Sometimes one can hardly sustain the constant repetition of a favored story or game, a roll-the-ball marathon with an infant. Then one day it is over. Never again. Well, not really never again. The game may reappear weeks, months, even years later, transformed, elaborated, more sophisticated. Or the story can be reread later when new and unsuspected layers of meaning are uncovered. (Sometimes older children like to rediscover the stories that were read to them and read them for/by themselves.) Or the trip to the circus that ended in tears may be a rousing success a few years later.

Children Think Differently

Even adults who live with children, who talk and play with them every day, are often surprised by the strange ideas they have, the startling gaps in their knowledge and the equally startling bits of information and misinformation they produce in their play. This may be unnerving for those who see a child only at intervals. On the one hand we are all aware that young children have everything to learn, on the other we are beguiled by their apparent sophistication.

We forget how much the play of children is influenced by books, television, movies, and other media. A child may talk about elephants and one thinks she knows about elephants. But in fact she has a picture-book image of an elephant and is stunned to see the enormity of the creature on her first trip to the zoo.

Not only are children unfamiliar with a mass of facts that most adults take for granted; more important, they do not use the same kind of logic, they work from a different set of premises about the world. What may amaze us doesn't surprise them; what we don't question puzzles and confuses them.

I once saw a group of children watching a magician. He pulled a silk handkerchief out of someone's ear, a rabbit from his pocket. The older children were enthralled, but the three- and four-year-olds squirmed in their chairs. They liked the rabbit, but they didn't see the performance as magic because they didn't have a firm understanding of why and how people and objects appear and disappear in everyday life.

Playing usually involves some conversation, and a chance to get a grasp of the youngster's thinking style by asking questions—"Why?" "Why do you think so?" "What do you mean?" Don't assume that the child means what you mean.

Children appreciate having their thoughts taken seriously. Especially as they grow older they don't want to be treated like cute little puppies. Sometimes their misconceptions and mispronunciations are so funny that it is hard not to laugh, but they are almost inevitable byproducts of the child's taking in information, stretching vocabulary, trying to make sense of the world.

Young children's dramatic play often reveals how much of their world is confusing, even frightening (see "The World of Make-Believe," page 159). A child may be scared of shadows or of a picture in a book—a storm, a crocodile. He or she may avoid the book, or want to skip that particular page, or sometimes peek at it and quickly turn the page. We do not know what associations are brought out by a particular image or perhaps a misunderstanding of words. Some young children are afraid of department store Santas. Does the oddity of his appearance, his size, the surroundings and the atmosphere of unreality frighten them?

Children's grasp of what is real and what is imagined is more precarious than that of adults. The fantasy or representation may loom as ominous as a realistic threat. But, without pushing, there will come a time when the child can enjoy the delicious shiver that comes from reading a scary story, or listening to ghost stories in the semidark, or wearing gruesome Halloween masks. One learns to sort out the real from the symbolic. Still, the boundaries are never completely firm; adults can be terrified by horror movies or waken in fright from a dream.

Playing with the Growing Child

In general it is the adult who has to adapt the style and substance of play to the changing needs, demands, and desires of the growing child. Playing with babies is usually fun and need not strain anyone's ingenuity. We don't expect too much from babies, and it takes little effort to get a glowing response. Babies get pleasure from watching interesting happenings and making something happen; and an interesting happening may be as simple as hearing a clicking sound, dropping a spoon, rolling a ball, seeing a shadow move, hearing a melody.

As the child grows and becomes mobile and verbal, there are dramatic leaps in the complexity of his or her activities. Young children work intensively on perfecting physical skills. They don't think of it as "practicing"; there is intrinsic pleasure in learning to pull oneself up to walk, in holding a cup, in learning to stand on one foot, in skipping. Clapping and singing games, hiding and retrieving, rhyming and nonsense songs are opportunities for sharpening skills while learning and enjoying. When adults participate in these rituals they can heighten the child's pleasure.

Young children like to pretend; they mimic, they invent, they dramatize. The classic "You be the mommy, I'll be the baby" has countless variations; sometimes all the adult need do is accept the role and add a bit of dialogue. These dramatic interludes can be serious or silly, realistic or fantastic, novel or repetitive. For the child this kind of interaction is a way of learning about the social world while at the same time stimulating the imagination. For the adult a child's drama can sometimes be embarrassing or distressing—but instructive, as when a child playing "father" screams vindictively at wife and children. The ideas and feelings expressed in dramatic play can come from the child's own family but also from families he or she has visited, television programs seen and perhaps only partly understood. The adult should not interpret the child's improvisation too literally; role playing is not real life. But the child may use the opportunity to become what he is not—a person of power, a ruler, a boss, free to express anger or dispense rewards.

The Basic Toys

In these commercial days, when many people think of playing as inevitably involving objects, a visit to a well-stocked toy store can be an overwhelming experience. It is true that children like and need toys (see "Toys: The Learning Tools of Childhood," page 29). It is also true that some of the simplest toys are the most versatile, that children too can be overwhelmed by "things." There are marvelous toys and books, objects that provide hours of enjoyment and can be passed on to others. But there are also gimmicky toys and games, packaged to look twice as big and interesting as they are, that just add clutter as they thin the pocketbook.

Toys that last have to be well made—sturdiness and versatility are perhaps the most useful criteria. For babies and infants, safety is a crucial consideration—no small removable parts, no toxic surfaces, because everything will go into the mouth. A ball is probably the prototypic toy. It intrigues the infant as pushable and rollable; it works for the preschooler learning to push, roll, bounce, and throw, and for the older child perfecting these skills in countless games. Blocks, too, have a long lifespan. And although plastic toys generally don't last, there are exceptions, like Lego, which lends itself to the capability and imagination of the constructor. The basic set, added to over the years, can be a household staple.

Many toys can be reproduced or simulated with materials in any home. Learn from the nursery school teachers, who are notorious savers and scavengers. Milk cartons get cut off and transformed into train cars; coffee and juice cans become containers or drums or bird feeders. Bits of cloth become doll dresses, cushions for doll houses, or parts of collages. Old spools make necklaces or doll furniture. Cardboard cartons are good to hide in, pile up, make into houses. Children enjoy recycling familiar odds and ends.

Sometimes the basic activity is constant over many years but the means or the materials change as the child matures. Drawing, for instance, may progress from doodling pad to sketch books, from crayons to Magic Markers to subtly colored pencils and drafting pens. The challenge is to match the means to the child's level of skill.

Another thing to think about when buying toys for children is what kind of message you are expressing about what you consider appropriate for girls and for boys. Do you give dolls only to girls, trucks only to boys? Of course the adult who is not the parent has to respect parental values and wishes, but that does not mean one should reinforce values one doesn't accept. We should look at toys and books with a cool eye, alert to stereotypes of sex and race.

Some toys that are designed to attract for a relatively short time are so well matched to the child's state of development that they are well worthwhile. Push-pull toys are just right for toddlers learning to walk; they get a thrill out of trailing something noisy behind them, an accompaniment to the newly acquired accomplishment. And there are occasions like birthdays and holidays when convention demands flamboyance, some jazzy absurdity that everyone knows will last only a few hours. Here, as in all things, it's a matter of balance.

Board Games

One of the great pastimes of childhood is playing board games. The commercial variations number in the hundreds but the basic format is simple: a place to start, a route to follow, and a goal to reach. Perhaps you begin with one of those simple ones that is color-coded or all in pictures so that reading is not required. Each player has a "piece" to move, you spin a dial, go a specified number of spaces past evil swamps, monsters, back six spaces, back to START, and finally someone comes to the palace, the honeypot, delivers the message, THE END. Children take these games seriously, count out the spaces with total concentration, shudder at dangers avoided, giggle at their opponents' mishaps. Adults tend to move the pieces in leaps—they can glance at the board and see where the next purple space is, where the counter will be in five spaces. Children need to count each space, figure out the number of dots on the dice, examine each box; they are enjoying the process and also reinforcing needed skills. Adults tend to get bored with these games pretty fast. One reason is that to us there is no challenge. It is all in the spin of the dial, the toss of the dice. At the same time, the very fact that both are subject to the laws of chance puts adult and child on an equal footing, an unusual circumstance for the young child, and one that he or she cherishes.

But when we move on to games that require remembering past moves, strategy and forethought, the adult has a clear advantage and has to come to grips with her or his competitiveness. Even so simple a game as checkers asks a lot of the players—one has to plan one's own moves and also take account of what one's opponent will do. Some plays may require three moves to complete. Will the opponent not be aware of one's play? The answer quite often is no. Children find it difficult—at early stages impossible—to see events from the point of view of another person. The adult needs to be able to handle these situations with some grace, to help the child learn and enjoy the game without feeling either up against unbeatable odds or hoaxed because the grownup "always lets you win." Until the child is on an even footing with you, you can make some concessions without really giving away the game. When the child makes an obviously disastrous move, you can say "Are you sure you want to do that?" Give the child a second chance as well as a small lesson in strategy and equity. It is not so different from playing ball. You don't use your most powerful overhand pitch when throwing a ball to a four-year-old. Perhaps it's easier to restrain the power because you are afraid of clobbering the child, but the issue is the same.

Children do like to win when they play games. Losing is hard on the ego. Some adults also have a hard time losing; they get so involved in the game that they can get a kick out of beating a five-year-old at checkers. Adults who feel like this should probably be straightforward about it: "Look, I must warn you, I am going to play this game all out, no holds barred, no concessions."

Even the more challenging games get boring much sooner for adults than for children. Like favorite books, children like to repeat them over and over again, each time with freshness and enthusiasm. Some children like to make up their own board games, usually modeled on a game that they have played many times. They will spend hours drawing the board scene, cutting out bits of colored paper to serve as currency of the game, devise and write the rules. Copying too is a way of learning to know, a kind of creation that signifies a mastery of the genre, and a small victory over the commercialization of play.

Sports and Physical Games

Another kind of play that is bound by rules and conventions is active sports. Here the adult has to judge his or her own competence and stamina in deciding how and when to participate. Even those who are inept on the playing fields can help a preschooler learn to throw a ball, and there are many physical activities that are not inherently competitive—swimming, hiking, jogging—in which the mildly active adult of any age can keep pace with the young child. In these early years adults can be most helpful by accepting the child's level of competence, tolerating errors, and encouraging improvement without stressing competition.

When children get to be about nine or ten, they usually want to play with their friends, and the adult's role may change from active participant to observer and facilitator (chauffeur and spectator). Watching some of these games can be instructive; many times more time is spent arguing about the rules than in actual play. The game itself and codes of fairness are of comparable importance.

The Uses of Play

A child can learn a lot from games. In the child's earliest play with a ball he learns about acting on an object separate from himself and the joy of making something happen. Dropping an object into a slot and seeing it disappear, then opening the box and seeing it there, can help to solidify ideas about coming and going, appearance and disappearance.

In taking imaginary roles and playing pretend games, the child may be imitating what adults do, or what she thinks they do. By joining children in these activities adults can feed information into these playful imaginings.

Puzzles help one to notice differences in shape, size, and color. Board games often have incidental information—one can pick up useful facts from a game with a geographic locale or one that is based on historical events or that involves buying and selling. Such games give a chance to practice arithmetic and mnemonic skills, to solve problems, to learn rules, to accept failure and success.

Sports promote physical development and usually involve social relationships. Children learn strategies, planning, risk taking. And as they grow, the sense of accomplishment and satisfaction becomes more subtle.

But more important, for children playing is a medium for learning, and it should be synonymous with pleasure. Playing should be fun, and sharing that fun with adults should intensify the pleasure. Perhaps the most important things that children learn from the adults they play with are what they learn about people. They learn about helpfulness and about cheating. They learn about sharing, about giving in, about sympathy. They learn about faking. They learn how different people behave in a playful competitive situation; how it feels to win and lose, how to accept the fall of the die. They learn about rules —following them, bending them, breaking them, adapting them. Playing is a social situation, and as an adult who plays with children you are the one who defines the nature of that situation and the kind of behavior that is appropriate and encouraged. Since play is part of life, the way one lives affects the way one plays; and conversely, the way one plays can shape action outside of play.

Communicating

BETTY D. BOEGEHOLD

People are verbal animals; we communicate with each other through words. Of course we send out a lot of nonverbal messages too, and our body language sometimes contradicts what our words say. When Johnny spills soup on Aunt Milly's skirt and she says with a sickly smile, "That's all right, dear, Aunt Milly doesn't mind a bit," we can bet that Johnny knows how his aunt really feels. On particularly trying days, when our kids act their worst, they are responding to our body language rather than to our entreaties to "please be quiet."

How can we use words to communicate our thoughts, feelings, and needs more honestly? How can we use language to establish better relationships with others, especially our children?

In our communication with children, they need to understand that no adult is all-powerful, all-knowing; that learning is a lifelong process; that adults can admit mistakes. Such attitudes can only strengthen communication and help children understand that they too have the right to be wrong sometimes.

The process of looking at oneself and trying to understand one's real motives in acting and speaking is a long, humbling task. Most of us need help in communicating with those we love, especially with our children. We need simple, everyday techniques that can be used, not only in intense emotional moments but in the quieter everyday exchanges. And thank goodness there are many such tools, discovered in the field of "general semantics," a few of which we can explore here.

Listening

The basic tool is *listening:* listening first to what the child is really saying to us; then listening to what we are really saying to the child.

Todd comes slamming into the house with angry eyes and a tight mouth. He throws his books on the table and yells, "I hate that lousy, no-good school! I'm quitting, hear me? Just don't try to make me go back again!"

We could respond to Todd's anger with our own: "You'll go back to school tomorrow! No son of mine is a quitter! And don't yell at me like that!"

Cool common sense tells us that this angry exchange can only escalate into more lack of communication. But who uses cool common sense when confronting strong emotion? We need another instant tool ready to use.

Reflecting Back

Sympathetic "reflecting back" of Todd's angry feelings is a quick and easy way to respond: "You must have had one terrible day. Something really bad must have happened to you."

Todd: "You're not kidding! Like having Mr. Morrison chew me out in front of the class for making fun of him—and I didn't even do it! I tried to tell him, but I was so mad I began to stutter. Now I've got after-school detention for five days, for something I didn't even do!"

Us: "No wonder you got mad. Would you want to try explaining to him again tomorrow? Or would you want us to go with you?"

Todd: "Naw. That would only make things worse. People don't like to be put in the wrong."

Us: "But you are being punished for something you didn't do."

Todd: "Oh well, there are lots of times I *was* doing something when they didn't catch me!" (Exit laughing.)

In this second exchange, we were listening to what Todd was really saying rather than the words he was using; his tone of voice, his facial and body language were showing his anger and upset, and we reacted with sympathy. We didn't go to the other extreme of overprotection; children must learn that unfairness exists and has to be dealt with. But Todd, relieved by our understanding, can take this minor upset in his stride.

Labeling

In labeling people we deceive ourselves as well as denigrate others: "Honestly, that Jean is a slob." "Johnny is plain lazy! He doesn't even try."

Such labels may not only be perceived as truth but be acted upon as true. If Jane is told she is "babyish" or "dumb," she may well act that way—it's a self-fulfilling prophecy.

Labeling often begins in fun but it is usually endured in pain and self-denigration for the recipient. We all have the power to stop it in our own lives and to help our children recognize the cruelty inherent in labeling others.

Generalizations

When we are angry we often resort to using sweeping statements that are usually gross exaggerations. A tendency to use "absolutes" often accompanies labeling: "Jean is *always* so sloppy!" "Johnny *is the laziest* child in his class."

If you're the *laziest* one, why try to catch up? If you are *always* sloppy, no use to try for order and neatness.

When William disrupted the class, Marvin said, "William is *always* acting up. He's bad."

The teacher asked: "He is *always* bad? He wasn't this morning; he studied very hard."

Marvin: "Yeah, he was okay then. But I think he's bad now."

That was a good beginning for more accurate characterization, for expressing specific observations. Marvin has taken a giant step toward assessing his peers more realistically.

Expressing Feelings

Yet we do form beliefs that we want to make known. How do we express strong convictions without raising hackles and with a better chance of being heard? By stating our beliefs as our opinions in words such as "To me," "I think," "It seems to me." This allows other people the right to their beliefs and opinions and makes fruitful discussions possible.

Children can easily accept this technique in everyday communication.

Joanne: "I think vanilla ice cream is the best."

Jerry: "It is not! Chocolate's the best."

Joanne: "To you, chocolate's best. To me, vanilla is."

And an incipient argument fades away.

Respect

We should not repress our real reactions, but we also need to show respect for the child. We should treat our children with the courtesy we would accord another adult. When offered something, we should respond; when asked a question, we should answer, as honestly as possible.

When a small child asks, "Where do babies come from?" the question should be answered in simple but truthful terms such as "They grow in a special place inside their mothers until they are ready to be born."

We honor the child's need to understand the world by giving as straight an answer as possible but always in the terms of his or her developmental stage; we don't overburden children, but neither do we deceive them.

Helpful Praise

Some overconscientious adults try to reply to every observation, every question, and are soon exhausted; others overrespond to children's questions and offerings.

"You must be the best clay worker in your group, Nancy. That's the most wonderful clay bear I ever saw!"

How can Nancy accept this overpraise? She knows she's not the "best clay worker" in her group. A more honest response would be something like "You made a bear, Nancy. I like its round little ears," responding to the article itself and not generalizing about it. Dr. Haim

Ginott describes this as "helpful praise," praise that is accurate and helps the child build a positive self-image.*

These few guidelines won't create immediate miracles, but as practical tools for everyday use, they can make family communication more thoughtful, more useful, and more pleasurable. They really can help us establish better relationships with those we love.

---

* Dr. Haim Ginott, *Between Parent and Child* (New York: Avon, 1965).

Part 2

PLAYTHINGS AND BOOKS

Playthings and books are the building blocks of childhood. Just as young children need good nutrition to grow strong and healthy bodies, they need materials that nurture their emotions and intellect. As providers of these necessities, parents have both the obligation and the opportunity to participate in their children's growth.

Toys: The Learning Tools of Childhood

NANCY BALABAN

Choosing toys for children: Could it be a secret method for adults to relive some of the endless, absorbing play of their own childhood?

"Won't this toy sailboat be perfect for Laura? I used to have one just like it when I was six. Now we can sail it together in the park." The smoothness of the boat's enameled body, its shiny deck, the glisten of its white cloth sails bring back to Laura's mother a childhood memory suffused with pleasure. Laura may or may not like the little boat equally, but the sharing is certainly worth a try.

The play of childhood is long and full. It occupies many hours of a child's day and contributes a store of memories, feelings, and experiences which adults draw upon all through life. Childhood play is not a totally hidden resource. It appears on the surface of the adult mind with only the lightest prod. A passing glance at a musical top can remind one of very early joys. Remember that ragged, lovely bunny which was dragged everywhere? Remember those endless games of Parcheesi? Remember playing?

Toys have existed as long as children. A child, for lack of a toy, will make one. Archeologists have unearthed toys from all parts of the world that are also familiar in most modern households—dolls, spinning tops, balls, drawing implements, and many others.

What is this need to use toys, to play, that we see rising throughout childhood like steam from a kettle? What is this powerful force that impels children to pick up two sticks and say, "This big one is the mommy and this little one is the baby," and then proceed to play house in a square drawn on the ground?

29

From the earliest moments of life, young human beings want to hook into their environment. They want to have an impact on it. They want to move it, shape it, and know it. They go about that passionate task by chewing and tasting; by feeling, pulling apart, poking, shaking, rubbing; by gazing, peeking, staring, blinking; by smelling, sniffing, nosy-ing; by listening, hearing, eavesdropping.

Yet they do something else in their undisciplined search for understanding the things and people around them. *They play.* They invent. They substitute something at hand for something out of sight—a stick for mommy, a bottle cap for a plate, a bit of rug for a bear. They are engaging in the ultimate human function: making symbols.

Children's compelling need to make sense out of the "blooming, buzzing confusion" that William James called the world out there seems to be the fuel that fires their insistent drive to play. No wonder they usually stop playing only when they are sick or asleep or have watched excessive amounts of TV.

Toys, then, are not the frills of child life. They are more the substance. It is by means of toys and playthings that children take hold of reality, which often "wears slippery shoes." "I don't really understand what the doctor is doing, so let's play hospital," a preschooler seems to be saying. A doctor bag, a flashlight, a paper hat bearing a red cross are the toy props that feed this hungry curiosity.

"It seems to me that rules keep society afloat and I'd like to have a hand in trying to make some myself," eleven-year-olds seem to be saying as they become embroiled in games like "Capture the Flag," "Dragons and Dungeons," chess or Monopoly or other board games.

Playthings and games need not be elaborate. In fact the less elaborate the toy, the more the child must elaborate, and "elaborate" is here synonymous with "think." To invest a simple rag doll with life, to be able to stretch the rules of a game or to incorporate ever more complex rules requires diligent mental effort. There is intrinsic reward in this intellectual work. Perhaps that is one reason why adults are able to recall bits of childhood play. It not only felt good emotionally but was satisfying intellectually. There is no one direct path to creative thinking, but some of the beginning stirrings and some of the roots lie in using toys imaginatively.

Clearly some playthings are better than others. Some are more suited to meet the powerful need of children to have an effect on their world. Some have more enduring qualities, more universal appeal to the nature of child life.

How can parents faced with an overmerchandized, supermarket collection of toys make wise, cogent, appropriate, and economically sound choices of playthings for their children? How can parents counteract the loud, ever present voice of commercial TV seducing the child consumer?

Here are some guidelines for parental choices:

Self-Confidence. Does the toy help a child feel competent and complete as a boy or girl? Children are very aware of packaging; the package should indicate that the toy is suitable for either sex.

A set of play dishes is popular with a group of young boys in a home-visiting preschool program. Since the package did not show girls, it was accepted with pleasure by both the boys and their parents.

Do you, the parent, feel that toys are "for girls" or "for boys"? Are you willing to buy a doll for your boy or a fire engine for your girl? The toys you give your children carry your unspoken stamp of approval—or disapproval—about appropriate boy or girl behavior. Shall boys be encouraged to be nurturing, assertive, curious? Shall girls be encouraged to be scientific, experimental, caring? The toys we provide speak to our children in a language that transcends our words.

Pride in Heritage. Does the toy contribute to children's pride in belonging to their particular racial, ethnic or religious group? If it doesn't contribute, does it at least not detract? Does the packaging say, in effect, "for whites only"? Do the pictures or parts of the plaything reflect the varieties of people who inhabit this country? Are any representations of people insulting or degrading? Subtle messages of this sort need to be censored by vigilant adults.

Enduring Appeal. Does the plaything truly appeal to some enduring interest of the child or is it merely an adult gimmick? A gimmick is something that has short-lived novelty, like a toy used for promoting a product or an event. Once action has been "done," the toy has been used up. Novelty, research tells us, wears off rapidly, even with the youngest infant.

Children are interested in motion, in putting together and taking apart, changing things, inventing, trying out roles, practicing what they already know, and collecting things. Playthings that address lasting interests like these speak to the core of child life.

Flexibility. How many variations can be demonstrated in playing with this toy? How many ways can it be used? A mechanical robot that works only with batteries has much less flexibility in the hands of a child than a floppy rag doll, which can be bent and placed. Conversely, too much variation, like a game with rules that even an adult can't understand, is a less happy choice than a game with comprehensible but not immutable rules. The proper amount of flexibility allows a child to experience power and control.

Age Appropriateness. The toy must clearly match the child's age-level capabilities and interests. Three-year-olds who are just becoming aware of themselves as individual people need toys to clarify the daily events of their own lives, like what mommies and daddies do all day, what it looks like outdoors when it snows or rains or becomes night. They need toys that are comfortable for plump hands with small fingers, eyes that are not yet fully developed, curious minds that comprehend only a small portion of a limited "here and now" world. Not fantastic make-believe, not outer space, but the everyday event is the preschool métier.

Middle-years children of seven to ten are another story. They need toys which allow them to explore the world of getting along with others, of going beyond the bounds of the preschool "here and now" to the "long ago and far away" or to the fantasy places of imagination. They need games and toys to test and expand the skills of their rapidly developing bodies and minds.

Look at the child: What can this child do? with body? with mind? What does he or she care about, talk about, try out? The child will reveal a host of capacities and interests if adults take the time to listen.

And for a child of any age, ask yourself whether the toy will outpace his or her abilities. Is there a comfortable mental stretch in using this plaything? Children tend to disregard toys that are either too simple or too hard. The secret lies in a toy that offers challenge without frustration, that rewards effort without defeat.

Interest Match. Is the toy consonant with the real interests of the child? A ball and bat to encourage a child who perceives himself or herself to be a poor athlete may reinforce feelings of not measuring up. A loom for a girl who would rather ride a bike, a football for a boy who would rather sketch, a chemistry set for a girl who would rather knit, are avoidable adult errors. Rather than relying on a salesperson for a "toy for a ten-year-old boy," adults would be better advised to find out directly what the child is interested in.

Durability. Is the plaything durable? Is it made of sturdy, unbreakable materials? Some plastics and metals are flimsy. Wooden toys are often strong but are becoming increasingly hard to find, especially for very young children. Record players for very young children should be selected with a tone arm that is built for unintentional abuse.

Durability means that the toy will have a long life. If the toy is one with many parts, such as a construction toy or a game, the container should provide lasting storage. It is frustrating for both parents and children to find pieces of Tinker Toy or Lego in various corners of the home. If necessary, find some sort of special, inexpensive container—a used plastic ice-cream container, a plastic shoebox, or a woven basket.

Function. Does the toy do what it purports to do? Do moving parts move? If it uses batteries, are they included? Do stable parts remain stable? Will it continue to work after several weeks? Try it out before purchasing and make sure.

Safety. Is the toy safe? The safety of a toy is predicated partly on the age of the child. For example, a Monopoly set would not be safe for an eighteen-month-old who might swallow any of the tiny parts, but clearly is not inappropriate for sale. On the other hand, children under three are protected by a recent regulation that bans a toy which is, or has parts that are, of a size prevalent in accidents among children of this age.

Toy safety is one of the primary concerns of an organization called Public Action Coalition on Toys. PACT's booklet, *Guidelines on Choosing Toys for Children,* contains the following vital information for parents:

> *Suggestions:* Ask yourself some questions about the toy—
> Are there no sharp edges or points, exposed nails, sharp
> wires or straight pins?

Is it large enough so it cannot be swallowed?

Is it free from detachable (or poorly glued) small parts that can be removed and lodge in the windpipe, ears or nose?

Is it made from unbreakable material?

Is it labeled "nontoxic"? (Avoid painted toys for infants, who put everything into the mouth.)

Is it free from parts that can pinch fingers or toes or catch hair?

Are the cords for crib toys no longer than twelve inches?

Is the projectile toy (rocket, dart, or airplane) capable of inflicting dangerous eye injuries?

Does the toy require electricity?

Will the toy be safe when used in its surroundings?

Are there any hidden hazards?

Is the toy easily cleaned?

. . . Although the U.S. Consumer Safety Product Commission has reduced the number of hazardous toys on the market (over 1,500 toys have been on the government's banned toy list), some banned toys are still available, and other dangerous toys are not yet banned. Children are vulnerable to injuries from toys. They are involuntary risk-takers, who often cannot or do not read or understand warning instructions. Children can be unpredictable in their use of products, and they lack experience to evaluate the hazards associated with toys.

Most of us are naïve. Despite toy labels saying "Fun, SAFE for child of any age," and despite recent consumer legislation, the statistics are shocking: at a minimum, 134,000 children end up in the emergency rooms of hospitals every year due to accidents involving their toys. This government statistic, based on data from the National Electronic Injury Surveillance System, does not include bicycle or playground equipment injuries which account for more than a million accidents every year, many of which could be prevented with safer products. What does it do to a child's world when a top explodes, as described in the book *Toys That Don't Care,* or when an eye is lost from a dart gun accident?

Think about the whole toy, not just one aspect, such as educational value or physical attractiveness (for example, blending with a child's room). Be especially watchful for the stylish but poorly made toy. Read *Consumer Reports* or other consumer testing reports before buying big expensive items, like bicycles. (Bicycles are number one on the list of products associated with injuries, partly because of poor brakes and chains and lack of reflectors.)

Avoid buying dolls and stuffed animals with wires, buttons, or Styrofoam stuffing; paper or plastic caps above 128 decibels; toy stoves and ovens with high temperatures or poor electrical outlets; glass mirrors in vanity sets; pellet guns; water-powered rockets which can zoom 200 feet into the air (or go horizontally).

Avoid buying the too-powerful toy, gas-powered toys, including airplanes and cars, mini-bikes, chemistry sets for young children.

Avoid buying easily breakable, cheap toys. Although a name brand is no guarantee, one precaution is to buy well-made toys from reputable companies in reputable stores.

Avoid buying balloons for preschool children. They can cause death.

Avoid buying any toy when the manufacturer is not stated and the number is not clearly marked.*

Aesthetic Quality. Is the toy attractive? Are the colors true, unmuddied, clear, bright, or gentle as appropriate? Is the plastic, wood, or metal of high quality, well finished, smooth, enjoyable to the touch? Will it remain attractive after use?

Is the design appealing? Does it have simplicity, grace, some air of elegance without pretension?

---

* Reprinted by permission of Public Action Coalition on Toys. Prepared for PACT by Myron Kaplan, Patricia Powers, Todd Boressoff, with the assistance of Victoria Reiss and Minnie P. Berson. Copyright © 1976, Public Action Coalition on Toys.

It may seem as if such a toy should be in the Museum of Modern Art rather than in a toy shop. Yet these are not out-of-bounds requirements. Children's aesthetic sense develops very early. Order, color, texture, sound, patterns are all experiences to which even newborn babies respond. Children can appreciate playthings of beauty that have been selected for them with care and discrimination. Taste is learned in the nursery and developed throughout school-age years. And attention to this aesthetic nature is a natural partner to communicating to children a toy's value, which is also the rationale for cleanup and putting away.

Make-Believe

Watching children use toys, games, and playthings in a relentless exploration of their environment is a very special pleasure for parents. Children seem to use toys on behalf of their own development, as though they were privy to some mysterious universal wisdom. They make-believe; they play games with rules; they perfect large and small muscle skills; they learn "science," "mechanics," and "mathematics." Certain sorts of toys support these nascent capacities in our young discoverers.

The bud, flower, and fruiting of pretend play occurs somewhere between the ages of two and five. Early childhood is the crèche of the imagination. For this reason, toys that encourage and support toddlers' and preschoolers' make-believe are an investment in their later mental richness and intellectual flexibility.

Young children need to "pretend" those activities which are most real to them—going to sleep, eating, being a mommy, a daddy, an uncle, a teenager, a doctor, a baby, a dog, a storekeeper, a firefighter. Through such pretend play children come to terms with basic aspects of their lives—nurturing, anger, health and illness, death, rescue from danger, love, dependence and independence.

Many young children are lured by the hypnotic quality of TV and tend to act out what they see on the screen. Some of this TV imitation is repetitive and sterile in comparison with the elaborated and extended play that revolves around real-life themes. Parents can do much to foster richer imaginative play by entering roles themselves when invited ("Oh, thank you, this coffee is delicious," as one sips from an empty cup), and by providing simple props and some small, protected place to play. Some parents may want to limit TV play to a few minutes at a time, or to redirect it to the outdoors, to encourage a richer and more complex kind of play.

Here is a suggestive, rather than a comprehensive, list of props that support productive "let's pretend":

> shoes and boots (women's and men's)
> handbags
> small suitcase
> kitchen ware
> lengths of cloth
> dolls, stuffed animals
> eyeglass frames
> stethoscope
> clothing for dress up (women's and older boys')
> cardboard boxes

The true fun for parents of young children lies in seeing their youngsters seriously engaged in assimilating reality and internalizing new ideas through their play. Such insight into the child's mind at work provides parents with both amazement and amusement. A word of caution, however: Keep the laughter low. It may seem funny to an adult that the child firefighter brings the fire to the building in the truck, but it is not funny to the child. It is simply children's way of trying out an idea about which they're not totally sure.

What parents learn as they watch and listen to their young at play is how children wrestle with concepts in their long, hard struggle to understand their environment. Play is a form of child thought. To listen to it (discreetly) is to learn how children think.

Make-believe doesn't stop with the preschooler. Children continue to fantasize well into their middle years and preadolescence. The activity goes underground, however. Where preschoolers delight in adults' pleasure in their games, six-to-eleven-year-olds are likely to shut the door against parental intrusion. They often become involved in constructing miniature worlds with tiny figures, construction toys, or reduced-in-scale props like doll houses. Children of this age construct societies with rules patterned after their own. They have strong opinions about how the game is organized, who does what and how.

Often much of their playing time is taken up in organizing and laying down the regulations and not all that time is necessarily harmonious. Yet through such play children of the middle years create the opportunity for working out their social relationships with one another, as well as trying out for themselves a variety of real roles like printing a newspaper or running a store.

The older children grow, the more private and interior their make-believe becomes, until it emerges, silently, in the form of the day-dream or reverie that is so familiar to adults. This capacity to day-dream is a highly worthwhile endeavor which feeds both the intellect and the emotions.

Parents can share some of their own childhood make-believe games in conversations with their children. This not only binds the two generations with a common thread but lends approval to the child's own daydream activity, which society often brands as "useless." Pretending to be a lion tamer, putting on a play for family and friends, day-dreaming while staring out the window should be valued along with reading or doing math homework. Parents will want to foster both types of activities (see "The World of Make-Believe," page 159).

Games with Rules

For children between six and twelve, rules of the game are, by and large, synonymous with the rules of friendship and the rules of life. What is fair and unfair is of crucial importance. The development of children's ideas about rules comes slowly, as does the development of their ideas about almost anything. For example, it takes a lot of time to really understand the setting of the sun. Children need various experiences with sunsets, many opportunities to try out several explanations of the phenomenon in their heads, and a long period of intellectual maturation before they understand. Similarly, involvement in games with rules nourishes and fosters children's development as moral and socially responsive beings. Repeated opportunities with their peers in a variety of game situations force children to understand points of view other than their own and demand that they coordinate their thinking with the thinking of others. Failure to develop such a moral and social stance leaves a child of this age on the outside of the peer group.

Games with rules have recently been expanded by the appearance of electronic computer-based games. Interestingly, many of these games, intended for children, have been appropriated by adults. There are many attractive features about these small, portable, brightly colored toys that appeal to and stimulate human intelligence more than the teaching machines of the past. With these toys, the object is not getting the right answer, but rather acquiring intellectual strategies and giving the player the experience of "thinking well."

These new developments are challenging for parents and children because machines can be seductive, luring with their glitter. It would be wise for parents, while exploring the exciting computer toys, not to totally replace the old-fashioned games. Despite all the innovations in playthings, human relations change very little, and old-fashioned games provide an essential opportunity for children to learn about themselves and others. In playing games of these sorts with school-age children, parents will enjoy the awakening intellectual abilities of the children as well as their companionship.

Playthings for Physical Skill

Children develop physically from gross control of their bodies to ever more fine and delicate control. The eighteen-month-old's pat on the back of the family dog is more likely to be an uncontrolled smack, while the ten-year-old can caress and tickle the pet with finely directed movements. Appropriate toys encourage and stimulate development and coordination of eyes and hands as well as the skillful use of the whole body. Proficient use of the body is, in the mind of the child, a sign of special triumph. The baby's first successful grasp of a ring, the toddler's first walk across the room, a preschooler's jump from the second step, the eight-year-old's riding "no hands" on a bike, the twelve-year-old's shooting the basket are all signals to the children of their growing competence.

Playthings designed to assist the emergence and elaboration of physical skills are very important. The child must be able to do something *to* the toy—be the effective initiator of the toy's action; and the child must be able to eventually make the toy "work."

Here is a list of some playthings that foster development of both small and large muscles:

First year. Mobiles that move or sound in response to the child's grasp or swipe; safe on-the-crib toys like the musical Crib Gym; rattles, clutch balls, stacking toys, drop-and-find toys, push-and-pull toys.

One to two years. Nesting toys, pounding bench, one to five-piece puzzles, pull toys that move or sound, dumping and gathering toys, large pegs and boards, foot-propelled riding toys, rocking boat, stairs, low climbing things, space to walk and run.

Two to three. Large cardboard blocks, wooden unit blocks, shape sorting, box, large Lego, large stringing beads, four-to-ten-piece puzzles, nesting toys, construction toys with large connectors, linked floor trains, tricycle, climbers, sliding board, stairs, swing.

Three to five. Construction toys like Lego, Tinker Toys, Constructo-Straws; real working tools (not screwdriver); puzzles over twelve pieces; wooden unit blocks, small table blocks; small peg boards and pegs; sewing on burlap, needlepoint canvas, or sewing cards; tricycle, sled, climber, beginning roller and/or ice skates; slide, swing, stairs for climbing and jumping.

Six to nine. Wooden unit blocks; woodworking tools; construction toys; bead looms, weaving looms; sewing, knitting; jigsaw puzzles; jacks, marbles; model building; jump rope, bicycle, scooter, pogo stick, stilts, roller and ice skates, sled with runners and steering apparatus; opportunities for climbing, swinging, hanging, chinning, "skinning the cat," bat and ball, hockey stick, badminton, tennis racquet, cross-country skis.

Ten to thirteen. Jigsaw puzzles; complex model building; tools of various sorts; whittling; volley ball, basketball, soccer, and other sports equipment; bicycle, skates, unicycle, snowshoes, hiking shoes, cross-country skis.

Many of these playthings lend themselves to joint parent-child use. If you love to ride a bike, do it with your child now and then. Did you love to play jacks? Engage your child in a contest. Is puzzle solving a pastime you enjoy? Set up a puzzle table in a corner of a room. Are you a basketball "pro"? Take your child out to shoot a few baskets. Teaching a youngster the rudiments of tennis, skating, biking, skiing, and such can be rewarding for both the teacher and the taught if it is understood that learning takes time and includes failures on the way to success. Parental praise for all attempts, even those that fail, will spur the child along the difficult and sometimes frustrating path to achievement.

Toys That Move: Nongimmicky Gimmicks

Many toys have only one function; they are labeled "automata," "optical," "ephemeral," and so on. Many of these are ageless playthings that contribute to mechanical, mathematical, and scientific knowledge. Through playing with such toys children come to know, experientially, such principles as gravity, rotation, flotation, and levers.

Spinning tops—from the smallest, propelled by a rapid thumb and forefinger action, to the largest, activated by a pumped handle—provide experience with rotation and gravity. The gyroscope, an illustration of centrifugal force, is another intriguing toy.

What better way to learn such scientific fact as floating and sinking, water displacement, notions of volume, the principle of the siphon or how a pump works, then to play in a sink full of water with a funnel, plastic bottles, plastic tubing, a baster, a ketchup pump, or both metal and wooden objects?

Think of the possibilities inherent in using common toys for learning about wind, levers, gravity, friction, prisms and light refraction. Think about the pinwheel, about wheels and gears, pulleys, a seesaw, a bouncing ball that returns to the ground, a yo-yo, a Slinky, a sparkler, a kaleidoscope, a periscope. They will lead to thoughts of other toys that, although they have but one function, provide children with the physical experience that underlies all true knowledge. By using these toys repeatedly, over a span of years, children begin to unlock the mysteries of the physical world.

Holiday Gifts

In our zeal to please children we need not deprive them of the pleasure of giving as well as receiving. We have all seen children reduced to hysterics by a flood of presents. We have seen them at the end of the gift-giving day complaining about "not enough" or "is that all?" while disgruntled adults fume about their "ingratitude."

One way to solve the problem is to make sure everyone in the group, toddlers included, shares in the gift giving. Each person might have a turn to give a gift to each assembled family member while everyone watches. As each gift is opened the receiver can thank the giver and everybody can enjoy the gift, whether it is a two-year-old's drawing or the most sophisticated store-bought item. What is needed is an atmosphere of calm and joy, both graciousness and appreciation.

Wise Selection and Good Care

Toys, it is clear, are children's tools for thinking, children's glass for peering into the inner workings of the world, children's companion on the uncharted sea of human relations. Parents can help children value these important assistants in growing up by selecting toys wisely and cautiously. Indiscriminate buying tends to devalue toys. A throwaway attitude tells the child that the toy is a bauble. A surfeit communicates that toys are frivolous.

Selecting toys carefully, enjoying them with your children, and providing attractive storage space for them place a value on them that children will understand. If at the end of the day everything is scooped up and thrown helter-skelter into a toy chest, the message is clear: "Let's get this junk out of the way." How many families would store their canned and boxed groceries or their dishes and silver in such a fashion?

On the other hand, if there are shelves that children can reach, then parents and children can clean up together, hunt for missing pieces, and make sure the toys are in good order. Children can then find what they want to use when they want to use it. Order in storage teaches children respect for their belongings, as well as a system of classification. Cooperation in putting away helps children know that such working together is a lot more fun than struggling alone or having a contest of wills, that it can be a rewarding part of playing with toys.

Toys for thinking, toys for growing, toys for unlocking the secrets of the world, toys for developing creativity! As children and parents enjoy their playing partnership, they are all developing their intellectual and imaginative capacities.

Books: Playthings of the Imagination

ELEANOR KULLESEID

Books, like spinach, are supposed to be good for us. In this push-button age they are still the primary vehicles for educating our young. Many of us associate books and reading with early schooling, struggling to "crack the code" because adults think it's important. When we become parents ourselves, we are admonished to introduce our infants to the wonderful world of books as early as possible, and we respond with enthusiasm.

But what books are best? Where can we get them? How can we help children to expect from a book the same degree of fun and involvement that is promised by the TV or the playground? And first of all, what are our own roles as adult models and mediators between books and children?

Reading Survey

What are our own reading habits?

How many books do you have in your home right now that you would want to pick up and read for pleasure?

Where are most of your books? Do you have a special area with bookshelves? Do you leave books lying around on a bedside table, the living room table?

When did you last pick up a book and read for the fun of it? When did you last buy a book on impulse from a bookstore, supermarket, newspaper stand?

44

When did you last visit your local library to borrow a book for yourself or someone in the family?

How often does your child interrupt you when you are buried in a newspaper, magazine, or book? How often does your child see you reading?

How often do you read or tell a story to your child? How often does your family discuss or refer to the books you are reading?

Getting in Touch with the Child in You

After this quick self-survey, some of us would have to admit that we don't read for pleasure and relaxation as much as we think we'd like to. We have such busy schedules, or we can't afford the expense of building a personal collection and don't feel comfortable about borrowing books, or we are overwhelmed with obligatory reading on the job—memos, instructions, forms, reports—and are hardly in the mood to face another printed page when we reach the refuge of home.

And there is still another obstacle. Living deep inside many of us is that small, rebellious child who repeats the question one six-year-old asked as he pored over a first-grade primer: "But why do I have to learn all this scribble-scrabble?"

Why indeed? Did we learn all that "scribble-scrabble" so we could pass an exam, fill out a job application, or make a gourmet chocolate mousse? Yes, certainly. Literacy is a minimum requirement for economic and social survival in our society. But that's not all. We want to provide children with an environment and books which stimulate a love for literature and reading. We can hope for greater success if we can get in touch with our own present and past reading experiences—not the struggles but the joys. Now let's ask a few more questions.

Do you remember hearing an adult read to you when you were young? What impression did it make? Were there any good storytellers in your family? Any teachers who loved to read aloud to the class? What stories remain in your memory?

What were the sources of reading pleasure for you as an

older child? Did you go on reading jags or have a favorite type of book—mystery, science fiction, dog stories?
Did you ever read one book over and over again because
you hated to say goodbye to the characters in it?

Can you think of one book from your childhood that you
would like to read again or share with a child today? Do
you still have it?

Young children are often understandably inarticulate about their
responses to pleasure reading, but as adults they may have vivid recol-
lections about their childhood reading. One day my four-year-old
daughter and I were looking at picture books in the library. She
pulled from the shelf *The Story about Ping*, a little duck who lives on a
Chinese riverboat. I recognized it as one of the few books I had
owned as a very young child. Flipping through the pages together, we
came to the part where Ping, lost from his family, is captured and im-
prisoned under a rope basket on another boat. I had a shock of recognition. Kurt Weise's illustration of poor Ping, looking out to daylight
and freedom from inside the basket, had the same claustrophobic effect it had had on me as an asthmatic child. My child and I both had to
read on, to share Ping's joy when he finally got back to his family.

A parent I know has not bothered to wait until his seven-year-old
twins are ready to understand all the subtleties of *Alice's Adventures in
Wonderland*. Other books are shared too, but Alice occupies a special
place in his heart because his mother read the book to him in his own
childhood.

Of course children's classics are not the only sources of literary
pleasure. Any childhood experience involving play with language
may be regarded as literary, whether it is "silly talk," clapping games,
listening to a record, or singing a hymn. D. H. Lawrence confessed
that "the dull Nonconformist hymns I learned as a child . . . mean
to me almost more than the finest poetry. . . . They are the same to
my man's experience as they were to me nearly forty years ago."

Choosing Books for and with Your Child

There are many resources available to help you pick out a book for
your child:

Libraries, both school and public, can be helpful in matching children's reading interests and abilities with appropriate books.

Bookstores that offer a wide selection of children's books usually have a friendly, knowledgeable salesperson to help you match your child's interests to particular titles or types of books.

Publications, many in paperback, offer annotated lists of recommended titles, usually categorized by age level, type of book, and content. Many have excellent introductions or chapters on children's literature: Three of the best are Nancy Larrick's *A Parent's Guide to Children's Reading* (Doubleday); Josette Frank's *Your Child's Reading Today* (Doubleday); and Abby Campbell Hunt's *The World of Books for Children: A Parent's Guide* (Sovereign).

A good annual bibliography is "Children's Books—A List of Books for Preschool through Junior High School Age," compiled by Virginia Haviland and Lois Watt. It can be obtained from the Superintendent of Documents, U. S. Government Printing Office, Washington, D.C. 20402. "Children's Books of the Year," selected by the Child Study Association Children's Book Committee, is also an excellent annual list; you can buy it for $2.00 from the committee at Bank Street College, 610 West 112th Street, New York City, New York 10025. (Your own public library will undoubtedly have its own lists of favorite children's books.)

Some newspapers and magazines have columns that review new children's books.

These information sources cannot substitute for a direct, three-way communication between you, the child, and the books. Browsing together is the best way to become acquainted with a range of titles, to experience and discuss them together, to observe your child's responses to them, and to make your own judgments. The following may help you get together your own guidelines for selection:

First, take your clues from your children. Watch what books attract them. Do they seem to want picture books, filled with illustrations? Do they go for the nonfiction "big books" of trains or planes? Are they drawn to books like Richard Scarry's "all about" books with their many small busy animals? Do your older ones want sport books? Mysteries? Outer space? Comics? If you can, start where they are—time enough for widening their horizons later.

Second, look at the words in the books you examine. Do you think they are what you consider good writing? Are there sentences that make you feel strongly? Imagery that brings vivid pictures to your mind? Is the plot something your child could understand? Do you think it will hold his or her attention? Is the theme true to real life? Will the book extend and confirm your child's feelings and experiences? Is the information accurate? In picture books, do words and pictures enrich each other? Will you enjoy reading the book aloud?

Third, look at the pictures. Are they strong and appealing to you? Are they beautiful, expressive, humorous, moving in some way? Are they intelligible to your child? Will the pictures intrigue, stretch the imagination? Do you think they are authentic and accurate?

Fourth, think about the social values presented in the book. What is the author and/or illustrator's *conscious* theme or message to the reader? What kind of implied statements or generalizations come through about children, adults, feelings, behavior, race, sex, human values? What will the book contribute to your child's social development, awareness of others, knowledge of groups other than those he or she belongs to?

Not all these guidelines can apply to every book, but they will help you ask the basic questions, remembering from your own childhood how deep an impression images and words leave with young children.

But, you may object, your child isn't interested in reading good books at all. She's stuck on schlock! Should she be forbidden to waste time on her comics, her TV or movie magazines? One parent grumbles about her daughter's passion for horse stories. When she asked me reproachfully why I couldn't lure her preteen daughter into richer fare, I asked, "What did you read when you were your daughter's age?" The women paused for a long moment, then replied ruefully that she remembered reading nothing but dog stories those two or three years before adolescence, and before high school plunged her into Dickens, Steinbeck, and Julius Caesar.

Some parents may ask, "Do I have to let my kid drown in that stuff? Can't I at least expose them to some good books?"

Of course, leave them around. Or even read one aloud if anybody wants to hear it. But don't force it like medicine down unwilling throats, and believe that the day will dawn when your child will be seen reading other kinds of books. The more children read, the better they read, and the sooner they tire of schlock.

Libraries

Most communities in the United States have some form of library resources for children. Your tax money supports these services and it makes good sense for you to use them.

Some parents mention the problem of returning borrowed books on time to avoid fines. One way to get around this is to make library visits a regular activity, incorporating a half-hour weekly or biweekly visit to the public library into the family's schedule. Regular visits will increase your child's acquaintance with books, demonstrate your interest in both, and encourage a regular turnover of borrowed material. One parent, a man who works at home, meets his nine-year-old daughter and seven-year-old son at the public library every Thursday afternoon. He makes a point of spending some time with them in the adult section, checking references for his own work and selecting a book to read for pleasure, and then accompanies them to the Children's Room.

Regular visits are often not enough to jog the memory. Children and grownups need other reminders to take due books back to the library, if only to renew them for another few weeks. One family keeps all library books on a special shelf near the hall door. This "Going Out Shelf" catches all books, mittens, and other stray objects that have found their way into the family's clutter. It is comforting to know that most public libraries have a sensible upper limit for fines on borrowed books. You can return a long-lost book without fear of expensive reprisal.

It may sound pedantic, but an additional benefit of the library ritual is the opportunity for the child to accept responsibility for shared community property, as well as accepting the consequences of neglect. Whereas older children should be expected to keep track of their own borrowed materials, the younger ones need your support in this area. For one thing, their time sense is less well developed, and the length of a lending period means very little to them. For another, the idea of borrowing, as against possessing, is sometimes difficult to get across.

Five-year-old Sabrina and her mother selected a pile of books to take home from the school library for spring vacation. She showed them proudly to her father at bedtime. "Do you think we'll be able to read all these books before it's time to take them back to the library?" he asked. "I don't have to take them back," she replied firmly. "The library lady said I could keep them. I signed my whole name on the card and I didn't need any help." It took a good deal of patient explanation and a few more library visits to help her comprehend the process. The fact that she could take out favorite books over and over again also made parting from them easier for her. Soon her parents made a book bank out of three-ply cardboard (in the shape of a book, naturally). When the bank was sufficiently filled, they made a special trip to the bookstore to buy one old favorite and one new book for keeps.

If you haven't cultivated the library habit, ask yourself why not. What were your childhood library experiences? Did the place seem austere and a little frightening? Did a stern librarian demand utter quiet so that you were afraid to turn pages? Or did no one teach you to find your way around, how to locate books you wanted? Did you feel so like a bull in a china shop that it was easier to depart than to stay?

If these impressions still linger, you'll be delightfully surprised at today's libraries. Your child will find warmth, friendliness, and an enticing feast of books to browse among.

Bookstores

Helping your children build their own personal book collections is an important long-term project. The decisions you make will depend to some extent on the costs of books and your budget, as well as family preferences. Oddly enough, in many parts of our nation it is harder to buy a good children's book than to borrow one from a library. However, there are a number of potential sources, the most obvious being one of the 14,000 retail general bookstores in the United States.

A few devote their efforts exclusively to children, but most have only a small juvenile section.

One of the easiest ways to find a good retail bookseller is to check your phone book or ask your local librarian to recommend one. When you find one you like, make friends with the sales staff. Once they see that you intend to be a regular customer, they may make special efforts to order books that are not currently in stock. Libraries, however, have books whose dates of publication go back a number of years, and some of them are either hard to find in stores or out of print altogether.

Other Sources

Most department stores have book sections, and many stationery stores, newspaper stands, and supermarkets have racks with children's books in cheaper paperback editions. Another excellent source of books is an annual school book fair. If your child's school doesn't hold one, you might encourage the P.T.A. to sponsor such an event. For help, write to the Children's Book Council (67 Irving Place, New York, N.Y. 10003) for Sarah Chokla Gross's useful pamphlet, *Planning a School Book Fair*.

Some good buys on books occasionally turn up at garage or white elephant sales, community fairs, and church bazaars. Then there is Aunt Jane's attic, or your own. If the mice haven't gotten there first, you may find some long-lost treasures to pass on to your child.

Paperback or Hardcover?

Many good books are available in both paperback and hardcover editions. Children are often attracted to the smaller, more portable paperbacks, perhaps because they look less formidable, and their lower prices offer more reading enjoyment for your money. On the other hand, paperbacks have what librarians call a relatively brief shelf life because of the cheaper bindings and grade of paper and ink. Most paperback editions of picture books are reprinted in reduced size, with some loss of clarity and aesthetic impact.

Perhaps the best approach to building a home collection would be to select for hardcover purchase the special books you know will be

handled over and over again with love, books you may want to preserve long enough for another generation to discover and enjoy.
Birthdays, Chanukah, or Christmas could be celebrated with the gift
of a hardcover book. Other purchases could be of paperback editions
that will be read once or twice, enjoyed throughly, and then passed
along or left on the shelf.

Grandparents and other older gift givers may be shocked at the rising cost of new children's books, but comparison shopping for toys or
the electronic marvels touted on TV—which start at around thirty
dollars—restores the balance. An elegant ten-dollar picture book will
probably last longer than a similarly priced toy, and be enjoyed over
and over. Books for older children often seem to be a better investment; adults are prone to believe they are getting more for their
money and may not be so reluctant to purchase them. But we can't
scrimp on the youngest child's needs; indeed, as we remember from
our own earliest days, books may make a deeper impression on the
very young than on any other age.

The Joy of Books

The wonderful thing about good children's books is that they do
not go out of style like fashions in clothes or TV toys. There is always
a new audience for *The Story about Ping*. And a good children's book is
versatile: it can be shared first as a look-at experience, second as a
read-aloud, then as a private read-to-yourself. Almost every family interest and activity can be enhanced through books—a trip to the zoo,
picnics on the beach, a quiet walk in the woods, a visit to grandma's, a
birthday party, a new pet. Matching reading with the rhythms of family life and feelings can open up new avenues of communication between parent and child.

Never underestimate your impact on the reading interests and
tastes of your children during their formative years. What you like
and find appealing they will strive mightily to enjoy. However, plenty
of books that they find alluring will not meet your standards. Seven-
year-old Greg, asked why he was renewing *Green Eggs and Ham* for the
umpteenth time, replied in a tone of resignation, "My mom and dad
won't read *any* Dr. Seuss to me at home. They say if I want to read
Green Eggs and Ham, I'll have to read it to myself. So that's what I'm
doing."

Reading with children is important, but so is sharing your reactions to books with them, including books that you are reading for pleasure yourself. Reading is a two-way communication, a creative act shared by author and reader. It is that special empathy, the discovery of common bonds between the self and others, that we must rediscover for ourselves in books if we want to share them with children in a joyful and meaningful context. A fourth-grader summed it up very well. "With a good book," he said, "it's just like somebody else was talking to me, telling me a story in my head, and if I like it, we're both making it up together."

The Dewey Decimal System

The Dewey Decimal System, invented in the late nineteenth century by Melvil Dewey, is the most commonly used method for cataloguing books in United States libraries. It is a handy road map for finding your way to topics of interest to you and your child. Fiction is generally classified alphabetically by author. In the nonfiction section, libraries that use the Dewey system number books this way:

100–199   Philosophy and Psychology
              People think about themselves: books on feelings and behavior.
200–299   Religion
              People think about God and the beginning of things: books on various religions, Bible, etc.
300–399   Social Sciences
              People think about other people—living and working together in social groups in cities, nations, etc. Includes books on government, careers, transportation, festivals and holidays, folk tales.
400–499   Language
              People learn to use words and to communicate: includes dictionaries, books on history of language.
500–599   Science
              People study and learn about the forces of nature: includes books on mathematics, astron-

omy, chemistry, physics, earth science, geology, biology and zoology.

600–699   Applied Science and Technology

People learn to use the forces of nature to make their lives more comfortable: includes books on tools, electronics, medicine and sex education, space travel, cooking, pets and domestic animals, etc.

700–799   Fine Arts and Recreation

People create art, music, and amusements: includes books, about sculpture, painting, architecture, dancing, sports, games, etc.

800–899   Literature

People from many countries create stories, poetry, and plays. (Most novels by American and British authors are in the fiction section.)

900–999   Geography and History

People describe the world around them and try to understand their own history by reconstructing past events: includes biographies and autobiographies—books about real heroes, people who have overcome obstacles and made contributions to society.

Reading Aloud: How and What to Choose

BETTY D. BOEGEHOLD

Reading aloud to your child is one of the best ways to prepare him or her for independent reading, and will create moments of shared pleasure in your busy days. Don't stop when they are old enough to read to themselves—being read to is always something special. Good advice, but not always easy to follow.

"What's really so great about reading to kids?" people ask. "They don't want to sit still or listen to anything but television." Other people may feel shy and uncertain. "I don't know how to read out loud," an uncle confessed. "I'm so used to reading to myself, I feel silly reading out loud. I stumble over words and I know my voice is a monotone— what kid would want to listen to me? Yet I'd like to read to my nephew and niece when they visit; I think it would be nicer than just looking at television together."

But reading to children *is* important, which is probably why it has been around so long. And it really can be fun for both you and your special child. It's a good bet that children will respond to the age-old custom.

But why are such experiences one of the best ways to prepare a young child for independent reading? The child specialists say that children must actively use their imaginations to picture the written events, rather than passively receiving changing images, as from television; that concentrating on language patterns imprints these rhythms on their own speech; that listening to the sequence of sentences and the development of plot line sharpens children's perception and understanding of "words in action"; and that children are

55

engaged in the inward processes of abstracting ideas, forming concepts, and expanding their horizons.

Aside from these impressive theories, some other important things are going on when you read to your child. First there's the joy of a shared experience; and second there's the value you are placing both on books and on the reading process. Equally important, the close physical and emotional contact creates an intimate bond between you and your child.

Of course the earlier you begin reading to a child, the easier it is for you. But the toddler may not want a regular story at first; he or she may want to sit on your lap and look through a magazine, pointing out to you the "kitties" or "daddies" therein. Photograph books are a great hit with this age, especially those that include small children or babies. And as they usually don't have a story line, it doesn't much matter if you look at them backwards, the usual way small children approach books.

"Told" Stories

For a child of one to two, the best stories are "told" stories, especially about the child himself (see "Storytelling," page 68). Small refrains about or accounts of the child's activities—"Johnny puts on his hat! Johnny puts on his shirt! Johnny puts on his shoe!"—bring delighted smiles. And when you deliberately misidentify the object, picking up Johnny's hat while saying, "Here is Johnny's shoe!" that smile turns into a broad grin. You've initiated your child into the world of humor.

Starting the Habit

However, most children seem ready to hear a "real" story, one with a beginning, middle, and end, any time from the first year up, whenever they have the necessary degree of patience to let the reader turn one page at a time, instead of ruffling through to look at favorite pictures. And they are ready to have a certain time of day as the "reading" time. This can be bedtime or after-bath time, or whatever fits best with your schedule. The important thing is that it be a time of relaxation; you shouldn't have to jump up to stir the stew or put toys away.

Sit as close to your child as you comfortably can—perhaps on the bed, or holding your child on your lap. Hold the book so you both can see the pictures. You may want to underline the text with your finger (going from left to right, the way we learn to read), if the child is interested in reading the words. One can ask questions about the pictures—"Where is that young mouse hiding?" "Which bear looks very cross?"—if they fit naturally into the mood and don't sound like catechizing. After the child knows the story, asking, "And what does the rabbit say next?" or, "Then what did the troll say?" gives a chance for the child to share in the reading process.

This is a great time for cuddling (though some children prefer to cuddle with a bear, blanket, or thumb; as in most matters, it's best to follow the child's lead), and it's a learning time for you as well as for the child. You'll get an insight as to what your child likes, what puzzles him or her, what concepts or misconcepts are forming in that charming head.

Over and Over

Almost always the young demand repetition. There you are, having a great time reading, say, *Goodnight Moon;* then, when you come to the triumphant conclusion and start to close the book, your child says, "Read it again." And again. Night after night.

Relax. This repetition is probably producing many of those results the experts predicted. And sooner or later, every child does want a change. So stick with it, enjoy your child's enduring interest—and you'll probably begin to discover why your child is fascinated by this story. A young father, reading Arnold Lobel's *Owl at Home* aloud for the umpteenth time, suddenly realized that the story was speaking to him as well as to his children. In one chapter Owl is trying to be upstairs and downstairs at the same time. The best he can achieve is sitting halfway up (or halfway down) the stairs. The father said rather ruefully, "I guess I'm like Owl—that's where I'm sitting." Of course his children demanded an explanation and this led to some new insights and interpretations of this seemingly simple little story.

And On and On

But what happens when your child learns to read? Doesn't the kid want to take the reins in his or her own hands now?

No. Please don't stop when someone is able to stagger through a first easy reader. Would you stop playing your recording of Beethoven when your child can play the scales? This is a great time to explore the finest of children's books together, stretching your minds and imaginations. Children are as intelligent and have the same wide range of emotions and aspirations as adults do; they just lack adult experience and store of knowledge. Children and adults can dip into the inspired wisdom of the great stories; and beyond the enjoyment you will share, just think of the language, the ideas, the insights, the human emotions you will both experience.

Books for Reading Aloud

Children learn best through their senses. A baby turns an object over and over, banging it, rolling it, biting it, shaking it; the baby needs to test his new experience by feel, touch, taste, hearing. This use of the senses is evident in the physical drive youngsters have to explore their world by climbing, running, tasting, pulling, etc. Thus a book that speaks in vivid verbs and similes, that explores how things look, sound, taste, is speaking directly to the child's own natural way of learning. The list below mentions books that use this method directly, but good writers for any age use the same language: a fresh, original choice of sensory images, to appeal to the child's equally fresh view and to reawaken our own forgotten visions.

Sensory Appeal

These books are centered on what we hear, see, feel, touch—sizes, shapes, colors, sounds, and feelings. We've tried to select those that offer more than a superficial scanning; some, indeed, have fine texts and are genuine classics.

> Margaret Wise Brown. *The Color Kittens,* Young Scott (Addison Wesley). Libraries and old books stores may carry this treasure; it is worth searching for. The text is lively and the pictures delightful, and the combination ex-

presses the joy youngsters take in discovering and mixing new colors.

_____. *The Noisy Book,* Harper & Row.

_____. *The Country Noisy Book,* Harper & Row.

_____. *Indoor Noisy Book,* Harper & Row.

_____. *Quiet Noisy Book,* Harper & Row.

_____. *Seashore Noisy Book,* Harper & Row.

_____. *Summer Noisy Book,* Harper & Row.

In the many "Noisy" books, a small dog named Muffin experiences the world through his senses. He is not able to use some of them for one reason or another, and thus must identify his surroundings in other ways. For instance, in the night he does not see clearly, so he must smell, hear, feel what is the object of his concern. Ms. Brown's inimitable poetic prose and Garth Williams's flowing pictures make these books a many-generational hit.

J. P. Miller and Katherine Howard. *Do You Know Colors?,* Random House paperback. This inexpensive book is fine for young children with its clean clear colors and simple direct pictures.

Lucille Ogle and Tina Thoburn. *I Hear: Sounds in a Child's World,* American Heritage. Appealing clear pictures, only two to a page, invite adults and their young children to use the book for sound and listening games. Suggestions for parents are included.

_____. *I Spy: A Picture Book of Objects in a Child's Environment,* American Heritage. Almost 400 objects are clearly pictured, with suggestions for using the book for games. The pictures are those within the experience of most very young children.

Virginia Allen Jensen and Dorcas Woodbury Haller. *What's That?,* Collins. This charming book designed for the sight-handicapped will intrigue all children and allow them the chance to "read" through other senses; a picture book with words but with shapes to explore and a plot to discover.

Tana Hoban. *Look Again,* Macmillan. Small cutouts showing

a bit of a covered photograph allow the child to guess the whole. This ant's-eye view fills us with wonder at the marvels around us.

———. *What Is It?* Macmillan.

———. *Shapes of Things,* Macmillan.

———. *Push Pull Empty Full,* Macmillan.

Other concept books by Hoban also use her marvelous photographs to extend children's visual concepts.

Barbara Brenner. *Faces,* Dutton.

———. *Bodies,* Dutton. With George Ancona's fine photographs and Ms. Brenner's equally fine text, children experience the variety of humanity's faces, colors, bodies, postures, and emotions. The visceral feeling of both text and art helps children identify with those other than themselves and strengthens their sense of belonging to the human race.

Poetry

Poetry is full of sensory language that speaks directly to the child's whole-body learning experiences. You may want to add some of your favorite poets to this list.

Eve Merriam. *Bam! Zam! Boom! A Building Book,* Walker and Company. Full of street and work noises, lively verse recreates the sounds that surround city children.

Delmore Schwartz. *"I Am Cherry Alive," The Little Girl Sang,* Harper and Row. A poetic celebration of childhood's sensory awareness of life, of "being me," illustrated by the celebrated Barbara Cooney.

Margaret Wise Brown. *Nibble, Nibble,* Addison Wesley. Poems full of sensory imagery and crisp rhythms.

Claudia Lewis. *Up and Down the River,* Harper and Row. Rich with imaginative images.

Mother Goose Most versions are illustrated with large bright pictures and are available in inexpensive editions. One fine edition is Random House's *Mother Goose Book,* illustrated by Alice and Martin Provensen. If you wonder why these old rhymes have pleased children for so many years when they don't always make sense to you, just read them aloud to the very young. Note their delight in the bouncy rhymes, the fascinating words. Children delight in word play, in strong rhythms and juicy words; Claudia Lewis in her book *Writing for Young Children* (Doubleday) calls these nonsense words "kribble krabble" (from Hans Christian Andersen's story, *The Marsh King's Daughter*): special kinds of nonsense syllables that sparkle in a child's imagination.

Look for the poems with "kribble krabble" as well as those that touch deeper feelings; you may find your child inventing "kribble krabble" too.

Self-Discovery

Young children are already fully engaged in discovering their own identity, their feelings, their fears and joys, and where they fit in the scheme of things. These books will help them find some of their own strengths, and your own explorations will probably find many more.

Margaret Wise Brown, *Goodnight Moon,* **Harper.** This small classic has captivated more young children than any other children's book. The slumbrous words, the felicitous rhymes, the fascinating pictures appeal to children as young as one year old, and even reach older autistic children. The book's secret may be that it depicts one kind of power than even the powerless young child may use—putting things and people away from you, instead of being taken away from them. The young rabbit in the book, instead of being "put away" to bed, is putting away the things in his room, becoming the master rather than the mastered!

Marie Hall Ets. *Play with Me.* Viking.

———. *In the Forest.* Viking.

———. *Gilberto and the Wind.* Viking. Ms. Ets' books have appealed to young children for many years; they mirror children's feelings, wishes and dreams.

Ruth Krauss. *The Carrot Seed.* Harper. An old favorite, spare but full of triumph for the smallest member of the family.

Ann Herbert Scott. *Sam.* McGraw Hill. The youngest member feels left out of family activities.

Lucille Clifton. *Everett Anderson's Year.* Holt, Rinehart. Children can identify with the daily happenings in a small black child's life.

Margaret Wise Brown. *The Runaway Bunny.* Harper. How the desire for independence conflicts with the desire for security. Children have strong reactions to the relationship of this bunny with his mother.

Norma Simon. *How Do I Feel?* Albert Whitman.

————. *What Do I Do?* Albert Whitman.

————. *What Do I Say?* Albert Whitman. These titles may sound slightly Victorian, but the books have a modern urban setting and charming pictures.

Arnold Lobel. *Owl at Home.* Harper & Row. Owl can show only or lonely children the fun and activities of solitariness.

H. A. Rey and/or Margaret Rey. The *Curious George* series. Houghton Mifflin. Children love the adventures of this lively little monkey because he does exactly what most children would like to do themselves.

Stephen Kroll. *That Makes Me Mad!* Pantheon. It helps to discover that you are not alone in having angry feelings and to be reassured that they won't last forever.

Betty Boegehold. *The Castle of Cats.* Unicorn Books, Dutton. A reassuring fantasy about the great adventure of leaving home someday.

Elsie Hoomelund Minarik. *Little Bear* series. Harper and Row. Gentle depiction of home life.

Jean Merrill. *The Elephant Who Liked to Smash Small Cars.* Scholastic. The difficulty of empathizing with others is delightfully resolved in this saucy little book.

Marjorie Flack. *The Story about Ping.* Viking. A Classic about the dangers and delights of being on one's own.

Maurice Sendak. *Where the Wild Things Are.* Harper & Row. A modern classic fantasy about triumphing over one's own internal "wild things" that children from five up want to hear again and again. This book may be too frightening for children younger than five; they may still not differentiate between reality and fantasy.

William Steig. *Sylvester and the Magic Pebble.* Simon & Schuster. A gripping story of loneliness and separation that has a most satisfying resolution.

Esphyr Slobodkin. *Caps for Sale.* Addison Wesley. A favorite folk tale. Young children identify with the teasing actions of the mischievous monkeys.

Judith Viorst. *Alexander and the Terrible, Horrible, No Good, Very Bad Day.* Atheneum. Children who experience the same off days that we all do, but are more devastated by them, will find relief in Alexander's misfortunes.

Friendship (and Other Relationships)

We often forget how difficult the process of making friends may be for a young child. Yet having a friend is a deep need of childhood; often the first friend is a stuffed toy, who won't reciprocate if clumsily treated.

Margaret Wise Brown. *The Golden Egg Book.* Golden. A fine, simple "first friendship" book for the youngest; in poetic yet spare text, it shows the loneliness of being by yourself, the satisfaction in finding another.

Miriam Cohen. *Will I Have a Friend?* Macmillan. A small child conquers his anxiety about his first school experience.

_____. *Best Friends.* Macmillan. Jim and Paul learn that, despite misunderstandings, they can still be friends.

Chihiro Iwasaki. *What's Fun Without a Friend?* McGraw Hill. The sadness of missing a puppy touches a responsive chord in young hearts.

Satomi Ichikawa. *Friends.* Parents. Beautiful illustrations and humorous text of what friends can do together.

Russell Hoban. *Best Friend for Francis.* Harper & Row. This

time, cheeky Francis has trouble holding on to a best
friend.

William Steig. *Amos and Boris*. Simon & Schuster. A whale
and a mouse prove that differences are irrelevant when
it comes to friendship and helping one another. The
language is just right for reading aloud.

Barbara Brenner. *Cunningham's Rooster*. Parents. Music inspired by friendship makes a book spiced with humor.

Betty Miles. *Around and Around—Love*. Knopf. A felicitous
text helps children recognize that love blooms in a variety of relationships; the pictures will be enjoyed by children eighteen months and up.

Arnold Lobel. *Frog and Toad Are Friends*. Harper & Row. All
the books in this series for beginning readers make fine
read-alouds too, and present an amusing, appealing picture of friendship. For once the young child knows
more than the protagonists in the book—a lovely feeling of superiority!

Phyllis Hoffman. *Steffie and Me*. Harper. Although the characters in this book of black and white friendship are
slightly older than the preschool audience, their lively
actions and true-to-life language and thoughts have
great appeal.

Joan Lexau. *Emily and the Klunky Baby and the Next-door Dog*.
Dial. Another "real" story that will appeal to youngsters
with younger siblings.

———. *Striped Icecream*. Dial. A family story for reading
aloud or learning to read.

Martha Alexander. *Nobody Asked Me if I Wanted a Baby Sister*.
Dial. The youngster in the story tries to give away his
baby sister. Children may deeply approve.

Betty Boegehold. *Pippa Mouse* series. Knopf. Pippa, a spunky
girl mouse, learns how and how not to treat friends.

Eveline Ness. *Sam, Bangs and Moonshine*. Holt, Rinehart. An
imaginative girl's fantasy lands her friend in real danger.

———. *Do You Have the Time, Lydia?* As an older sister races
from activity to activity, she forgets to help her younger
sibling.

Gunilla Wolde. *Tommy and Sara Dress Up.* Houghton Mifflin. Ms. Wolde's books appeal to the youngest children in their depiction of everyday life, friendships, and non-sexist activities.

Animals (Real and Imaginary)

Why are animals the main characters in so many books for young children, especially animals who act and dress very much like children? Many adults are not only puzzled but resentful. Why not have real children? Why these false pictures of animals who are really children in fur coats? Why not just have real children and real animals?

Some books do have real children and real animals. But others don't—and for some good reasons.

First, most young children identify closely with animals. Animals may seem less puzzling than people; certainly animals live more simply and often seem to enjoy just what young children enjoy. Pet animals are uncritical and never give orders. Their soft fur makes them comforting to hold.

Second, stories about animals represent one safe remove from reality. Peter Rabbit can be chased with evil design by a bewhiskered Mr. McGregor, but how frightening it would be if real children were being pursued to make a pie filling! A story of an abandoned or lost kitten can arouse catharsis and compassion in a child listener who might be terrified if the abandoned one was a child. And in less dramatic tales animals can still do many things forbidden to children, but which they can readily identify with.

Third, fictional animals usually exist in a world with no cultural mores, racial or ethnic identity, or sex biases. The child can freely relate to the actions, emotions, and feelings of the protagonist without the need to compare life styles.

And last of all, animal characters provide humor and zaniness in their take-offs on human ways; a child may have his or her first perception of the absurd when viewing taken-for-granted human activities enacted by animals.

A word to the wise: when choosing animal character books, look for those that also have the flavor of real animals; even though the characters represent "humans in fur coats," they shouldn't violate too strongly the prototype animal.

Many good animal stories have already been mentioned. Here are some others:

> Richard Scarry. *Best Story Book Ever.* Golden. Scarry's books are extremely popular with very young children. All his characters are animals; all have human jobs or pleasures. A must for children of four and up.
>
> Beatrix Potter. *The Story of a Fierce Bad Rabbit.* Warne.
> _____. *The Tale of Squirrel Nutkin.* Dover.
> _____. *The Tale of Two Bad Mice.* Dover.
> Young children should all have a chance to see, hold, and hear more of Beatrix Potter's classic tales than the famous Peter Rabbit. They are quaint but tough, which children appreciate.
>
> Jane Feder. *Beany.* Pantheon. Small clear pictures brighten this everyday story of a boy's love for his cat, told in "real-child" language.
>
> Alice and Martin Provensen. *Our Animal Friends at Maple Hill Farm.* Random House. Real animals in real activities but with lots of humor and great pictures.
>
> Michael Bond. *Paddington Bear.* Random House. The many books about this popular bear are preschool favorites.
>
> Robert McCloskey. *Make Way for Ducklings.* Viking. A classic favorite about real ducks finding their way in a real city, Boston.
>
> Don Freeman. *Corduroy.* Viking. For youngsters with a special affinity for Teddy bears, this is a lasting favorite.
>
> Leo Lionni. *Frederick.* Pantheon. This fantasy may give a young listener the first hint of the importance of art and imagination.
>
> Arnold Lobel. *Mouse Tales.* Harper & Row. Seven zany tales that children love.
>
> Barbara Seuling, *The Great Big Elephant and the Very Small Elephant.* Crown. Another "self-identity" discovery in the guise of two elephant adventures.
>
> Bernice Freschet. *Bear Mouse.* Putnam. Like all Ms. Freschet's books, this brings to vivid life one of the small creatures who share the earth.

Dr. Seuss. *The Cat in the Hat.* Random House. Another classic in the comic-strip mood. Every youngster should see it.

Norman Bridwell. *Clifford, the Big Red Dog.* Scholastic. Great fun with a pet dog who is bigger than a two-story house.

Edith Thacher Hurd. *The Mother Deer.* Little, Brown. In a series of "Mother" books Ms. Hurd depicts the lives of wild animals in simple, beautiful prose.

Steven Kellogg. *Pinkerton, Behave!* Dial. Children will delight in the Great Dane Pinkerton's first schooling and will identify with his nonconformist approach.

Susan Bonners. *Panda.* Dial. Soft-as-fur water colors illuminate this gentle account of a real panda.

Howard Knotts. *Winter Cat.* Harper. A realistic story of a stray cat and concerned youngsters, simply told.

Margaret Wise Brown. *The Dead Bird.* Addison Wesley. This classic, beautiful but composed, reflects the way children begin to explore the facts of death.

Judith Viorst. *The Tenth Good Thing About Barney.* Atheneum. A more personal experience of grieving—the death of a pet. A gentle tale that helps youngsters undergo this sad event.

This list is the merest beginning. As you and your child compile your own, these criteria will help:

Does the book speak to the child's interests?

Is the language vivid, but simple?

If nonfiction, is the information correct, simple enough to grasp?

Does it appeal to you too?

If fiction, does the story move right along with plenty of action?

Would your child identify with the hero?

Do *you* like the theme?

If all these questions can be answered affirmatively, your choice is probably a good one, whether the book costs a lot or a little. A book that speaks to a child's deep need, that offers reassurance, or that brings the special magic only books can create, may have an effect on your child that is lifelong.

Storytelling

CLAUDIA LEWIS

For the Love of a Story

Why tell stories to children when it's so much easier to read them aloud out of a book?

Don't we all begin as storytellers with our infants when we chant, "This little pig went to market, this little pig stayed home"? Or when we repeat with our preschoolers those nursery rhymes—actually small stories—that we all learned as children?

Think of those little narratives that come so naturally in the course of a day with a very young child: "This arm goes in this sleeve. Now this arm in the other. There we are. Here we go. Debbie's going with Mommy out to the store—"

Of course these aren't the full-blown stories children want to hear later on, but they are the narrative beginnings that not only give delight but encourage participation. How easy to join in on "Down we go, down we go," "Home again, home again," or catchy, funny words like "Mumble grumble," "Hoity-toity"—all offering repetitions that help children learn to talk well.

Still, why tell a story like *Chicken Little* or *The Little Red Hen* or a fairy tale when it's written so well in the book?

There are a few reasons. First, people tend to talk more naturally than they read aloud. Reaching a child across a book may be harder than through direct contact, eye meeting eye and a natural voice speaking. And of course it is through direct contact—face-to-face telling and laughing and enjoying—that we establish the bond that enriches story time for both child and adult.

Those of us who have listened to good storytellers know that this is an experience unlike any other: close to being in the theater but even more spellbinding. The story characters take on life; we are transported into the background scene; we are there, listening, living, feeling. When children have this experience it can propel them into a love of story, of language, of searching out stories in books. Perhaps, too, seeing and hearing an adult venture without a book into imagination's vast arena offers an incentive to children to become storytellers themselves. Sometimes these are accounts of happenings wonderful to remember:

> When we went to the park today we had so much fun!
> We played with mud and then we rolled in the grass
> and we were running up and down the hills
> and we had so much fun that we always felt like skipping
>   down the hill again.
> We were running like little cats down the hills. . . .

Sometimes flights of imagination related to a picture just painted:

> It's a dark and stormy night
> and the moon is shining bright,
> while the frog ribbits to the moon.

Some are stories with plots and characters that represent the emotional complexities a child is trying to deal with. The following story, dictated by a six-year-old girl, expresses some kind of burden or dread that is demanding relief. It is easy to surmise that a measure of relief, or belief in a happy outcome, was found just through the satisfying effort of inventing the right symbols, and organizing and telling such a completely rounded little story:

Timmy the Tugboat
Once upon a time there lived a little tugboat and he had a mother and father. But he couldn't pull a boat. One day he saw a fairy but that wasn't a real fairy. That was a witch and the witch took him away and he didn't know—he kept walking backer and backer and he thought he was walking home. And when he got to the witch's house he was scared because the witch wasn't really a fairy. Before he thought she

was a fairy and when they got there the witch said, "I will kill you, if you don't pull a hundred tugboats at one time." He knew he couldn't pull that many boats and then right before his eyes a hundred tugboats came. He tried to pull them and he could because a fairy was helping him.

The fairy appeared before his eyes and then the fairy said, "The witch must be turned into a rock." And so the witch turned into a rock and then he lived happily ever after.

There are innumerable testimonials to the importance of the story that is spontaneously told. Parents often manage to sooth restlessness, either at home or on a trip, by telling, not reading, a story. And there are times when a book simply is not available. Suspense, crackling word-sounds, and an imaginary character who quickly jumps into action—these are some of the simple ingredients that are just right for young children. And they are the ingredients that can make the first attempts at spontaneous storytelling very easy for the beginner. Almost any adult in a playful mood can pull suspense and a few magical word sounds out of the air and build them into a story with the smallest of plots involving no more, say, than

> losing and finding
> trying and succeeding
> going away and coming back

So much the better if the imaginary character is an animal, easy for children to identify with and to love, but with the safety of a little distance away from the character's troubles, mistakes, or misdeeds. And equally effective is the personal story that is simply telling about something that once happened to you as a child—something exciting, mysterious, wonderful. Plenty of room for suspense here, too, and for repetitions, guessing, and words that are fun.

If any of this sounds difficult, remember that the very young child is most receptive and will welcome anything you try—literally anything that has the slightest suggestion of a story in it. Begin with the youngest children, stumbling if you must, and find yourself growing with your listeners. They will support and encourage you every step of the way.

Of course we don't stop reading aloud to young children the beautiful picture books with their short tales of laughter and friendship, wonder and discovery; or to older children E. B. White's *Charlotte's Web* or Scott O'Dell's *The Island of the Blue Dolphins,* and a great many other books that an adult can help a child savor. But sometimes we also drop the book—no matter what age the child—and venture out, and *tell* a story.

Books about Storytelling

Bauer, Caroline Feller. *Handbook for Storytellers.* American Library Association, 1977.

Carlson, Bernice. *Listen! And Help Tell the Story.* New York: Abingdon, 1965.

Ross, Ramon R. *Storyteller.* New York: Charles E. Merrill, 1972.

Sawyer, Ruth. *The Way of the Storyteller.* New York: Viking, 1942.

Reading Just for Fun

SEYMOUR V. REIT

This is the story of how a knotty problem was solved when a purse fell off a table.

A young woman volunteered to help some eleven- and twelve-year-olds with their reading in an after-school program. But after weeks of struggle the three girls in her group still failed to respond. No matter how much Ann tried to interest them in the books supplied by the remedial reading counselor, their attention wandered, they talked and giggled and were obviously just plain bored. Ann was in despair and ready to give up when, in the middle of another frustrating session, she knocked her purse on the floor and it spilled open. Glad for the distraction, the girls rushed to help her pick everything up and were instantly fascinated. Ann was attractive, personable, well dressed—a model whom the girls yearned to emulate—and the things in her purse were automatically of interest to them. In no time they were reading, or trying to read, what they had picked up—a brochure from a beauty shop, a recipe for chocolate brownies, a driver's license, and so on. Ann, recognizing her opportunity, went over each of these items with the girls, who were suddenly and for the first time deeply involved in the reading process.

From then on Ann brought to her sessions things such as clippings from fashion magazines, TV reviews and articles, recipes, menus, beauty and make-up brochures, small boxes with interesting labels. She had particular success with a letter from a friend who had gone with her husband to work in North Africa. Even a bus timetable proved of interest; the girls had never had the opportunity to examine one.

The purse opened the way to an important learning dimension. Most children, even poor readers, will enjoy reading something if it is relevant to their own concerns. Naturally, the material has to be simple enough, and roughly within their decoding capacities, but motivation is all-important. *Success is easier when the interest is high.*

As Dr. Jane Ervin, an expert on the reading problems of children, writes,

> You will find, if you use your child's special interests as a vehicle for teaching him, or even getting him to do something he doesn't want to do, you will have much greater success. If you want to improve his reading comprehension and he is mad about football, go and get him an autobiography of a football star.*

Do you have an avid reader in your household, who latches on to almost anything that comes along? Or are your kids indifferent or hostile toward reading? Do they read—if at all—in spurts? Do they count on the TV set for all their fun and information? Kids—like their parents—come in different shapes and sizes, mentally as well as physically. But the potentialities are always present. If your children don't read as well or as much as you think they should, don't despair. There are ways to help them.

The simplest route, of course, is by example. Kids in homes where books are valued and plentiful—and read for the sheer fun of it—usually develop similar interests. Their special tastes, interests, and preferences can serve as handy springboards. Is your child a sports fan? Try a subscription to a good sports magazine. Are cars important? Many publications are available. Do you have a fledgling cook in the family? Cookbooks are the obvious answer. And of course there are myriad "how-to" books that cover everything from health and beauty tips to hobbies and crafts. Don't be hesitant to share this material as well as provide it. Look up sports statistics with your youngster, try a recipe from a cookbook, help build the model airplane.

---

* Dr. Jane Ervin, *Your Child Can Read and You Can Help* (New York: Doubleday, 1979, p. 19).

One ten-year-old with no interest at all in books developed a great interest in camping and scouting. Encouraged by his parents, he soon began thumbing through the Scout manual and was soon reading it avidly. In addition to example and motivation, availability is another basic factor, and the boy's parents had made the manual available.

Our end goal is to establish a good relationship with books, but children approach this goal by various routes. At a certain point many kids read nothing but comic books, and devour them voraciously. Some comics, heavy on violence, are admittedly atrocious, while others are harmless and quite entertaining. Among the popular ones are "Tin-Tin" and the "Charlie Brown" series. Younger children enjoy "Casper," "Bugs Bunny," and the various Disney creations. For preteens, the "Archie" series is acceptable; these comics generally present wholesome situations and emphasize decent values.

Alan Fern, Director of Special Collections at the U.S. Library of Congress, likens comic books to the old medieval "block-book." He points out that the technique of drawing people, with words in baloons to represent speech or thoughts, and arranging these pictures in story sequence, goes all the way back to the fifteenth century. This technique has been adapted to modern adult themes by author-artists such as Jules Feiffer and Shel Silverstein.

Because they are highly visual and use dialogue exclusively, comics appeal to children in the same way that photographs with short, lively captions appeal to adults. There are also comics which "reinterpret" classics such as *Moby Dick, Call of the Wild,* and *Treasure Island.* Certainly these aren't a "pure" form of literature, but such illustrated stories often stimulate young readers to delve deeper into specific subjects and authors.

Of course it's up to adults to monitor comic-book material and exercise a reasonable degree of control. But the most important thing is to remain flexible.

In addition to the beloved comics, some children go through phases in which nothing interests them but humor magazines—*Dynamite, Bananas, Mad*—TV fan magazines, or joke books. Sometimes the only reading seems to be what's on the box of morning cereal. But even that can fortify the habit of reading and, with tact, be expanded into other areas.

Surveys show that quite a few youngsters hooked on *Star Wars* and similar space movies have gone on to become fans of science fiction. One father whose child developed this interest made a habit of sharing a chapter of a good sci-fi book with her every evening. Father and daughter took turns reading, and the ritual become so enjoyable that they're now on their fifth book.

Think back to your own pattern, to the time in your growing years when you began to discover the pleasure of "real" books. Some of today's most dedicated readers were weaned on pulp magazines such as *Flying Aces* and *Dime Western*. Others read series books such as "Tarzan," "The Bobbsey Twins," and "Bomba the Jungle Boy," with their high excitement and cliff-hanger chapter endings. However banal and simplistic, those stories helped nurture a love of reading which grew into an abiding interest in genuine literature.

The psychiatrist S. L. Warner and his collaborator, Edward Rosenberg, in their book *Your Child Learns Naturally,* point out that the word *learning* comes from the Latin word *lira*, which means a furrow in which seeds are planted. "Learning," they say, "means every kind of activity that results in a change, from the development of the first muscle skills to the highest intellectual accomplishments. Learning is as natural as growing. Parents can facilitate it or interfere with it."*

As parents, we can help or hinder the discovery of reading for fun. By setting examples, providing motivation, making suitable books and magazines available, remaining flexible, accepting our children's own reading pace, and sharing their interests with them, we can help them find the joys inherent in the printed word.

---

* Silas L. Warner and Edward B. Rosenberg, *Your Child Learns Naturally* (New York: Doubleday, 1976).

Part 3

LIVING WITH CHILDREN AND TELEVISION

Of all the subjects covered in this book, perhaps none is as complex or as ubiquitous as television, a relatively new factor which has profoundly influenced modern family living.

The Bank Street College of Education has been involved in television for many years, both in preparing special children's TV materials and as educational consultant to major networks. In pursuing this role and responsibility, the college staff has developed some principles and content guidelines that we hope will be helpful to parents and other people responsible for children's use of television. These principles are outlined in the following chapter and practical, painless ways to use them at home are given in the subsequent ones.

The Electronic Member of the Family

WILLIAM H. HOOKS

The Bank Street philosophy is that "education" refers to the "whole child"—his or her physical, mental, emotional, and social development—and that children and adults together are a community of learners. Therefore we are deeply concerned with the effects of the communications media within the family. Of all the media, television is, for better or worse, a prime "educator." These guidelines are our ways of analyzing programs designed for children, as well as the many other programs they watch.

Physical Violence

We are concerned with the obvious form of violence that manifests itself in *physical violence:* harm which is inflicted upon persons, property, or the environment. It is not our aim to merely eradicate all evidence of violence, since this would be a denial of reality; but rather to consider this form of violence in context. If the violence is used clearly as a dramatic example for what should *not* be done, and clear, negative consequences are demonstrated as resulting from such violence, we would in all likelihood not suggest deletion. But gratuitous violence is always unacceptable; as is the glorification of brutal acts or characters. We are particularly concerned that violent characters in children's shows are not made attractive to viewers.

Violence to the environment through carelessness, neglect, or willful intent concerns us, particularly the attitude expressed in children's

79

shows about these matters. We want children to grow up to be aware, concerned adults, realizing that they live on a small, finite planet that must be treated with great respect.

There is a special category of comedic physicality in animated shows for children which may or may not spill over into the area of unacceptable violence. With the magic and fantasy elements of animation, characters often fall, crash, bang, and splatter for laughs. Here again each action must be examined in its particular context; but in general we find acceptable those actions which do not appear *hurtful*. If a cartoon character falls from a plane and splatters to the ground in a flattened shape with an accompanying sound track of canned laughter to indicate this is meant to be funny, we could consider this objectionable despite the fact that the animation artist resuscitates the character in the next frames. However, if an animated character is established as able to reshape itself and then pour through a keyhole to re-form on the other side of the door, we would find such action acceptable. In general, we do not support the actions of characters, animated or live, who are deliberately put through hurtful actions with the intention of humor.

Emotional Violence

Emotional violence is a subtler but perhaps even more important matter. It is here that implicit messages about behavior come into play. The simple question "What is this show saying to children?" should always be asked. With a sensitive application of this question, one can determine whether violence is being done to the emotional development of children. We are especially concerned with the language and actions of characters as they relate to each other. If the characters tend to denigrate people and things, or to contribute to a diminution of positive self-image, the dialogue or action is destructive.

Language and actions that denigrate physical attributes, intellectual capability, or one's cultural or social background are primary concerns. Such negative language when attractively packaged stands a good chance of youthful emulation; and the power of such usage in television, as in print, is that for the child the medium sets a seal of approval on this usage. Often these denigrations have settled into classic stereotypes which have traditionally been used for humor, without regard to the effects of the humor. "Fat lady" and "four-eyed egghead kid" jokes are examples of denigrating physical attributes; put-downs of the mental capacities of "natives" or "dumb blondes" illustrate the intellectual concerns; and insensitive references to ethnic backgrounds or home conditions for the sake of a laugh are absolutely out of bounds for our new generations of viewers.

Along these same lines we have concerns about some traditional uses of imagery. For example, the color black has long been used to denote what is sinister, evil, frightening, etc.; nevertheless, it is now known that this constant referencing does something damaging to children who are black. The same applies to yellow, red, and brown to lesser degrees. All stereotyped referencing must be carefully examined to insure that no segment of our population is being treated in a derogatory manner.

Sex Roles

Sex-role factors are linked to emotional and even physical violence. Here too we look for ego strengthening and the building of a positive self-image. Girls should not be relegated to passive traditional family- and child-related roles, but neither should these roles be neglected. Boys should not be made to feel inadequate or uncomfortably different if they do not fit the traditional male role prescriptions. A whole range of options should be covered in any well-balanced network grouping of children's programs. The guiding principle is not to pass along to young children the restrictive taboos which in the past have often denied equality to both sexes, or have encouraged stereotypical behavior.

Role Models

A great deal of role modeling has to do with sex, but there are also other important areas. In our pluralistic society it is essential to provide adequate role models for *all* our children. There is an implicit but strong message to children who never see (or too infrequently see) their own kind (color, sex, ethnic background) in roles they can regard as positive, favorable, and indicative of leadership. It is not enough simply to be included, the more important question is how the role is portrayed.

Age Appropriateness

We need to look at television for children in terms of its appropriateness for the developmental stages of the particular child. Since viewership is broad based, and invariably cuts across more than a single developmental stage, this appropriateness has to be centered— with some loss at either end of the age range. In judging appropriateness we look at such factors as language, content, and concepts. We are seeking content which entertains children, and which informs them in ways that are open-minded, fair, and caring.

Respect

"Respect" is a catchall term that relates to all the categories we have discussed, an overarching principle to be applied to all children's shows. It pulls together all our discrete concerns, and its cumulative effect is a major factor in establishing moral and ethical value systems.

Some of the major "respects" are:

Respect for the individual
Respect for differences
Respect for religious beliefs
Respect for cultural backgrounds
Respect for ethnic qualities
Respect for all animal life
Respect for the environment
Respect for private property
Respect for public property
Respect for moral values—one's own and those of others
Respect for feelings and sensitivities of others
Respect for oneself

The Great American Tube Challenge

SEYMOUR V. REIT

You may recall reading about the Luddites, working people who rioted throughout the industrial centers of England in the early 1800s, breaking into factories and smashing machinery. The Luddites believed, quite sincerely, that British technology would wreck the fabric of their lives and would, by doing away with manual skills and labor, cause vast unemployment.

The Luddites never got very far; the Industrial Revolution had obviously come to stay, and people soon realized that problems had to be solved not by smashing machines but by effectively harnessing them. In due time, of course, technology added far more jobs than it ever destroyed, and in the process raised living standards for millions everywhere.

Today we face a host of similar bugaboos—and one in particular worries all parents concerned with the welfare of their children. Boob tube, idiot box, one-eyed monster—whatever you call it, the fact is that television in the modern world, like the dreaded machinery of the Luddites, is here to stay. Attitudes toward this great new force range from indifference to irritation, from despair to a furious desire to pull the plug on the whole thing. Some people hail the tube as the greatest invention since the wheel. Some look on it as a nightmare, spewing out endless mental junk food. And others (including many parents) have more or less surrendered to the tube with an "if you can't lick 'em, join 'em" viewpoint. The TV set is accepted passively in these homes as a built-in kid sitter, and little if any effort is made to monitor programs or control viewing hours.

But experts now believe that, between these various extremes, there's a solution to the Great American Tube Challenge. Teachers, psychologists, educators, and social scientists are discarding their early negative attitudes and accepting the fact that TV can be a valuable tool—one to be shared and enjoyed creatively by both parents and their children.

Eda LeShan, a noted educator and family counselor, wrote recently of television, "Selective turning on is just as important as selective turning off. Television has added a rich dimension to the lives of our children." She added that "television can and does open windows on the world. It can stimulate wonder and curiosity; it can help young people gain a broader perspective and clarify their own goals. It can invite the mind to new adventures."*

Certainly the medium, good or bad, is a major factor in today's family life. There are now TV sets in 73 million households, which means that well over 200 million Americans—97 percent of our total population—have access to what the networks offer. According to surveys, many families average between three and six hours every day in front of the TV set, and some children spend more time watching the tube than they do in any other activity except sleeping.

Excessive, certainly, and hardly helpful to a child's healthy growth and development. The best answer, according to the experts, is simple, though not easy: parental guidance and discretion. No parent would let a youngster eat nothing all day but candy bars, or play in the middle of a highway, or toss lighted matches around the house. Children obviously need—and deeply depend on—rules and regulations set by parents and other caregivers. We teach our kids at an early age how to dress themselves, how to brush their teeth, how to use knives and forks at the table. We make sure they get adequate sleep, fresh air, a nourishing diet. We encourage them to study, to learn and grow. All these things—vital parts of every child's protective environment—happen almost automatically; but for some reason the tube (until recently) has been largely exempt from rule making. Eda Le-Shan comments, "It is hard to know just why parents allow a kind of anarchy where television is concerned that they do not allow in any

---

* Eda LeShan, "Wanted: Parents Who Are in Charge," in *3 to Get Ready,* (New York: Bank Street College of Education, 1978). Reprinted by permission.

other area. . . . My guess is that it has something to do with the fact that the television set is there in the house, that the programs are free, and as a baby-sitter, it seems quite irresistible."

Fortunately, the laissez-faire tide is turning. Mothers and fathers are beginning to take charge of the one-eyed monster, beginning to set firm limits, and to monitor what their kids are watching on TV. Through organizations such as Action for Children's Television adults are also letting the networks know when they are angry or dissatisfied with the quality and content of the programs.*

But meeting the TV challenge goes beyond that. Instead of being quietly exploited by the medium, parents are learning how to become the exploiters—how to turn this powerful and exciting tool into a real asset. To achieve this, A.C.T. recommends T.L.C.:

> *T*alk about TV with your child.
> *L*ook at TV with your child.
> *C*hoose TV programs with your child.

A.C.T. has taken a strong stand against violence, sexism, and other antisocial TV factors, but its attitude toward content is realistic, moderate, and full of common sense. Peggy Charren, its director, says, "It's relatively irresponsible in this day and age to tell a child not to watch any TV—there are a lot of good programs." The approach she favors is limiting the number of hours a child watches television— perhaps to seven hours a week instead of the average of twenty-five or more. But she adds, "Be flexible about it. If there's something really special, add that to the seven hours. Don't let the rules run your lives."

Another strategy might be called the "three S" approach: *selectivity,*

---

* A.C.T. was launched in Boston by parents who wanted to improve the nature and quality of what their children were offered on television. It now has branches in almost every state in the Union, as well as Canada, Mexico, Australia, and Japan. It sends representatives to congressional hearings and FCC meetings, and floods TV network bosses and advertisers with mail and phone calls. Largely because of its efforts, the commercial message time on children's programs has been cut almost in half; the host or hostess on children's programs (therefore an authority figure) cannot be used to sell the sponsor's products; and advertising of vitamins and other candy-coated pills to children is no longer permitted. A.C.T. is now battling to cut back on the advertising of heavily sugared breakfast cereals, candy, and other sweets which are harmful to youngsters. For information or membership, write to Action for Children's Television, 46 Austin Street, Boston, Massachusetts 02160.

supervision, and *sharing.* By being selective, and by supervising the use of the set, we can help our children separate the TV wheat from the chaff. And by sharing what the tube offers, we can enjoy the real magic of television. Sharing a program with one's youngsters turns the passive act of tube watching into a dynamic process, opening new channels of communication between adult and child. It can help to allay a child's fears and provide answers to questions. Sharing can also inspire family projects that grow out of what has been seen on the tube.

Does this mean that a parent has to sit through endless Saturday morning cartoons, watching sly mice outwit imbecile cats or super-heroes fly through the air to foil mad scientists? Decidedly not. And let's face it—the mediocre kiddie fare pouring from the tube in the morning hours is part of our children's world. Kids as well as adults need "escape," and watching this type of show (in moderation) is a harmless enough form of relaxation. This is particularly true now that the networks, thanks to both public pressure and self-regulation, are making an effort to eliminate violence and sexism and to rule out objectionable commercials. Of course if you do have a spare hour on a Saturday, it's an excellent idea to sit in front of the set with your youngster and monitor some of the programs. You may find food for discussion, and in any case you'll have a better idea of what he or she likes to watch. Keep in mind that Saturday morning TV, for today's kids, is pretty much what pulp-magazine fiction was to children of an earlier generation. Like bubble gum, it's totally without nourishment and fairly harmless if taken in small doses.

But the important part of sharing—and the fun—does mean a bit more work for parents. Just as we plan dinner parties, outings, and other events, the art of TV sharing also requires a certain amount of planning. It means checking TV listings regularly, scanning the daily ads, and earmarking appropriate programs. It means offering children options to the usual junk fare. Every network now has special "flagship" programs for kids, prepared with very high levels of content and quality. There are also superb dramas and documentaries well worth the attention of the whole family. Yes, time can be a problem, but time is also a vital factor in meeting the tube challenge. Why not let the dishes go, postpone phone calls or household chores, and sit down to enjoy a special program together?

The results of this kind of selective sharing can far exceed your expectations. Besides the pleasure of sharing, a good TV show helps youngsters develop what some educators call their "viewing skills." In these days of high nonlinear communication, the new art of looking is second only to the venerable, cherished art of reading, requiring the ability to sort out and decode the moving image as well as the printed word. And a shared program can open channels of exchange in a smooth, effortless way. A recent program on adoption, for example, sparked many solid discussions between parents and their adopted offspring, conversations which might not have taken place without the crucial TV springboard. Similar programs deal with knotty subjects such as race, sex, nuclear power, ecology, and divorce; and of course such series as *Roots* are a gold mine of good discussion possibilities.

Science documentaries are also fun to watch together, and can spark new activities. One little girl, after watching a Jacques Cousteau underwater drama, was so excited she used her birthday money to start her own tropical fish tank. Documentaries dealing with outer space have led kids to take an active interest in astronomy, with family visits to museums and planetariums. Television of this sort gives our children a chance to peek through fascinating "windows on the world" and to share with us what they find.

Any approach to TV must of course be flexible, and worked out according to the needs of each family. A few simple tips may be of help:

Discuss the week's TV listings with your child or children. Offer options, draw out their own preferences, steer them if necessary toward worthwhile programs. For example, "This show on dolphins looks interesting; let's watch it."

Plan ahead of time. Build up a sense of anticipation. It's a good idea to arrange your home schedule in advance, just as you would for a movie or a party: "We're going to have dinner early tonight, so we'll be ready for our program by seven o'clock."

On occasion, try steering the table talk to TV. Along with "What did you do today?" you might ask, "What did you watch on television this morning?"

After a good program, discuss it. Ask your youngsters what they thought of it, and welcome their opinions. Encourage discrimination by comparing the show with others. What did the child like or dislike about it? Why?

Such discussions can be priceless tools. Use this chance to communicate, to sort out and clarify moral and ethical points. Were there heroes in the show? Did people act kindly and lovingly toward one another? Were violence and hatred portrayed? Talk about these things to make sure your kids know how to sort out the good from the evil. Help them to express themselves and to build their own value structures. Even poor, bad, or violent shows can thus be turned to advantage.

Use these discussions as springboards to other activities. Depending on the age of your child, this may involve taking a book out of the library, drawing pictures, writing a fan letter, starting a scrapbook or a new hobby. The possibilities are endless since TV is, as educators have noted, an amazingly strong motivator.

These suggestions aren't meant to gloss over the serious excesses of television. The psychologist Werner Halpern reports that many of his young patients who are hyperactive are heavy viewers of TV, drawn especially to programs with fast-paced formats and loud music and voices. Other studies have found that frenetic action and some detective shows tend to make children's behavior more aggressive and more antisocial, even at the nursery level. Some experts say that much of television is "too much, too fast, too loud."

Such charges further emphasize how vital it is for parents to become personally involved in what their children see on TV. Television is a "loaded" medium that requires adult guidance. But it's also a simple reality of life, and its value as a learning tool is enormous. One recent survey found that in the nine-to-eleven age group, 83 percent can correctly identify the President of the United States, 36 percent can identify Martin Luther King, and 24 percent know about the Equal Rights Amendment. These are surprisingly high averages for young children.

Many surveys report that TV is children's favorite source of information, followed closely by books, then movies and newspapers. Contrary to popular belief, TV doesn't always take the place of reading; in a broad-based sample of 1,156 kids, 79 percent said that they also read and enjoyed books. And the children added that they enjoy watching TV much more when their parents participate. Clearly the little box is part of modern life, and it can be either tyrant or servant.

The problem is soluble and the benefits are tangible. Properly used, TV can help our kids learn how to communicate, how to sort out values, how to cheer the good and reject the inferior. It opens up boundless worlds, quite unavailable to earlier generations. So the solution is not simply to pull the plug, but to monitor programs and to share the viewing experience.

And Now a Brief Message—

A friend tells the story of going to church with his young son. Russ was intrigued with the minister, who gave a short, lively sermon complete with dramatic flourishes. On the way out he said, "Dad, the minister sure gave a good commercial."

Like or dislike the fact, the truth is that TV commercials are part of every child's—and every adult's—social landscape. The average youngster sees about 25,000 commercials a year, and children's commercials cost advertisers some $400 million annually.

The sales pitches that bombard us (except on public and educational channels) have been called "the best shows on television"—and with good reason. The finest and most expensive talent in the media goes into those audiovisual dramas, the country's top actors, directors, animators, song writers and cameramen. The result is lively, tuneful, often highly entertaining—and very hard to resist.

How can parents and caregivers help children cope with all this pressure to consume or buy this, that, and the other thing? Again the solution calls for time, patience, and genuine adult involvement.

Taming the commercial gorgon involves a two-pronged effort, one *internal* and the other *external*. Internally, it means changes in the television industry itself, brought about by public pressure on network policy makers, the sponsors who foot the bills, and government regulatory agencies. Today, for example, the Federal Communications Commission requires a short introduction (known in the industry as a "bumper") for each commercial, a brief change of pace which in effect says to the child, "This isn't part of the show you've been watching, but a separate message from an advertiser." For younger viewers, such a separation is important.

Externally, it means tackling the problem in the home—at the receiving end. It means alerting our kids, raising their consciousness, so that they can handle TV pressures. "I.D." is shorthand for identification—and our kids need mental I.D. cards, first to gain *I*nsight, and then to *D*iscriminate.

Insight is especially important for very young viewers. Does your youngster really understand what a commercial is and what it's for? Does he or she realize that it's simply a method of selling? That, no matter how tuneful or entertaining, it is no different from a billboard poster or a printed ad in a newspaper or magazine? This kind of knowledge, simple but necessary, can give kids a better perspective. It can detach them from the "fun" part of a commercial and help them to judge what is being said.

Insight also enables us to reinforce our own personal and family values, and to remind our kids of what we consider important. TV commercials are totally "thing oriented." They deliver topheavy doses of materialism, urging us to constantly use more and buy more. To counter this kind of subtle brainwashing, we can remind our youngsters—and ourselves—of our real values, reiterating that the latest toy/game/candy bar/breakfast food/eighty-speed bike isn't really the magic answer to everything.

Modern advertising agencies use elaborate market research and expensive testing methods to make their sales messages irresistible. That's why discrimination is also required. Can your child tell a truthful message from an exaggerated or slanted one? Does he or she pick up the underlying theme of the commercial? No, it isn't easy, but it can be done with a little guidance from us.

Educators Dorothy and Jerome Singer point out that parents need to take a more active role in helping children understand that commercials are often inaccurate and sometimes misleading. The Singers recommend "a certain amount of watching of children's television and monitoring of commercials, so that the adult can talk with some authority to the child about these issues."*

For parents this sometimes means walking on thin ice. We don't want always to be heavies, constantly denying our kids the pleasures

---

* Dorothy and Jerome Singer, *Partners in Play* (New York: Harper and Row, 1977).

and playthings that they think they want so badly. It isn't enough to say, "No, you can't have that," or, "We have enough junk in the house." Kids are entitled to simple, fair reasons for our decisions. It helps them to discriminate when we explain that a certain cereal is bad for their teeth and can lead to cavities, or simply that a particular toy is too expensive or a certain game much like the one he or she already has and rarely uses. Postponing is also a form of discrimination: "Let's keep this in mind for your next birthday," or "Why not put that on your Christmas list?"

The Singers warn: "Simply to pooh-pooh whatever appears on commercials creates confusion for children. They are too young to be exposed to a cynicism that they can scarcely comprehend, and which may instead create a feeling in them that their parents are negatively oriented."

We adults have to be inventive, but we can encourage understanding by being fair and explicit, and by using good plain common sense.

One young mother fought back in her own effective way. Her eight-year-old seemed to want every plaything he saw advertised on the tube. She knew that most of these were cheaply made, that the claims were unreal, that the toys would prove very disappointing. But she wanted Peter to find out for himself. The youngster had saved his birthday money plus other small sums earned at household chores. A decision was made that he could buy any toy he wanted, provided he used his own money. Peter, delighted, promptly sent away for an elaborate plastic item—which predictably broke after three days of use. Several weeks later he tried again, and the second toy also quickly bit the dust. Peter, wiser if poorer, is now much more discriminating. He's learning what he really wants and expects for his money.

Does this mean that all commercials for children are necessarily bad? Not at all. Many of them—responding to consumer demands— offer valuable messages showing kids how to eat balanced breakfasts, or practice good dental hygiene. Many of these little dramas offer rich role models, showing helpful interaction between children and adults or children and their peers.

But our kids do need guidance, and perhaps the best rule-of-thumb is an adaptation of A.C.T.'s recommended T.L.C.:

> *T*alk about commercials with your child.
> *L*ook at commercials with your child.
> *C*reatively evaluate commercials with your child.

Alternate Channels

The TV set, that voracious time devourer, leads us to the jackpot question: What are the alternatives to television, and how can parents steer children toward other interests?

The most obvious alternative to TV, of course, involves a simple "no" coupled with the use of the OFF button; but this, carried to excess, casts a parent as an ogre, a spoiler of fun. At times a "no" is certainly necessary, since rules for television—like rules for sleep, meals, hygiene and so on—are essential to any well-run household; but the healthiest approach is to develop other ways in which youngsters can fill their time successfully and enjoyably. And surveys show consistently that in families where there are good parent-child relationships, where the family has other lively, creative interests, the set is used less frequently.

Many TV alternatives are simple enough. In good weather, they can include outdoor games and sports, kite flying, hiking, picnics, bike riding, chores in the yard, skate boarding, walks, trips to the store, or (oil shortages permitting) a drive in the family car. Indoor alternatives are reading, playing with toys or games, helping with household duties, working on models or other hobbies, writing letters to friends or relatives, helping to prepare a meal, or drawing pictures. And, of course, doing homework. Remember too that it's often flattering and exciting to a child to be asked to help a grownup with his or her own project. Most kids will respond eagerly to a suggestion such as "How about helping me bake cookies?" or "Would you like to come outside and help me put up the new swing?"

Most parents don't have to invent such projects; usually there's something on the back burner that will fit the needs of the moment. One father had volunteered to patch up a whole carton of broken toys for a local charity bazaar. On a cold, rainy afternoon, while his nine-year-old daughter was disconsolately clicking the TV dial, he decided to tackle the repair work and asked her to help. "You know a lot more about toys than I do," he said. The little girl, who had assumed that the project was strictly for grownups, was delighted with the suggestion, and became so absorbed that she had to be coaxed away from it when it was time for dinner. Another young parent, planning a children's birthday party, decided it would be fun if each guest had a personal place mat complete with name. She had a stack of colorful construction paper tucked away, and she lured her two children from the noisy tube to help make the mats. The children got some practice with their printing and spelling as well as the prestige of working with a grownup.

Offering interesting alternatives to TV is part of the larger problem of coping with TV itself; and for this every family finds its own answers. Of the families interviewed for this article we chose three to illustrate the diversity of solutions. These consisted of a mother, Sally, her husband, Daniel, and a girl of eleven and a boy seven and a half; Myra and Don, a young couple with an only child aged six and a half; and Arnold, an engineer who is a divorced father with two preteen boys whom he sees on week ends and during summer vacations.

Sally is a poet and teacher married to a psychiatrist. She began with a little background information:

> We didn't have a set until Abby was maybe five and Benjie two, at the very earliest. I actively didn't want to have one in the house. And then one day the kids came to me and said, "We want to have a television set like the other kids." And I said, "Yes, that's right, if you want one like the other kids, then we'll get one"—feeling my heart sink and saying to them right then that of course we would have rules about how much it could be watched and what they could watch.
>
> *But you finally said okay because you didn't want them to feel deprived?*
>
> Yes, it seemed unfair to me. I don't know enough about human communities to take the responsibility for having my kids be the only kids in the neighborhood who don't have a TV. . . . And I had no doubts about my ability to regulate the time they watched.
>
> *What are your rules? Have they changed? Do they work?*
>
> They work! Benjie is now allowed to watch an hour and a half of TV, three days a week. Not a great amount, but

more than it was in the beginning. Actually, Abby hardly watches television at all. When it was first allowed her, it was an hour a day three days a week—something like that—but not two days running. It's Monday, Wednesday, and Friday, since we go to the country almost every weekend and there's no TV there.

Does one of the children like television better than the other does?

Yes, Benjie likes it a lot more than Abby. At seven and a half he's reading well, but he's not reading chapter books. He can't get a galloping amount of information and fantasy through books yet. As soon as Abby was able to do that, her interest in TV went way down. I understand Benjie wanting it more. Recently he had a nightmare, first nightmare he'd had in years, and he knew it was from *The Three Stooges,* which he had chosen as one of his programs.

They do the choosing and then check with you?

Yes, it gives them a kind of control. But they aren't kids who like to be scared. Benjie (and Abby was the same at his age) believes what he sees. A week later he had a second nightmare about *Gilligan's Island*—this man took a pill and was going to *pretend* to die, and they laid him on a pyre and started the fire. Benjie still can't tell about that without getting all choked up. When he came to me about that, I told him I admire his kind heart. He said, "How could grownups make a show like that?" And then he said, "*I* know, *they* don't believe it," and that's true. Now he realizes TV can give him nightmares. The second nightmare wasn't so bad because we'd talked about the show before he went to bed. I said to always talk to me, that you don't have nightmares so much if you talk about what scares you. He's less hot for TV since those two bad dreams.

It does seem that your children are atypical of the problem, the overwhelming obsession to watch. They appear to be moderate, not constantly besieging you to watch television.

Maybe it's because of the games we've always liked to play together. In one game, Abby and I would sit together on the couch with two pads of paper. She would draw something—this was before she could draw representationally—and I would draw something, and we'd trade. Then I would try to copy what she had drawn, and she would try to copy what I had drawn. She would have these amazing complex, abstract doodles and I would have very simple drawings, like a face with two eyes and a mouth. It was really harder for me to copy hers than for her to copy mine. I liked doing that because I like to draw.

Do you have other activities, alternatives to TV?

Well, I keep memory scrapbooks with pictures of the kids, of Daniel and me and our family and friends. Sometimes there are pictures that don't turn out well, or I may have a duplicate. I give them those pictures and we play "Doing Scrapbook." Daniel and I also play little games with them, math or spelling or simple word games.

Do you watch shows together?

Yes, if it's a point in the day when I feel I have time to spare. I do it because it's something to *do* with Benjie. And I tell them what I dislike about programs. When Benjie discovered *The Brady Bunch* it was a wonderful universe opening for him, and that was great, but I told him I really didn't like that particular show. He asked, "Why?" and I said, "I hate canned laughter, first." He said, "What's canned laughter?" and so we talked about how canned laughter works, how it's faked to make people think something's funnier than it was. And I hated the easy solutions to problems that we know in our family—problems like grumpiness, jealousy. Those aren't solved in half an hour. I felt it was a sexist show, too, and we've discussed that at various times. I wouldn't tell him not to watch, but I do tell him why I dislike it.

Do you also have positive ideas about TV?

> Oh, sure. Benjie loves the cuteness of TV animals. He
> knows that when a baby duck or mouse comes on *Tom
> and Jerry* I like him to call me. I understand the cartoon
> thing—the freedom, and how the little one is the one
> who's making a fool of the big one. Benjie knows I don't
> like the amount of violence in *Tom and Jerry,* but he ex-
> plains to me that they don't feel anything and they're
> just drawings.

Sally also "talks back to commercials" when she watches TV with the
children. She feels that this gives them a more realistic approach to
sales pitches. "Now the children have started talking back, too," she
said.

Another approach is described by Arnold, the divorced father who
sees Timmy, aged ten, and Sloan, aged twelve, on weekends. Arnold
lives in a roomy loft studio, sectioned by dividers, and the boys use a
double-decker bunk bed on their visits.

How do you deal with TV when the kids are staying with you?

> Well, my loft is really one large room—you just can't get
> away from the set. I have to be careful. We have rules,
> and the boys accept them.

What kinds of rules?

> On Saturday nights when we're home, they're allowed to
> watch one and a half hours of programs. We try to agree
> on these in advance, and I often watch with them. On
> Sundays, if the weather is nice, we're always outside, in
> the park or something. If the weather's bad, they can
> watch a little extra, but not much. And whenever there's
> a choice between staying in and going out, we go *out*.

Do you ever have conflicts over what programs to watch?

> Oh, sure. But we manage to compromise. If they can't
> agree, I let Timmy pick one program and Sloan the
> next, and I get a turn too. They know that parents also

have rights when it comes to television. Sometimes there's a little bickering, but we always iron it out. In my experience, if you're firm with kids and they know the setup is fair, they're content. Life is made up of compromises, right? I'd like them to learn now, get some practice and understanding.

What kinds of shows do the kids prefer?

Well, there we're fortunate. We're all athletes, very sports minded, and there's a lot of sports stuff on TV. So we can almost always find something we like and can share. In summer, we have baseball. In the fall and winter, football. And in between there's plenty of basketball, hockey, tennis. Last year the kids got really turned on by the tennis matches. So I bought them both rackets and next spring we're going to get out on the courts. Sloan is getting interested in cross-country skiing, which we saw in a program about Colorado. We may try that later, when the boys are older.

It sounds as though television actually brings all of you closer to each other, in view of your interests.

It does, it's very much a shared thing—a tool I try to use. You know, watching is a chance to communicate. It triggers conversations, we talk about things like sportsmanship, fair play. If we see somebody behaving badly in a game, it gives us a chance to sort out our own values. And there's one other point. I'm an activist and so are the boys. We like watching TV, but that's a passive situation. When it comes down to it, we'd much rather be out doing our own sports than just watching someone else have fun. Our real alternative to TV is activity.

Myra and Don, the parents with the only child, are, respectively, a social worker and an educational administrator. Their daughter, Ellen, is six and a half. Younger than the children in the other two families, she is less "structured" in her watching, but she is developing a special interest in music programs. Her parents are somewhat more permissive about TV, less negative toward its influences and possibilities, than Sally and Daniel. They are also very attuned to its cultural aspects.

Is TV important in Ellen's life?

Don: It's a major force, there's no question about that. It's used in many ways, especially as a place to unwind and to "not think."

Myra: We're willing to go along with a certain amount of that.

Don: I think it's a time for being passive, and some of that has to do with what else she does in school and after-school activities.

What does she like to watch?

Don: She likes cartoons, the kiddie cartoons, but she doesn't care any more for *Sesame Street*. She thinks that's "baby stuff." And she'll avoid *Electric Company* unless there's no other option. Certain cartoons, the superhero things, we don't like because they're so violent. So we said no. Certain kinds of shows we simply eliminated— said she could *not* watch.

How does she react to that?

Myra: Sometimes she'll get very angry, very huffy and puffy. But we say, "You have a choice. You can either watch something that in our family we think is acceptable for children, or you can go do something else."

Don: She's grown to like certain things that we really don't like but feel are comparatively harmless. Dumb but harmless. For some reason *The Brady Bunch* appeals to her. Maybe it's an opportunity for her to fantasize an extended family, something different.

Myra: But she's not the kind who gets hooked. She doesn't *always* watch *The Brady Bunch*.

What else does she find of interest?

Myra: Well, she has sat and watched opera and ballet.

She'll watch a whole three hours of ballet without moving.

Don: Last night they showed *The Sound of Music,* and she
really wanted to watch that, so we said she could stay up
until ten. I wish they'd schedule those shows at a more
reasonable hour.

How much TV does she watch, on the average?

Myra: She watches, oh, about twelve hours a week, most of
it Saturday and Sunday morning. If we allowed it, she'd
probably watch from early morning until noon—until
she ran out of cartoons. But when we let her watch too
much she gets very grumpy and cranky. We have weekend rules, like no TV until you're fully dressed, and
your other chores are finished.

What programs do you watch together?

Myra: We watched *Wild Kingdom* and she enjoyed that,
and was getting a lot of information. But we enjoyed it
too, and talked about it with her.

Don: She loved the series *Edward the King,* and she asked
us a lot of questions about it. It was really after her bedtime, but we let her stay up.

Myra: She gained a sense of history out of that which I
don't think I could have given her.

What about cartoons?

Don: We've talked to her about the violence in some of her
cartoons. *Tom and Jerry* do tend to be a violent combination, but maybe they're no worse than the old nursery
rhymes.

*How do you deal with commercials? Does she want you to buy her
everything she sees advertised?*

Myra: No. We do a big number on TV advertising. Ellen
has two cynical parents, and she probably won't buy a
thing that's advertised on TV.

Don: Under the circumstances, we're lucky she'll drink
milk.

Both parents acknowledged that the most successful alternatives to TV were activities in which they participated. As Don put it, "It does require an interaction to get something to happen away from the set. When you're asking young children to do something else—well, they want you invested in it too, or they would just as soon be passive."

At the end of the interview, Don summed up his own impressions as an educator as well as a father: "Sure, much of TV is junk, and I have real questions about it as a teaching tool, but I think there are moments that are wonderful. When you see something like *The Ascent of Man*, there is no book including Jacob Bronowski's own that will take you that way. If TV motivates me to pick up a book like *The Ascent of Man* and really look at it, then I think TV is working at a high level. Or, if it motivates somebody listening to a concerto to say, 'I'd really like to own that concerto,' then that's a benefit. I think we need more debate about where the benefits are."

There are as many possible approaches to family television watching as there are families. The ideas and statements of the parents quoted here offer springboards to the search for suitable solutions based on your family's needs. The challenge, as Don points out, is to discover "where the benefits are."

A Family TV Bill of Rights

For PARENTS

I have the right to guide and supervise my kids when it comes to watching TV, and to protect them from harmful programs.

I have the right to my kids' company; to talk, interact, and play with them, instead of always sitting hypnotized in front of the set.

For CHILDREN

I have the right to count on my parents' guidance and help in this complex world of TV watching— a right to parental concern.

I have a right to my parents' company; to talk, interact, and play with them, instead of always sitting hypnotized in front of the set.

We have the right to enjoy and share the good things on television, and to reject the bad things.

I have the right to say "no" when my kids bug me to buy them the endless products they see advertised on the tube.

I have the right not to waste my allowance or birthday money on gimmicky toys and other products I see advertised on the tube.

I have the right to limit the hours my children spend in front of the TV set, and especially to curb their late-night viewing.

I have the right to be fresh and alert for my day in school, and the right to a calm night's sleep, with no nightmares caused by scary shows before bedtime.

When there's a conflict between the adults and children about who watches the family set, we have the right to discuss the problem together and try to arrive at a fair compromise.

I have the right to monitor the programs my children watch on TV, and to rule out any and all programs which I consider objectionable.

I have the right, when a particular show is vetoed, to be told why, and to be helped to understand my parents' decision.

I have the right to expect quality TV programming, and to watch it at times of my own choice, consistent with my other needs and duties.

I have the right to expect quality TV programming, and to watch it at times of my own choice, in keeping with the rules set down by my parents.

We have the right to ignore or veto TV when we wish—and to exercise this basic right by voting with the OFF button.

I have the right to have fun *with my kids,* in watching and enjoying appropriate programs together.

I have the right to have fun *with my parents,* in watching and enjoying appropriate programs together.

We have the right to our identities as human beings, working out our own values in our own family context, without undue pressures from television or other mass media.

Snack Snatchers

JOAN GUSSOW AND JAN DODDS

"Mommy! Captain Courageous is having Giggles and Bumps. Can I have some?"

"Not now. But help yourself to one of the little packages in the refrigerator. I just put them there."

"Are they those peanut things? Yea!"

You've learned that saying a flat "no" doesn't work. They're going to snack anyway in the face of those twelve-times-an-hour suggestions from the television set; so maybe you too have figured out how to save your nerves—and their nutrition—with a do-it-yourself treat bar.

Snacking has an undeserved bad name. It doesn't matter how often children eat—there's nothing magically healthy about three meals a day—but it matters a lot *what* they eat. So smart parents ban junk foods from the household and keep a variety of interesting and healthy snacks where they are easy to get at.

Here are some healthy ideas you may *not* have thought of to add to your snack-bar.

Children love to eat little pieces out of little bowls—so serve: individual cups of all kinds of nuts, popcorn, or peanuts-soybeans-raisins-sunflower seeds mixed—it's called *gorp*. Or, put out little saucers of whole-grain crackers, or quartered slices of whole-grain breads with peanut butter and jelly on them, or cheese chunks of Cheddar, Muenster or Swiss.

NOTE: Reprinted by permission from *3 To Get Ready* (New York: Bank Street College of Education, 1978).

When they're thirsty, bring out: ice-cold orange juice, apple juice, pineapple juice, V-8 or tomato juice, or chilled milk (flavored sometimes with chocolate, strawberry or vanilla), or yogurt with their favorite fruit added (blueberries? peaches? pears?).

When they want cool refreshing finger snacks, try: banana chunks on a popsicle stick rolled in wheat germ, or pieces of apple, pear or other in-season fruit dipped in orange juice and rolled in coconut, or orange pieces or grapes with toothpicks to spear them with, or frozen orange juice treats made in the freezer tray with a toothpick-speared fruit surprise in the middle, or pieces of celery filled with cream cheese or peanut butter, or green pepper or carrot sticks with cheese or yogurt dip.

And then for a *special treat* (and they are going to find out cookies are special, no matter what you do), pull out some of those oatmeal or peanut butter cookies you stashed in the freezer.

What all these snacks have in common is that they are made from whole, natural foods. Each of them will contribute something to your child's daily nutrient requirements. By your careful selection of snack foods at the store and by your thoughtfulness in keeping only good snacks accessible, you can constructively shape your children's food habits.

Children like good foods and enjoy the adventure of learning to eat new, wholesome foods.

And maybe one day soon your child will come to you and say, "Captain Courageous is having Giggles and Bumps. Can I have an orange, Mom?"

Won't that be the day!

Part 4

DAY BY DAY

Many of our casual and largely unplanned activities—preparing and sharing meals, caring for pets, cleaning the house, investigating nature, sports and games, exploring art and music—can be a great source of rich and abiding pleasure, with rewards for all members of the family.

How can we transform the day-by-day "ordinary" into something a little bit "special"? In the following section, let's explore these potentials and possibilities.

Plain Days

ALICE MILLER

The Ordinary Fabric of Lives

Nothing is more predictable than the day-to-day routines that take up most of our waking hours.

"Plain old days" is what one four-year-old calls those days when "nothing" really happens. They are the days unmarked on the kitchen calendar—days that lack the distinction of being tagged with a red crayon to indicate a family birthday, or even a visit to the dentist, or perhaps the day Someone is going to enter kindergarten. On plain old days you just don't do anything much, except perhaps grow another day older.

On those days, in most families, things of course do happen, but they are so habitual that they happen almost unconsciously. Very little real thinking accompanies these activities—and very little fun. Yet even on the plainest of days a great many events do take place. There are mealtimes, for example, and the routines of morning and evening with their baths, tidying up, and so on. There's the business of getting ready for school, doing homework, shopping, housekeeping chores, feeding the pets, taking out garbage, dressing properly for changes in the weather. And outside a big city, adults spend a lot of "plain old time" chauffeuring the young ones to school, athletic fields, and assorted social events.

All these are essential to the orderly fabric of family life, but they do eat up many hours of our time. How can we improve the quality of this time and make it more rewarding for everybody?

107

One thing to keep in mind is that small children are fascinated by things grownups take for granted—a hydrant, a mailbox, a wedding cake in a bakeshop window. Part of the pleasure of doing a simple errand with a child is the pleasure we get from seeing such things through the eyes of a child.

At the risk of sounding Pollyannaish, let's take a look at a few simple ways in which the plain old days can be made perhaps just a bit less plain. To many kids "Whistle While You Work" is simply one of the songs in *Snow White and the Seven Dwarfs.* But most of us really can whistle or hum or sing as we go about our household chores. Singing may not come naturally while you're watching laundry twirl around in a washing machine or stacking the dishes for an electric dishwasher. Those jobs don't take as much time and elbow grease as they used to, nor do they involve our own body rhythms in ways conducive to song. But there are quite a few household chores that can be brightened with a bit of song, and most parents can dredge up memories of dozens or even hundreds of great old songs like "Dixie" or "Old Mac-Donald Had a Farm" or "The Man on the Flying Trapeze." Your children will enjoy having them as part of their heritage too, if they hear them frequently in a setting where they can join in.

Do you play word games while driving the kids to an appointment? You might try a wonderful game such as "I Spy" (see page 217). A simple game like "Ghosts" (see page 110) can be fun, and helps to sharpen spelling skills. Sing-alongs are a great way to pass the time while driving.

One mother-chauffeur created a game called "Make a Story," which is popular with her seven- and nine-year-olds during short car trips. The story always starts with "Once upon a time there was a . . ."; then each of the participants takes a turn, round-robin style, adding one new sentence to the story. Inventiveness runs wild during these sessions. Another parent, whose youngsters help her make the beds, accompanies this tedious chore with a playful pillow fight.

Such ideas point the way to games that can accompany the most boring of chores. Similar pastimes can embellish dusting, vacuuming, putting away toys and books, tidying closets, shining shoes and folding laundry. Try arranging a "Laundry Folding Race" with your kids —the laundry may not get folded to perfection, but it will be done faster than you can believe.

An aunt of mine used to practice a bit of harmless bribery in getting her rooms cleaned up. She would hide a few coins here and there, then invite the kids to help her dust and clean. Any coins they found were theirs to keep, provided they kept busy.

So Darn Daily

But what to do when "nothing works," the weather turns bad, and the plain days stay plain and sulky? The rain in Spain may be more predictable, but it certainly rains a lot when one is housebound with small children. And when it isn't raining it may be snowing, or just too windy and cold to take the kids outside. At that point cabin fever (also known as "mother's disease") sets in. Children squabble and whine more than usual. The pet acts sick. The washing machine or, worse, the TV set may choose that moment to go on strike.

Well, here's a good time for some nice old-fashioned storytelling. With rain pouring down and black clouds brooding outside, it's a good moment to light a candle on the coffee table, group everyone around in chairs or on comfortable pillows, and try some favorite tales of mystery and adventure. You don't have to be a pro at it; all kids expect is your effort, your interest, and above all your participation. Grandparents are particularly adept at these story sessions, since they can regale youngsters with "how things were" when they were kids. Most youngsters will listen in wide-eyed wonder to tales of how life was lived back in "olden" times—the clothes people wore, the foods they ate, what schools were like, and so on.

Another antidote for cabin fever is the tried-and-true indoor picnic, guaranteed to delight. A checkered tablecloth spread on the floor, a plate of sandwiches or leftover snacks scrounged from the refrigerator—and an ordinary lunch becomes something special. One mother stage-sets this with a few potted plants placed around the cloth and bridge lamp nearby to provide "sunshine." "Our picnics," she says, "have everything but the ants." (For the fun of it, you can add a few "ants," too, by drawing them on paper napkins.)

Gloomy, housebound days are also a good time for children to catch up on school projects, reading, and hobbies, or to try some drawing games (see "The In-Between Times," page 216; "Pencil Tips," page 220).

Mealtimes are other daily occurrences that with a little tact and care can be made enjoyable. Around the family table parents and children can share events of the day, talk about friends, and plan activities. It's a time for everyone to participate, including the youngest of the children, whose opinions sometimes get shunted aside.

One family has a very amiable rule: the conversation (at least for starters) goes around the table in a fair and equal manner, and everyone has a turn to have his or her say. "When it comes to table talk," says the father of the tribe, "I guess you could call us an 'equal opportunity' family."

The maxim "Children should be seen and not heard" has gone the way of the buggy whip, and kids are now free to express themselves—some parents would say wryly, "Do they ever!" This doesn't mean, though, that parents and other adults are to take a back seat. Adult prerogatives and opinions have to be respected; and in a well-balanced family, all members are accommodated, particularly at these important mealtime get-togethers.

These suggestions won't transform every plain old day into a glamorous one, but thought and ingenuity can make a difference. Children are not toys to be played with only when the parent feels in the mood to play. Children have to be around the house even on the plain old days, and they can give us moments of pleasure when they're doing things as simple as trying to tie a shoelace or figuring out how to make a fortune by selling Kool-Aid for less than it costs to make it. If we help increase their enjoyment of the "dailies," they will give us even more pleasure, even when we all seem to be doing nothing but "growing one day older."

How to Play Ghosts

"Ghosts" is an all-time favorite among kids of ten and up. Keep in mind that it requires an ability to spell.

Let's assume you're playing with a group of four youngsters. Each takes his or her regular turn. The first player chooses a letter—say "A." The next child may say "U." Now each in turn adds a letter, gradually building a word. The player who gives the last letter of the word loses that round and becomes a "G." If he loses again, he becomes a "GH," then a "GHO," and so on until one player is a full-fledged "GHOST."

The trick is to extend each word cleverly, so that the final letter will fall elsewhere. In our sample game, player number three might add to the "A" and the "U" a "T." Now the next speller is up against it. If he says "O" he has completed the word "AUTO" and becomes a "G." But in this case he adds an "H," going for the word "AUTHOR," which will fall on a later player.

Bluffing is permitted; a player can give a letter without having a legitimate word in mind. But the next player is free to challenge him. If the challengee has no word, he becomes a "G." If he does have a word, the challenger is a "G" instead.

Living under One Roof

SEYMOUR V. REIT

"Environment" is a word that triggers strong feelings. We think of the battle against pollution, the problem of pesticides in our food, animals on the endangered species list, preserving clean air.

But environment isn't only global—it applies also to personal lives in family units. Whatever else we may or may not share with our kids, the *one inevitably shared unit is our living space:* a family, by its nature, is "in it together," whether "it" is a city apartment or a suburban home, a farm or ranch house, a villa, beach shack, mobile home, or houseboat. For adults and children, this business of living under one roof can be a success or a failure, a source of enjoyment or of daily irritation.

"Turf," according to the dictionary, originally meant "a surface layer of earth or sod containing a dense growth of grass and its matted roots." Later it was expanded to mean "the area claimed by a juvenile gang as its personal territory." Today the word has wider implications, in terms of personal space and how we go about sharing it.

Of course the answer depends a good deal on the amount of space available and the number of people involved. An only child in a large house, with his or her own room, represents one end of the spectrum. At the other end is the modest apartment that houses sisters, brothers, parents, and maybe a grandparent or two.

Today affluent families have basements or other play areas which can serve as the children's turf, and where bedrooms are shared by siblings there are bunk beds, platforms and built-ins to make better use of available space. In many homes the lone TV set in the living room or den has given way to individual sets in different rooms of the house (which adds to family fragmentation although it does cut down on conflicts and arguments). Many families, however, must use all their combined ingenuity to find a bit of turf for each member.

Whatever your own specific space arrangments, the basic principles of turf sharing are the same:

> Every child in the family needs some private area, however small, to call his or her own. Whether it's a whole room or part of a room, a toy chest or a shelf, or no more than a little bulletin board, it should be recognized and accepted as his/her personal place for his/her own things.
>
> Acceptance is a two-way street, and adults in the family are also entitled to their prerogatives. Kids for instance should know that when they blast their hi-fi rock music too loudly, they trespass on the quiet space of the adults.
>
> Apportioning turf in a house or apartment must be fair and consistent, but also flexible: at times priority must be given to certain needs or special events, with other members of the family cooperating. A familiar example is the preempting of the den for a teen-age party, at which time the adults are rightly expected to make themselves scarce.

The application of these generalities on a day-to-day basis requires tact and ingenuity. For example, the three Martin children aged seven, eight, and eleven, were constantly coming home from school with hand-made posters, drawings, and water-color designs. The kids were proud of their work and wanted to display and share it, but the Martins' house was elaborately furnished, with expensive wallpaper on most of the walls, and available space in the kitchen and TV den quickly ran out. To avoid competition and hurt feelings, the Martins finally set up a special "picture gallery" in one of the long downstairs halls, where each of the children was assigned a large area. This gallery was a big success, and visitors were immediately taken by the hand for a proud tour of the display. Coincidentally, the gallery added a lively visual dimension to the household.

In another family two preteen girls shared a bedroom: each had accumulated a favorite collection of photographs, patches, buttons, and pictures from fan magazines. The edges of the shared mirror were soon jammed, and there was endless bickering and jockeying for the limited space. The solution was simple: a separate bulletin board for each girl, with her name tacked to the top, where beloved personal items could be adequately displayed. A bulletin board in the kitchen also makes a good family message center. In households with older children, with independent coming and going, music lessons, sports sessions, and appointments to keep, a central clearing house simplifies communication.

. Family space means a lot more, of course, than simply a place to display art work and messages. "Free to be you and me" implies room to be you and me—and that means privacy. For kids living in the suburbs or the country, a tree house, a tent in the back yard, an old shack, or a grove of shrubbery can serve admirably as private turf or clubhouse. Wherever you live, if your child has his or her own room, that too allows space to arrange everything from aircraft models to school trophies, from dolls to day-glo posters.

Helping a child fix up his or her room can be fun for parents as well as the youngster. The big thing to remember is that it's your child's living space—and identity—which is involved, not yours. Different ideas and opinions are inevitable, and there's also the matter of cost. But by and large, when helping your child to decorate his or her room, keep in mind that a child's tastes and preferences are a vital part of growth and development.

It's also good to realize that your youngster may be going through a phase of intense identification with some current fad or cultural activity and will want this personal environment to reflect it. Are your child's walls covered with gruesome sci-fi posters? Garish ads for rock concerts? Is he or she a sports fan, with photographs of baseball and football players plastered all over the walls? Does the room look like a psychedelic disco hall? Well, why not? You needn't always approve and certainly don't have to share every enthusiasm; just wait for the phase to run its course, or to develop into a lasting interest that is all the more to be respected.

Separate rooms simplify things—but what if the space in your home isn't very lavish? Cramped quarters, especially in city apartments, are a fact of life, and siblings sharing a room—or even a house —are invariably going to bicker (look at TV's ideal Partridge family). When a household has to share a single bathroom, there's also bound to be squabbling. In these cases you may need an extra rule or two: a schedule, for instance, as to who uses the bathroom first on busy mornings. It isn't easy, but it can be done. A simple axiom to follow: *The smaller the space, the better the organization.*

The aim is a reasonable degree of privacy for each person, regardless of the space available. Privacy also involves respecting a child's inner life—for example, not opening a young person's mail, or prying into his or her precious diary.

Finally, there's a subtle difference between privacy and isolation. We all need time alone, yet as members of a family we also have to live and share with one another. Children need to learn this, and effective cooperation tells a child that he or she isn't the only pea in the pod. It reinforces a sense of self while encouraging fairness and respect for others.

Children and the World of Work

CAROLINE ZINSSER

During a stay in a small Spanish village I observed the children and thought of how their perceptions of work differed from those of children I knew in the United States. The Spanish children walked the short distance to school each morning at the same time their fathers were going to work in the fields or shops. As the children studied in the schoolroom, they could hear the sound of farm machinery through the open windows and were reminded of their fathers working nearby. When the children played in the bare dirt schoolyard, their mothers were likely to pass by on the way to the bakery for a fresh-baked loaf or to the flat stones where women washed clothes together.

At noon children left school and went home for three hours of lunch and siesta. During this time they helped their mothers slice fresh-picked tomatoes, saw their sweat-drenched fathers return from the fields to wash the dust from sunburned arms, and walked to the communal well to refill the heavy water bucket. During siesta time all shops closed, the church door was locked, and the village square emptied; the village was at rest. At three o'clock the village stirred, people resumed their work, and children too went back to their work in the school, the work of becoming literate as preparation for further work as an adult.

The Spanish child, much like the child in nineteenth century America, had a clear idea of his parents' work and his own. He could understand the need for fields to be plowed or for the shopkeeper to open his shop. He could understand his mother's household chores, how scattering the grain for the backyard chickens was related to frying the egg in the pan for breakfast. He saw himself growing up into a man or woman who would perform similar work. Work was an all-important part of life; serious, difficult, yet satisfying.

In contrast, the contemporary American child is in many ways separated from the world of work. Mommy and Daddy go off in the morning to "the office," a place the child has never seen and may not even be able to envisage. What do they do there? Well, they do everything from "systems analysis" to "space sales." In fact, the *Dictionary of Occupational Titles* lists over fifty-thousand different jobs! The work of American parents is increasingly specialized and often deals in complex processes which cannot easily be explained to children.

When parents return from "the office" they are tired and cranky. They say they have had "a hard day," but the child knows little of what makes the day hard. What he does know is that it is not a good time to ask for an increase in his allowance. He has learned that "the office" and "the hard day" are somehow linked to a very potent subject in family circles, "what we can afford." The child has found that the answer to "Why can't we have a car like that?" is that "We can't afford it," but he doesn't really understand why some people "can afford it" and his family cannot. It has something to do, he realizes, with what happens at "the office."

Adult work, with its pain and its satisfactions, including wages, is a central part of family life, and children need to learn about its nature and value. How can this be accomplished in homes where the places and kinds of work are so far removed from the child? Parents justifiably worry about this.

Connecting to Adult Work

Although the end of the work day may sound like a good time to share concerns about one's work with family members, it rarely is. The parent often comes home tired, cross, angry or frustrated. Asked how his day has gone, he is likely to snap, "Lousy," and flip on the television hoping that the evening news of global disaster will at least distract him from his office hassles.

Children, on the other hand, have often been eagerly awaiting the parents' arrival home for sympathetic ears in which to pour accounts of teachers who unfairly accused them of copying, of basketball games won, and of other defeats and triumphs of the school day that need to be shared with an adult who is family. Faced with parents exhausted from their own work and seeking escape from the mental tangles of the day, children learn to stay out of the way rather than to attempt sharing.

What may help this situation is a period of transition for both parents and children that will help them to shed the day's stress and begin a more relaxed period at home together. Physical activity is a change from sedentary work for children and adults. Throwing a ball, taking a bike ride, jogging, dancing to records, or just roughhousing may help family members clear their heads of the day's tensions and listen and talk to each other with real interest and concern.

A more direct way for children to connect to the world of adults is by visiting their parents' places of work. Most parents have been told repeatedly how important it is for them to visit their child's school in order to understand and to share with the child his work there. What is also important is for a child to see the setting for a parent's work.

Parents can take children to offices on Saturdays or, even better, on school holidays when the child can meet the parents' fellow workers. The seriousness of work in the adult world is apparent, and children are generally at their best and most winning. At last they meet "the boss" and "the secretary" and have a chance to see "the files" and "the layout room," those mysterious people and places they have heard about so often at home.

Of course many parents work at sites where children are barred, such as an automobile plant. Ironically, these places are the ones likely to interest children the most, as they involve manufacturing processes, machinery, movement and change. Some companies, recognizing the need for families to connect to parents' work sites, sponsor family days, when children and other relatives can observe the plant under safe conditions. Companies sponsoring such visiting days are aware that having a worker's family make a closer connection to the place of work increases job satisfaction for the wage earner.

The most powerful way for children to connect to adult work is to actually share it. Although we are far removed from the Spanish village, sharing is probably more feasible than is supposed by a society that has come to accept a division between the child's world and adult work. In England, for example, truck drivers often take children along during work. A few working mothers in America can have children brought to the place of work after school and stay until both mother and child can go home.

This sort of arrangement was much more common in our grandparents' time, when helping in the shop after school or working with father on Saturday was expected. American parents moved away from children's direct participation in adult work for good reasons, including the dreadful exploitation of child labor during a large part of our national history. But as the nature of work and of family life changes, as more work can be performed through technology at home, and as working hours become more flexible, we may find new ways to show children the realities of their parents' work. They need to develop an understanding of parents as workers, and of their own future roles as workers.

Play as Work

Even the very young child is engaged in his own work. A child playing with blocks may be constructing a fire station, acting as a fireman, pushing a fire truck down an imagined street, giving or taking orders, and energetically producing whooshing noises as the fire is successfully extinguished. Children play house by assigning roles and tasks as mother and father.

Recently psychologists such as Jerome Bruner at Oxford have concentrated on analyzing the function of play for children. Bruner points out that the child's playful practice with toys and games is preparation for later problem solving. He explains that in play the pressure for achieving a goal is reduced, which allows the child to play around with different strategies for solving problems without the frustration attached to more formal problem-solving situations. Bruner concludes, "Although we do not yet know how important play is for growing up, we do know that it is serious business."*

We can see that the child at play is also going about his work—the work of growing up into an able, problem-solving adult. A "useful"

---

* Jerome S. Bruner, ed., *Play: Its Role in Development and Evolution* (Harmondsworth, England: Penguin, 1976.)

task in adult terms may not be as useful to the child's development as his play.

"Real Work"

In addition to play as a form of work, the child seeks "real work." He is eager to help with household chores such as carpentry or cooking. His independence dictates that he do it "all by myself" and yet his manual skills are limited, and his threshold of frustration at these real tasks is low. He imagines that he will produce a beautiful chocolate cake, or a cage for the rabbit, but at the first spilled milk or bent nail, his spirits falter and further setbacks soon lead to tears. His parents feel caught between wanting him to begin to do real work around the house and not wanting an emotional scene.

The goal is to work with the child in an atmosphere of acceptance. The first lessons in making cookies are not a good time for requiring perfection (see "Kids in the Kitchen," page 128). The need for care in making exact measurements can come when the child is more proficient. At these first sessions what is needed is large aprons and an adult to wipe the spills and hold the bowl steady as the child inexactly but enthusiastically tries his or her hand. "Take your time, there's no hurry" produces a much better climate than "Come on, we haven't got all day." The adult should also put aside his ideas of the "perfect" cookie or rabbit cage. Cookies and rabbit cages may be a little lumpy or lopsided, but their makers will have the satisfaction of knowing they did it themselves.

The most discouraging thing a parent can do with children who are learning to work in the home is to take over the project in exasperation with a "Here, let me do it." This leaves the child feeling incapable and unconfident. Deprived of his right as a beginner to make mistakes and to learn from them, he may withdraw from the task and refuse to try again.

In many families where both parents work, household chores are shared by mother, father, and children. Children in these families have the satisfaction of knowing that their work is really needed to enable the household to function smoothly. Everyone, children included, finds work more rewarding when it is not "make work," but is essential. This may be one of the reasons why asking a child to clean up his own room on a regular daily or weekly basis often turns into such a battleground between parent and child. The child resists cleaning up, does not see the point of picking his toys off the floor if he himself prefers a cluttered room. As adults we might feel the same way if someone ordered us to straighten up our desks, when we actually prefer our own personal and seemingly haphazard system of books and papers.

What helps in such situations is for parents to mentally back off from the struggle and try to see it with a little more perspective. From the parent's point of view, how much is a power struggle (If I give in, am I losing my position of authority?), how much is personal style (I'm a neat person living with slobs), and how much is really a question of work (Rooms have to be kept clean)?

By concentrating on the real area of work, some of the emotional struggle can be avoided. "All the rugs have to be vacuumed on Saturday morning" is an order less troublesome for a child to handle than "If this room isn't cleaned by Saturday, there'll be no television for a week." The first order describes work to be done in terms of needs of the entire household; the second is a threat.

Tasks that obviously need to be done, such as feeding the dog, collecting the dirty clothes for washing, setting the table, and taking out the trash, are jobs that are suitable for children. They have the advantage of having a start and a finish, of being required on a regular basis, and of being *simple but necessary.*

A job with more ambiguity, such as watering the plants when they need it, can be doomed from the start if the child has no interest in the plants. On the other hand, children who have shared a parent's interest, have planted seeds and watered them and observed the growth of a plant of their own, have gone with a parent to choose new potted plants, will be much more willing to share the work of plant tending.

Other tasks which give children satisfaction are those involving the world of adult work. In cities, children can run neighborhood errands, taking clothes to the cleaners, shopping for a single item that is needed in a hurry—the kitty litter, the quart of milk. Children who do not live within walking distance of shops can bicycle to nearby stores or accompany parents, taking on some of the purchasing themselves. Special occasions lend themselves to children's taking on whole projects. Older children can arrange entire birthday parties for other family members, choosing table decorations and baking the cake.

Helping a child to assume responsibility for performing household tasks is a form of teaching. The child learns partly from the example of his parents. If he sees them assuming their own responsibilities in good cheer, he is more apt to be cheerful himself. If his parents hate their work around the house, he is apt to pick up these attitudes also.

Fathers who take on their share of housework willingly and without resentment are good examples for both their sons and their daughters. Children brought up in families where work is not always performed according to assigned sex roles will be better prepared to assume the work responsibilities they will face as adults. When both parents cook and when both mother and father use the power tools, their children are more likely to acquire the wide range of skills that will be needed in the adult world.

One son, returning from his first term at college, announced proudly that he was the only person in his co-ed dorm who knew how to sort the laundry for washing. "It was a great way to meet girls," he said.

Children's work can and, even in the best-managed households, does often turn into a battle of wills. "How many times do I have to tell you to put the ladder away?" and "I shouldn't have to remind you to *please* take your sneakers out of the living room" are familiar pleas to most of us. Some of this nudging is inevitable, but parents can try to be as matter-of-fact as possible in dealing with children's work. Sarcasm only leads to resentment; it does nothing to bring about a more receptive attitude.

Children, like the rest of us, are procrastinators. Here's a familiar scene: Child is sitting on couch reading magazine. Parent, who is up and about, tidying living room, says: "When are you going to take that skateboard out of here?" Child replies angrily: "All right, all right, I'll *get* to it!" But he doesn't, he continues to sit and read. Parent reaction ranges from annoyance to fury (in which case he pitches the skateboard down the hallway).

The timing is wrong in this sequence. A child who is engrossed in his own interesting project will often resist a parental order. He has every intention of eventually getting around to doing what is asked; he just doesn't want to do it right now. A better plan is to announce,

"In fifteen minutes I'm going to start picking up in the living room and I need some help. Please finish what you're doing." This allows the child some time to make the transition from his own project to the work task, and gives him an opportunity to take responsibility for himself.

Problems arise when parents expect children to see where help is needed and pitch in without being asked. "Here, take these bottles, can't you see my hands are full?" may produce the desired result but puts the child in a position of blame. Children are often lost in thoughts of their own, and are not paying attention to adult activities. Asking directly for help—"Would you take these bottles, please, my hands are full?"—works better. We want children to be connected to adult work, but we can't expect them to be always oriented toward adults. They have rights to their own private distractions and thoughts.

School Homework

Another kind of work that children are responsible for is school homework. Parents shouldn't assume that very young children can perform homework as they themselves remember doing it (these memories may actually date from high-school experiences). Expecting young children to work for long stretches in isolation is unrealistic. Parents are often so scrupulous in not wanting to undermine the child's independent work that they fail to give the warm encouragement that is needed.

If a parent "helps" a child by going over his homework and correcting errors so that the homework is handed in letter perfect, then the parent is depriving the teacher of a diagnostic tool for discovering areas of schoolwork that are misunderstood by the child. This kind of "help" should be avoided. On the other hand, a child may show his parent a completed homework assignment and be told, "You've done a good job in finishing your assignment." Parents can also be helpful in sharing knowledge, getting into general discussion of the subject of an essay assignment without counterposing their opinions to those of the child or the teacher. This is helping with homework in the best sense.

To Pay or Not to Pay

As children approach adolescence—and today we tend to think of age ten as preadolescent—they become more eager to perform adult work. No longer content to hold the ladder steady, they want to paint the house. Instead of helping in the kitchen they want to cater a party. This is a time when parents find that the child who balks at raking leaves in his own yard will eagerly take on a full day's yardwork at the neighbors'. At home he may feel that he is only a set of helping hands, at the neighbors' he holds a real job. And some of this change in attitude has to do with being paid.

When children should be paid for their work and how much—whether, for example, a child should be paid for baby sitting for his own younger siblings—is a vexing question. Parents resent paying for services which they consider to be part of family responsibilities, yet children work with more satisfaction when they are earning money. What is important is to establish a clear value system, one that children understand and find reasonable, one that will help them take pride in their contributions.

For younger children, giving a set amount is often a reasonable solution. The child is not paid by the task or by the hour, which is difficult with the kind of work young children are able to perform; he is paid by the week with the understanding that he must have completed his assigned work.

Attaching some monetary value to household work is helpful to the child. He feels he is less "on the dole" and more of a contributing member to the family's well-being. Equating his own work in his home with work performed outside the home by teenagers and adults, he feels linked to the world of real work.

How much older children should be paid is another perennial problem. There is no one correct solution, but certainly parents should consider paying an amount comparable to what other children in the same school or neighborhood, and of the same age, receive (provided, of course, that this is a reasonable demand on family income).

It is fair to give older children more than younger ones, but the older child should be made responsible for more difficult tasks. In figuring allowances, parents also have to count in inflationary rises and squash the impuse to chide, "I only got a dollar a month when I was your age."

Raising Consumer Consciousness

Once an allowance has been made, how much should the parent have to do with how it is to be spent? Should parents point out the merits of UNICEF, Sunday School, and savings accounts? They can certainly point them out, but should probably not put restrictions on how the money is to be spent. It is hard for a parent to see the child's money go into a steady stream of junk food, baseball cards, rock albums, or sequined tee shirts, but these are exactly the items that children cannot wheedle out of their parents. Purchasing power is exactly that—power—and as such, a means of growing independent.

How children spend their own earned money becomes part of their education into the world of work. Money is more meaningful when it is gained by one's own efforts, and choosing how to spend is certainly one of the rewards of work. Should a parent remain silent when a child sends his hard-won savings off to a manufacturer whose advertising is clearly misleading? A reasonable solution is to provide enough information so that the child's expectations will not be so unrealistic that he will be terribly disappointed, or feel foolish and ashamed. Instead of protesting that the child shouldn't purchase "such junk,"a parent can point out the small type that states, "Batteries not incuded." If the child goes ahead and makes his purchase, only to be disappointed in the result, a parent can be helpful by sharing an experience from his own childhood—"I remember sending for an inflatable dirigible that turned out to be as big as a baseball"—to assure the child that his experience is common and should not be the cause for humiliation. The worst thing a parent can say in such circumstances is "I told you so."

How much guidance a parent should offer a child in spending money will differ, of course, from family to family and according to the child's age. By the time children reach the teenage years they should be trusted sufficiently to handle their own money and make purchases without adult censorship. What is of value to children is a systematic education in consumerism, starting with very young children as they go with parents to supermarkets, hardware stores, and department stores. Parents can explain their reasons for picking one product over another—"See, this bottle is taller, but it doesn't hold as much," and "This sweater can go in the washing machine, but this one has to be sent to the cleaner."

Such raising of consumer consciousness over the years is more effective than a showdown over whether a child is allowed to spend his entire allowance on a glow-in-the-dark plastic "authentic" Egyptian mummy. When a child has his heart set on a product, no matter how spurious, and the money is his own, even though it has just been handed to him by a parent as his allowance, it is unfair, in the child's eyes, to interfere. Money becomes a means of gaining independence from the parent. Money can buy fantasies, and the child's fantasy is different from what the adult sees as "best" for the child.

In the long run it is the parents' example that has most influence on the child; the values that have been emphasized, the time taken to explain and to illustrate through their own actions. These will most likely emerge as the guiding principles that children will ultimately adopt. The long-term training is well worth the effort and can be counted on for general guidance. An occasional foray into foolish expenditure doesn't mean that children have lost or abandoned the real values that have been demonstrated and instilled by parents during the early years.

Count Me In

Families living in modern America, though far removed from the simplicities of earlier times as exemplified in the Spanish village, can include children in the world of work. Our complex technological society can be one in which children have a working share. The fact that our work as adults accounts for so much of our lives, and that children face an adulthood in which work will be equally important for them, indicates how crucial this is for children's adjustment and success.

Only by sharing their working lives can parents provide the kind of modeling that children need. Keeping work as a part of parents' lives that is inaccessible to children deprives them of essential information and of experiences that will enable them to act with sureness when the time comes.

Children who see their parents as capable workers, as consistent over the long run in attitudes of responsibility and diligence, will be off to a good start in establishing similar attitudes of their own. Of course some work is tedious, and this is also valuable for children to learn from their parents and to experience on their own. What is of most importance, however, is to help children see that although work is hard, it is also rewarding; not something to be dreaded and avoided but something that can be interesting, challenging, the source of deep satisfaction. We would not thrive without work, it is the wellspring of much that nourishes our lives. Let us make sure that our children are not excluded.

Kids in the Kitchen

DORIS B. WALLACE

Preparing and eating food should be a pleasure. At an average of three meals a day, we go through the process well over 70,000 times in a lifetime of 65 years. Preparing and consuming food is associated with deep meaning, elaborate ritual, and acute pleasure, as well as human necessity. One of the tasks of rearing children is to induct them into these traditions.

Nearly all children are interested in food. They're interested in it when they are hungry (eating when you're hungry, after all, is one of life's greatest reliable pleasures). But children are also interested in food as objects to be explored.

Messing Around

From about eight to eighteen months, small children want to handle food. They are getting their first idea of what food feels like outside the mouth. Squashing and messing with food and playing with it is a delicious sensuous experience, and intellectually stimulating as well. Up to this point, except for the ubiquitous teething foods, such as Zwieback, they have always been spoon fed, so they have seen, smelled, and tasted food but rarely handled it. In spite of the mess, it's a good thing to let it happen. Messing about with their meals once hunger is satisfied extends experience. It also enables the very young to learn to feed themselves, first with the hand, fist, and fingers, then with a spoon. It gives them experience with texture and mass and also a feeling of control. It is good for jubilant laughter.

128

But what about you? At this stage, mothers, fathers, or other care-givers are presented with a real challenge. The child discovers the de-lights of overturning the food plate, wiping food over the high-chair tray, clenching and squashing food and reflecting on the results. A high point is dropping food over the edge and watching with devoted interest its descent to the floor. These actions are repeated tirelessly, the better to assimilate them.

When you clean up what has been dropped right away, the child's temptation to do it again is irresistible. Now *your* action has become part of the sequence of events the child is causing and observing with such interest. After the food has hit the floor, the child looks at you with alert interest, waiting for you to make your move. A game has been invented and your amusement at the inevitable repetition is ap-preciated and reciprocated. The problem is, how long can this go on? Contrary to popular myth, young children have a great capacity for prolonged and concentrated attention, especially when they are con-tributing to or initiating the action. To make something happen, espe-cially the first time, is for the child a creative act, an invention. Once the novelty has worn off, it sometimes helps if you let the child drop things without cleaning up immediately.

Here are some other useful tips that will make "messing around" more a joy than a headache.

> Limit the ammunition; give small amounts of food
> Remember that a bib is there to get messy
> Use the sponge cheerfully
> End with a cookie and a kiss

A relaxed approach at this early stage doesn't necessarily mean a sloppy child a few years from now. Letting the young child mess around with lots of different foods can be a help in developing a pal-ate for a variety of good foods, which nutritionists tell us is one of the most important aspects of a balanced diet.

What's the Right Amount?

The principle of giving small amounts also holds good later on. At my daughter's nursery school I watched as the teacher served lunch to a group of three-year-olds. Each child was given a small spoonful of meat, vegetables and rice. Each plate was a vast white space with three tiny islands of food. I watched incredulously, thinking, "How stingy!" But this teacher knew what she was doing. She knew how overwhelming it is (at any age) to be given mountains of food one can't finish. She was giving the children the chance to eat what they had and ask for more. She was also preventing them from associating eating food with wasting it. And, equally, she was developing an amiable climate for eating.

Unlike many adults, young children do not eat when they are not hungry, and the amount of food children need varies, depending on growth rate. Given a reasonably balanced diet, most young children eat what they need, in both amount and kind. Trying to force a child to eat when not hungry or pushing a food which has been refused usually doesn't work. Even when it does work it is not necessary. There is no need to stuff the child. It can be a way of passing on our own hangups about food and eating.

When a child doesn't finish, we often deal with it in a silly way: "Eat your peas or you won't grow into a big strong boy." Most nonhumans eat until their hunger is satisfied and we recognize this and accept it. But what happens if the young human animal doesn't finish a meal? Consternation. The adult has prepared it, lovingly and with care; if the child does not finish there must be something wrong. Why is he resisting the food? Why isn't he hungry "enough"? Why is he rejecting what he ought to want? To the young child, admonition makes no sense. He has eaten as much as he wants. Finishing the peas now as a tradeoff for later muscle has little meaning and no interest. He is full.

Special Notions

The way food is presented can be very important. There is a stage when a child may want each item strictly separated on the plate. During this period you may be ill advised to serve meat over rice, to mix two vegetables together, or even to serve gravy on the food. And heaven forbid that you should serve a casserole. Often there are abrupt changes. String beans, which have been a favorite vegetable for weeks, are suddenly rejected. Chicken may be requested and then not eaten. This is the time when adults can grow fat on the children's leftovers.

Sometimes these mysterious events are remembered and explained years later. Once string beans tasted funny—no more string beans. The texture of the chicken was suddenly repugnant. A tiny speck of fat disqualified all meat. Color, texture, shape, smell, temperature— all these are important and vivid. It is not just the taste of food that counts.

One of the best-known food faddists is the child who eats only one or two foods exclusively. Word of this spreads rapidly, through peers and family adults. "Paul," one is told, "eats only hamburgers and raw carrots. For every meal. Honestly! That's *all* he eats!"

A good deal of distinction attaches to Paul. Even though his eccentricity is not easy on his household, it is a marvel to his peers. Sometimes, just because Paul is so publicly and dramatically labeled (and hostesses warned ahead), he is locked into his state. Given the right moment, he might be willing to try some other food, but this is difficult for him because now his special identity is at stake. Paul therefore has two challenges to meet: to eat something else and to break with a rigid, publicized identity. The latter challenge is particularly hard because people are always watching him to confirm that he does what he is famous for. Being famous brings obligations.

Invariably, of course, the Pauls of this world do meet the challenges and change their eating habits. It is best not to worsen the situation by commenting or complaining about it. Simply give him what he wants without fuss, and make other simple things available (such as raw celery, fruit, cheese). And have faith that change will come. Often a Paul tries a different food at the house of a friend where the ahead-of-time warning has been forgotten.

Eating Out

In urban and suburban areas it is easy to take children out for a meal at an early age. Many fast-food chains cater especially to children. The speedy appearance of the food is a great asset. Children know what to expect there and they know that many of the items in such places are exactly to their taste.

The disadvantages of these restaurants is that the food does not provide well-balanced nutritional meals. They usually supply adequate protein but not enough fresh fruits and vegetables. Fast food is high in calories and tends to be monotonous. To children, monotony is irrelevant if they like the food; the relentless reliability of the thing is part of its charm. Once in a while is fine, especially when coping with groups of children, but it becomes boring to the adult. Change is also a good thing for children. It broadens the mind as well as the appetite.

Do, therefore, go to restaurants with a larger repertoire of items and take the children. Usually a restaurant offers dishes which you do not have at home (which is one of the reasons for going out to eat) and provides the possibility of expanding a child's gastronomic experience. Even if your kids stick to spaghetti and meatballs, they have the chance of seeing you have something different and perhaps sampling it.

Be aware that when you take children out to eat, things may not always go right. I once took a three-year-old to New York's Chinatown. In the modest restaurant where we were to have dinner, she was presented with rice, a familiar item, plus meat and vegetables in a new form. She immediately demanded tomato ketchup, an unknown item there. Upon hearing that there would be no ketchup for her rice —that there simply *wasn't* any—Olivia slid under the table shrieking with tearful rage. Visions of well-behaved Chinese children marched before my eyes as I alternately cajoled and ignored her. Eventually she returned to her seat and ate a bit. She had the air of having been mistreated and I felt that, on balance, she was right. Total unfamiliarity had put too much strain on her.

Eating with other families is the first and best step to eating outside the home. The child is there as a friend and will eat in an amiable atmosphere. However, the food is bound to be different from home. Some children can say, "I don't like eggplant"; others can only muster, "I'm not hungry." In most cases such responses are accommodated without fuss. In the end there will also be pleasant discoveries and you will be urged to make fried chicken "the way Willie's mother makes it."

Going to restaurants has the advantage of letting the child choose what to eat. But table manners also become important. It is a good thing for children to be put into a situation where they have to live up to more formal behavior. This is best done gently. It is important to recognize the efforts children make, even if their physical skills are still immature—for example, in handling a knife and fork—or if they drop or spill things. At the beginning, especially with young children, restaurants with a relaxed atmosphere are recommended.

When children are taken to restaurants on a special occasion, like a birthday, and when you want things to go well, go to a place they know and like, or one with a menu that won't be too unfamiliar. If there are children's portions, or special children's dishes, so much the better. If they are not feeling adventurous, they can feel safe.

Big-city street fairs are also fertile ground for trying new things in small quantities in the exciting ambiance of other cultures. Here the child is not pinned down at a table with the choice of ordering an unknown dish. In a street fair, you can see and smell the food before making a choice.

Cooking with Children

Children can become creators of meals rather than mere consumers. As early as possible they should take part in the functions of the kitchen. This includes learning to use all its tools when they are able to handle them safely and seeing the value of keeping things orderly and clean. Less popular tasks like doing the dishes and putting things away are part of the larger enterprise of cooking. However, most young children are fond of water play, which is only a step away from dishwashing. Eventually, as adults, some of us are bored with the routine of doing the dishes and putting things away. But there is also a quiet pleasure in it and some children love it. It helps if you don't convey a negative attitude about these tasks.

Cooking with children can be a marvelous experience. They go at it with verve and thoroughly enjoy the atmosphere of a busy kitchen. They like sharing in adults' tasks, especially those that interest them. Cooking is full of mystery, of miraculous transformations, of exacting physical effort, of waiting impatiently for things to come out of the oven. It is full of earned rewards. It is also a way of enticing the child who is reluctant to experiment with new foods.

The four- or six-year-old who for the first time beats a slippery viscous egg white and sees it gradually transformed into a mountain of solidly standing, snow-white froth, has lived through an amazing event. How could something wet and wobbly end up so foamy and beautiful? When you take some with your finger and put it in your mouth, there is nothing. What does it taste like? Nothing. Folding the egg white into another mixture makes it disappear. Add sugar and bake it and it becomes meringue. Mix it with egg yolks and other things and it becomes a soufflé that rises hugely in the oven. When it goes in, it hardly fills the dish. When it comes out, it towers over the rim. For a child the ordinary egg white is not ordinary at all.

Making cookies is one of the most popular kitchen pastimes for children. Have several kinds of decorations on hand, the gaudier the better. Decorating cookies can become a beloved party game tradition too. Children from three or four to about ten like it a lot. The quality of the cookie doesn't matter as much as the variety and quantity of decoration. Simply have a large table with a paper cloth and give each child some unbaked cookies and an enormous array of decorations. Accept the ensuing mess and everyone has a good time.

Cutting cookie dough into interesting shapes is another high point. You can buy ready-made cutting shapes, use the rims of glasses, or cut them free hand. Changes in the size and bulk of cookies during baking is something to be discovered and applied in the spacing of the unbaked cookies on the cookie sheet. Sometimes it is better for children to learn these things by making their own mistakes.

As children grow older, their taste in decorations may change and their passion for unnaturally green and brilliant red sprinkles may diminish. The decorations become less important and the cookies more so. Older children can also become very interested in why some foods are good for you and others not. Recipes may be sought and followed with this in mind. Only a light hand is needed to guide these activities. Other children may become specialists in one dish without necessarily taking a continuing interest in cooking. Parents can encourage the talent and hope, but not nag, for its expansion.

When a main dish is being prepared, many children like to feel part of this effort, genuinely contributing to its most important aspects. An interested eight-year-old can tell right away when being fobbed off on a relatively trivial task. But to know that you did the stuffing from beginning to end is to know that your contribution carries weight. It means chopping things, stirring them in the pan, mixing them, perhaps with bread cubes and egg, seasoning the whole, and finally actually inserting the delicious-smelling mixture into the bird and sewing or skewering the opening shut. Here too one learns that stuffing expands with heat so the cavity should not be filled completely, however tempting it may be to do just that.

My friend Olivia, of Chinese restaurant fame, was interested in the kitchen and its goings-on from an early age. Her first culinary exploit was at age two, when she spent an hour one lazy Sunday afternoon in taking all the spices from the kitchen one by one and emptying their contents in neat rows along the windowsills of several rooms in her apartment. This was discovered by her parents when they noticed an unnaturally long silence and a strong smell of cinnamon. Later on Olivia liked to do "experiments" in the kitchen. This meant taking interesting ingredients—say, flour, vinegar, ground cloves and a slice of cucumber—combining them in a glass jar, and watching what happened over days or even weeks.

Olivia loved cooking with her mother. When her mother was chopping parsley, she wanted some to chop too. With young or inexperienced children, there is an immediate dilemma here. Should you give the child some parsley with a blunt knife or a sharp knife? The sharp knife raises visions of a cut finger. The blunt knife will not cut the parsley. I'm in favor of a success with risk, namely the sharp knife, which is actually safer since it cuts without effort. In cutting parsley (and other things), the knife can be held by the handle with one hand and by the tip of the blunt edge with the other. The parsley can then be cut by chopping up and down rather than in a sawing motion with one hand holding the parsley. Some side-step the whole problem by using scissors, but this may not be easy for a very small child. The problem will come up in any case with, say, onions. Demonstrating the actual movement can be important. Stay with the child and help with the task until you are sure it can be handled.

The other main danger in the kitchen is burns. Do make sure the child understands that the stove is hot and keep hot liquids out of reach until children are old enough to deal with them efficiently. Do not let young children put things into or remove things from a hot oven.

Measuring, stirring, and mixing are all enjoyable for children, as they are for many adults. Measuring a cup of liquid can be the occasion for learning that a cupful in a cup measure seen from above is not a cup when you check it at eye level; that one cup is the same as eight ounces and also the same as half a pint or two half-cups. Asking a child to measure the various quantities of ingredients you are going to need is a very good way of starting things off. Measuring herbs and spices in the nest of spoon measures is fun even for the experienced adult cook.

Stirring things is another simple and popular assignment, especially when something is happening, like a thin mixture containing egg yolks gradually thickening as it is heated. Stirring is vital during this process and the child sees the value of it first hand.

Mixing things has many charms and is a useful activity for one or more children in the kitchen. It is sometimes hard to pry somebody away from making Russian dressing—by mixing mayonnaise and ketchup—especially if he's also tasting it a lot. Mixing things is also a good opportunity for handling food. Mixing herbs and chopped onions into hamburger meat and shaping it into meat balls or patties; or mixing flour, water, and fat for pastry dough are good tasks for any child. Mixing food with the hands provides special pleasure, an echo of earlier days. In the kitchen such activity is socially acceptable.

Cheerful Meals

Meals are a time for enjoyment, a social occasion in which children and adults are equal participants in a common activity. It is often the only occasion during the day when the members of a household are together. Ideally, it is a cheerful time.

Keeping cheerful is easy when you and your child want the same things. It is when the adult's wishes clash with the child's that tension mounts. Mealtimes can easily produce this kind of tension because they represent not only money spent, planning and time (shopping, cooking, preparing), but psychological investment—hope that the meal is a success, the food eaten and enjoyed and the effort that has gone into it appreciated.

When a meal is a flop, do we swallow our disappointment? Feel sorry for ourselves? Nag or yell? Here are some thoughts that may be helpful:

> Don't expect every meal to be a complete success—or com-
> pletely eaten. The reason for failure may have nothing
> to do with the cook.

Try not to let your disappointment make you a nag or a mar-
tyr. Both will make the situation worse.

After the first surge of annoyance, remember that clean
plates are not as important as relaxed or contented
people.

There are many meals ahead; don't give up.

Conversation at table plays a key role in making mealtimes pleasant
or miserable. Some families have a rule that no quarrels are to be
raised or settled during a meal. They are wise enough to know that,
apart from the social advantages, there are physical ones: tension and
turmoil are hard on the stomach. It is better to find some other time
to settle complaints. After a pleasant meal discussion is apt to be more
rational; the heat is gone.

Beyond Cooking and Eating

Introducing children to cooking early gives them a great deal of
pleasure and a feeling of competence. Whether they are aware of it or
not, they are also seeing many scientific and mathematical principles
in practice—increases in volume, the hardening or thickening of
things when heated, the importance of exact measurement and of different quantities. There is art in cooking too, and decorating cookies
and cakes is only one example. And there is sweat—chopping, beating, stirring, kneading. These activities are enjoyable because there is
always a visible upshot—triumphant or terrible or merely expected.
When they are cooking with you, children are making things happen.
They are having a good time while engaged in serious and important
business. And after doing all that, they get to eat the results. The pleasures of eating and cooking should not be snatched, but savored.

Bikes, Backpacks and Basketball Hoops

VICTOR BUSCH

Children have always been highly physical beings, reveling in their games and sports on city streets, in parks, on sand-lot fields and in suburban backyards. In our culture they are often joined by hordes of determined, muscle-conscious adults involved in running, biking, swimming, skiing, golf, soccer, and improving their tennis serves. And most kids and grownups love such ambitious projects as hiking, camping, fishing, and extended bicycle jaunts.

The value of such activities, done with appropriate moderation, includes a built-in fun component. They're pleasurable by their very nature, and special effort isn't necessary in order to insure enjoyment. But a few suggestions may help parents smooth out rough spots in planning and execution and guarantee an even higher level o.° pleasure.

Close to Home

Whether you live in a city, a suburb, on a farm, or even a mountaintop, your kids undoubtedly have their own favorite play areas and a whole roster of games to go with them. In cities there are scores of street games which require little more than a jump-rope, a small rubber ball and the side of a building, or a bit of chalk to mark a hopscotch grid on the sidewalk. Roller skates, bicycles, and the ubiquitous skateboards (descendants of the old-fashioned scooter) round out this street paraphernalia.

Every city now has its share of parks with playgrounds for the younger set equipped with slides, swings, and the like. For older children there are diamonds for softball games, fields for touch football, tennis and basketball courts. In the suburbs, a hoop attached to the side of a garage will provide hours of exciting one-on-one games, and badminton and volleyball nets can easily be set up in backyards. Many communities also have swimming pools, skating rinks and gymnasiums, as well as specifically marked bicycle and jogging paths. And of course, there are Frisbees everywhere. Kids have invented many variations of this toss game, including "Frisbee baseball" and "Frisbee golf." (In Frisbee golf, a receiver stands still in one fixed place. The thrower stands some distance away on the "tee" and aims the Frisbee. If the toss can be caught without the receiver having to move his feet, it scores as a "hole in one.")

All these activities are necessary to growing children. Their enormous energy reserves have to be invested properly, and as their bodies grow so too does the need for large-muscle coordination and healthy skeletal development. And naturally, vigorous physical activity is high on the growth agenda.

Where you as an adult come into all this depends chiefly on the age and interests of your child. When it comes to outdoor play, kids are highly self-sufficient and highly inventive. They need and welcome every opportunity to test and stretch themselves physically as well as mentally. But there is a place for adults in this busy active world. With younger children, an adult acts as guardian, supervisor, and teacher. Safety rules, even for the youngest, must be carefully laid out regarding traffic, climbing, going too near the edge of high places, and so on. Simple first aid (of the Band-aid variety) should also be introduced early. Naturally there will be scrapes, bruises, and other minor accidents—but with young children we adults are responsible for creating a sense, not of timidity but of safety and reasonable caution—as well as enjoyment.

As your children get older and become more involved in team and structured sports, your own role changes. Instead of acting as guardian or supervisor, you may at times become an active participant, joining in softball, basketball, touch football games, and so on. Here too the mature person's contribution is vital. Whether you're a bystander, a coach or a team member, it's your chance to promote the basic values of fairness and good sportsmanship. Fairness is something that children feel keenly about, and team sports are an excellent way to give this concept tangible form.

Competition is another factor. With peers, childhood competition —up to a point—is natural and healthy, but kids need to know that the real idea isn't simply to win, but to play as well as possible, and to have a good time. Only experience will help them learn that "you win some, you lose some." Time will also help them discover their strengths and weaknesses. Such discoveries are essential to learning how to compete rather than simply scoring or striking out.

Too often, parents and overeager coaches bring their own competitive yearnings to the ballpark. Some try to compete with their own kids on the playing field, instead of nurturing and encouraging the child's developing skills. Others want to fulfill their own frustrated dreams by basking in the glory of "my kid the champ." Remember, most youngsters have enough trouble measuring up to their own expectations and those of their peers. Having to "deliver" to satisfy an adults' needs will only add to anxiety and in some cases cheating. When kids have to play "like pros," a lot of the joy of playing ball gets lost—like a fly ball.

Respect for nature and the environment also need to be encouraged. Playing areas should be chosen well away from flowers and shrubbery, and cleaning up after a game is a must.

Is your child hesitant about certain sports? Here your role is a sensitive one, since the aim is to encourage, not to pressure. If you were once a whiz at touch football, or the champion skater or basket shooter in your neighborhood, that doesn't mean that your offspring will share these same ambitions and interests. In this area kids are excellent judges of what they like and wish to do; your role is primarily to support, encourage, and advise.

What about sports equipment? Again it's a matter of judgment. Obviously a child can't play baseball without a ball and bat, or go bicycling without his wheels, but athletic supplies can be kept to a fair and inexpensive level. Sometimes the danger here is too much, too soon. One twelve-year-old expressed a vague interest in skiing, and before she knew it her parents had loaded her down with a costly array of "the best" skis, poles, boots, clothing, and so on. The youngster's interest in skiing faded fairly soon, and all that expensive equipment wound up in her closet, gathering dust and cobwebs. On the other hand, Lee, a lad of eleven who kept pestering his family for more hockey equipment, was told at last to "get the money yourself for all that expensive stuff." He promptly rounded up the rest of his embryo hockey team and they gathered up enough castoffs for a "Super Dooper Tag Sale." Lee and his friends not only financed their equipment but learned to organize, to sell, to keep records, and to stick to a job despite discomforts.

Farther Afield

Many families enjoy hiking, camping, backpacking and bicycling together. See Suggested Reading at the end of this chapter for a list of some of the books that deal with these activities. Meantime, as you and your youngsters move farther from home territory, a few basic facts are worth emphasizing.

Biking

In many European countries bicycles are a major form of day-to-day transportation, but here they are usually associated with fun and leisure, and touring has become a much enjoyed sport. A bike trip for yourself, your kids, and a few friends can last for a day or be a longer one. In either case the principles of safety and common sense apply. Here are some generally accepted "rules of the bicycle road":

> Younger children on tricycles should always stay on the sidewalk, never in the street.
> For learners, training wheels are an excellent device.
> For older kids, the proper wheel height of a two-wheeler should be one-third of the child's height.
> When riding in traffic, always stay on the right side of the road, and ride in single file.
> Watch out for potholes, wet pavement, and loose gravel. Before coming out of a driveway, look both ways carefully; also look both ways at all intersections.
> Give hand signals when stopping or turning.
> Watch out for pedestrians, especially the older folks.
> When riding at night, be sure the bike has a headlight and rear reflectors.
> Don't ever overload the bike—and *don't* try to show off while riding.

Remember when biking on roads with traffic that single file is particularly important. Bike flags on high antennas and bright-colored safety clothing are also advisable. Avoid highways with heavy truck traffic (especially when you're biking with kids), since a big, speeding truck can literally blow a bicycle off the road.

Whether your trip is long or short, one recommended pace is forty to sixty miles a day. This allows biking for about six daylight hours at a speed of eight to ten miles an hour, plus comfortable time for eating, resting, and sightseeing. But if you and the kids are still neophytes, don't try to break any records. To carry your food and other small gear, there are many varieties of bicycle bags. Some bikers prefer the kind that fit over the front handlebar. Others go for large panniers that fit like saddle bags over the rear wheel. If you prefer to wear a backpack, *keep it small.* A large pack worn while you're riding your bike can make you topheavy and throw you off balance.

Planning is essential. Before starting you'll want to ask yourself a few basic questions:

> What will the weather be like? Do we need sweaters? Caps?
>   Light ponchos in case of rain?
> Do we have plenty of food? Water? Fruit juice or soda?
> Will we need a map?
> Do we have a small first-aid kit in case of emergencies?
> What about our route? Are there too many steep hills? Can
>   we stay away from heavily trafficked roads?
> Will the route take us through pleasant country with interesting scenery?
> And especially important: Are all our bikes in good condition?

Before starting a long bike trip with children, be sure you've had some sound experience yourself. Then you may want to try out the group enterprise with a short trip in or around your community. If so, find out all you can about local routes and bicycle paths. For the more ambitious there are carefully worked out bicycle trails in every state, and maps of these are available (see end of chapter). There are also organized bike tours with well planned routes, tour leaders, arrangements for food, shelter, and so on. Information on these trips can be obtained from:

American Youth Hostels, Inc.
National Campus
Delaplane, Virginia 22025
International Bicycle Touring Society
846 Prospect Street
La Jolla, California 92037
Bicycle Touring League of America
260 West 260th Street
New York, New York 10471

Perhaps the most important thing, for this and other vigorous activities, is to consider the age of your child. Biking and camping trips call for considerable muscular activity—even strain—and this can be traumatic for small bodies. Try not to be overambitious, and don't let yourself be talked into a trip that isn't appropriate to your child's age level and particular stage of development.

Camping and Fishing

Camping and fishing too require some personal experience before you undertake them with children.

Camping ranges from simply living in the woods with a knapsack and a sleeping bag to more elaborate expeditions complete with vans, cots, and fancy tents.

The right equipment, of course, is a must. Do you all have sturdy, waterproof boots? The right clothes? Will you have adequate shelter? Do you have enough food of the right kind, and the implements you'll need for cooking? Will you cook over an open fire or a small camp stove fueled by gasoline, kerosene or liquid petroleum? Have you worked with this stove so you can use it safely? Do you have a good hunting knife, hatchet and small digging tool? Do you have a good first-aid kit? A length of serviceable rope? Do you have one or more gasoline or propane lanterns? (Tip: Choose a stove and lanterns which use the same kind of fuel, which will simplify your fuel problems.) And finally, you'll need those small items which are essential but sometimes overlooked: a bottle and can opener, a metal mirror, a small sewing kit, personal toilet articles, suntan lotion, insect repellent, a hammer and nails, dish towels, toilet paper. If you plan to do any exploring, maps and a compass are also necessary.

Remember that in most parts of the United States, while the days may be hot and sunny, nights outdoors can be quite cold and warm garments are needed. And while you don't want to overload, make sure you have enough shirts, socks, and underwear to replace the ones being washed.

"Safety First" is a watchword on any camping trip. Do your youngsters understand how to use all your tools? How to build—and put out—a campfire? How to spot poison ivy and poison sumac? Gathering food from nature can be fun—but do your campers know how to recognize poisonous greens, berries, mushrooms? The operative idea here is: When in doubt, leave it out. It's foolish to take chances. If you plan to cook in a tent, make sure you have good ventilation. Most camping accidents with portable stoves occur in small crowded tents or cabins without enough circulating air. A burning stove in a confined space eats up oxygen and emits carbon monoxide, which is odorless, colorless—and very dangerous. If you're cooking inside, be sure you have a good air flow.

Next to safety, "Have Fun" is the second order of the day. This means fun for you too. Nothing can be more onerous than herding small fry twenty-four hours a day if your needs aren't met too.

Slip a paperback or two into your pack. Or tuck in a bottle of wine, some cans of beer or your special hors d'oeuvres. When the youngsters have been bedded down, you can enjoy your own "adults' hour" under the stars. Just be sure the safety rules are clearly understood by all before you do your relaxing.

Part of the fun of camping is learning and respecting the ways of nature, and every serious camper must be an ecology warden as well.

> Be careful about your water source, and never drink water where there is doubt about its purity. Organized campsites always have good water, and if you're traveling in a van you might bring along a good supply.
> Toilets should be located at least one hundred feet from water sources. For solid waste, dig a sizable hole or holes; afterward fill these up with loose soil and tamp it down.
> All washing (dishes, clothes and personal) should also be done well away from sources of drinking water. Soapy

water should be disposed of at least a hundred feet from
lakes or streams.

Burn all garbage (with care) or cart it away with you. If you
merely bury it, erosion or animals will probably bring it
out in the open again.

Don't camp close to the edges of lakes, streams, or rivers.
These shorelines are fragile and can be permanently
harmed by too much human activity.

Don't be a noise polluter. Leave those loud radios and tape-
decks at home, and enjoy the myriad sounds of nature
instead.

Show respect for wild animals and all growing things. This is
especially important for younger children who get excited at the prospect of pulling up great bunches of wild-
flowers or chasing after small woodland creatures.

Taking a cue from the Indians, always leave your campsite in
cleaner, better shape, if possible, than you found it.

Tom McNally, in his excellent book on camping (see Suggested
Reading, p. 147), concludes with a Camper's Code of Courtesy in
which he outlines the right kind of behavior for dedicated campers,
including respect for others, conformity to rules in public areas, and
so on. He ends with a logical point: "I will conduct myself as a responsible camper at *all times.*" McNally also lists the addresses of official
campsite agencies for all fifty U.S. states plus Canada. Organized public and private camp grounds are available almost everywhere, offering fresh running water, cleared sites, privies, fuel and food supplies,
and other amenities. These sites can make life for campers a lot easier
and should be investigated, especially by families new to camping.

Guidelines for fishing trips follow those used for camping, and very
often the two activities are combined. Again, your trip will be successful if you plan it properly and bring to it some prior experience.
Serious fishermen must have good knowledge of fishing sites, tackle,
and the kinds of catches available. And, of course, safety rules must
include precautions regarding sharp hooks and other tackle, and the
basic principles of boats and boating.

In all these cases: Don't take children who are too young. Don't be
overambitious. Arm yourself with information ahead of time. And
follow the rules of safety and common sense.

146   *Day by Day*

Backpacking

Backpacking is a great activity for hardier adults and older children. Backpacks can be obtained in scores of shapes and sizes, like sleeping bags and necessary items such as hiking boots, gloves, parkas, cooking equipment, and toilet kits. The difference between this equipment and the kind used for more sedentary camping is that backpackers must aim for total lightness and utility.

The best way to find the right equipment is to read up on the subject, talk to experienced backpackers, and then carefully shop around. You'll find heaps of gear and gadgets, some useful and many unessential. If funds permit, you're better off buying quality. After the initial expense, backpacking becomes one of the most economical vacations possible.

Here are a few pointers for successful backpacking:

> Don't choose boots simply because they're "heavy." A light, sturdy boot will make the hiking easier. According to veteran packers, a pound on your feet is equal to about five pounds on your back. Pick boots with fewer seams, so water won't leak in when the going is wet.

> Carry freeze-dried food in preference to canned food when possible. Canned foods contain water, which makes them much heavier. To save weight, get rid of fancy packaging and repack food items in light plastic bags and containers. On the trail a backpacker burns up twice the calories he or she would burn at home (this goes for the kids, too), so be sure you have enough food with you —or know where you can buy more.

> When packing your load, the heaviest items should always go high and forward. Surprisingly, this provides better balance and tends to relieve strain on the shoulders. Pack items on top which you need frequently, so you can get to them more readily.

> Ninety percent of all backpackers in the United States do their hiking in the month of August. If you and your family crave solitude, you may want to go at other times of the year; but trails are plentiful, and there's generally more than enough room for all.

Campsite agencies (see Suggested Reading) can supply information on suitable hiking trails and routes in your area. Here again planning is crucial, and no trip should be undertaken without full knowledge about the weather, nature of the terrain, presence of wildlife, and so on.

Since the aim is for everybody to have a fine time, all the members of your outing have to be accepted as participants. On a backpacking jaunt, for instance, even the smallest child (perhaps a ten- or eleven-year-old) should have his own *small* pack to carry, in order to feel like a full-fledged member of the team. On a camping trip the youngest can help with the washing up, or in gathering twigs for kindling. By sharing the work and responsibility—as well as the fun—adults and kids alike will find such adventures a time of great growth and inner rewards.

Suggested Reading

Freewheeling: The Bicycle Camping Book by Raymond Bridge, Stackpole Books, Harrisburg, Pa., 1974.

Bike Tripping by Tom Cuthbertson, Random House, N.Y., 1972.

Guide to Bicycle Trails by Robert Colwell, Stackpole Books, Harrisburg, Pa., 1974.

Camping by Tom McNally, Follett Pub., Chicago, 1972.

Camper's Guide to Woodcraft and Outdoor Life by L. M. Henderson, Dover, N.Y., 1972.

Campground Atlas of The U.S. and Canada by Bier and Raup, Better Camping Magazine Pub., Milwaukee, Wisc.

National Park Guide by Michael Frome, Rand McNally, Chicago, 1970.

Rand McNally Guidebook to Campgrounds, Rand McNally, Chicago, 1970.

Private Camp Grounds, U.S.A. by Glen and Dale Rhodes, Box 2652, Palos Verdes, Calif., 1970.

Fishing by Tom McNally, Follett Pub., Chicago, 1972.

Fishing with Small Fry: A Parent's Guide to Teaching Children How to Fish by Jim Freeman, Chronicle Books, San Francisco, 1973.

Fishing for Fun by Byron Dalrymple, Winchester Books (Scribners) N.Y., 1975.

Fishing From Boats by Milt Roske, Macmillan, N.Y., 1968.

Introduction To Backpacking by Robert Colwell, Stackpole Books, Harrisburg, Pa., 1970.

America's Backpacking Book by Raymond Bridge, Scribners, N.Y., 1976.

The Sierra Club Summer Book by Linda Allison, Sierra Club, San Francisco, 1977.

A Pet in the Family

BARBARA BRENNER

"Please, may I keep him? I promise to take good care of him."

These phrases could go into an anthology of "common litanies of earth children," they're so typical of all times and all places. The concept of sharing human space with an animal pet seems to have been with us for a long time. Toys, games, education—even values—may change. But the pet tradition remains intact, one of the rituals that helps parents to bridge the generation gap; to share and care with our children; to exhibit our values in action; and to just enjoy our kids.

Are Pets Necessary?

What is there about a kitten or a tank of guppies that has such enduring magic? Can the companionship of a dog or cat mean that much to the total of a child's life? Psychologists say it can, and everything we observe affirms it. Knowing and caring for another creature seems to home in on some of our deepest emotions—caring, nurturing, being needed and accepted. They're feelings we certainly want to encourage in our own kids, especially in a world where feeling for fellow creatures, human or otherwise, sometimes seems to be going out of style.

There's another less lofty but certainly as valid reason for the popularity of pets. They are, quite simply, great fun, as anyone who grew up with them remembers and anyone who shares the experience with a child observes.

When I was growing up, our family ran to dogs. Our first was a Bos-

149

ton Terrier name of Dotty, who was already old when we inherited her from my grandparents. We all loved her madly; when she died we bought Boston Topsy, a separate but equally wonderful experience. And she was followed by Boston Tuffy, in what was by now a family tradition. By this time I was married and ready to acquire my own pets. But it seems that pet-lovers not only produce pet-loving children; they imprint them totally. The first dog in my new home was a Boston terrier.

My own children's total commitment to animals resulted in our branching out in the pet department. We have kept snakes, lizards, turtles, rabbits, parakeets, tropical fish, guinea pigs, and dogs, to name a few. We've had pets for a brief time and for their lifetime. We've watched them being born and watched them die. That zoo parade has been a tremendous part of our boys' growing up and we are all enriched by it.

I have a bias in favor of keeping critters around. I think having a pet is good for everybody—like vitamins and milk and sunshine. However, this is not a hard sell. Before you leap into the great pet-owning stream, stop a minute and consider.

How Do You Feel about Pets?

Before you opt for hamster or hound dog, ask yourself what kind of animal *you* are. Do you like animals and feel comfortable with them, or does the very sight of a beastie running around make you twitch? Are you in a family that leans to casual housekeeping and is willing to deal with a certain amount of mess or clutter associated with pets? Or do you pale at the sight of animal hair on a carpet? It's not a question of how you think you should feel but how you do feel. And if you're going to be miserable having a pet "for the sake of the children," don't do it. Or do it in a way that will accommodate to your needs as well as those of the youngster. Discuss your reservations with your child frankly; he or she probably already knows. And if you decide that, for one reason or another, you simply can't tolerate a pet, stick to it. You can do other things. Like taking your youngster to the zoo more often, or establishing bird feeders outside, or taking food for the ducks in the local pond. You can even donate a pet to the school (first check with the teacher), if you feel you want your child to have the experience.

But maybe you're just not sure whether your family and a pet will be a good combination. Then the best thing is to go slow. Why not try a few pets for size? One pet test is to borrow a neighbor's cat or dog for a few hours or for a day. See how you like having an animal around. See how the youngsters react. Is your child thrilled or frightened? Is having an animal around a hit or a hassle? You can sometimes get a pretty good notion from this visit whether having a permanent pet is the right or wrong idea for your family.

Another pet test is to borrow from the wild. Spend some time outdoors with your child. Catch a cricket or grasshopper, or capture an earthworm, toad, or salamander. Put your captive in a jar with a screen on top or holes for air. Give it leaves, grass, and a sprinkling of water for moisture. Keep it overnight to observe. Do a little research on what it eats, how it lives. Then return it to the wild place where you found it. Assess how your offspring enjoyed the temporary visitor.

You'll probably discover that everyone got enormous pleasure from its presence. Perhaps after a few of these experiences you'll expand your collecting to snails, caterpillars, or small lizards. And then after a while you and your child will be ready to talk about having a permanent house guest, a real pet animal to keep.

Choosing a Pet

The important thing is that everyone should agree on what animal you're going to bring into the family. Try to match your choice both to your child's age and to your family's life style. If you live in a city apartment you may not want a dog, which needs to be taken outdoors three times a day. In this situation a parakeet, hamster, or kitten may make more sense. Check your lease before you adopt. Otherwise you may be faced with getting rid of an animal that everyone has already become attached to. At one point we found out, much to our chagrin (and after we had acquired our rabbit and hutch), that rabbits are prohibited in the deed to our house.

Climate, too, is a consideration. If you live where it's cold, you may have to rule out a tropical animal. Most lizards, snakes, and some birds need constant warmth. This means you'll have to figure on heating lights or some other device to maintain cozy temperatures in the winter. From both an energy and a budget point of view, it may rule out these exotica for you.

The age of the would-be pet owner is a big factor in your choice. Some animals make great pets for older kids, but not such great ones for toddlers. If your child is two or three years old, you're going to have to figure on doing most of the maintenance yourself. If it's a hairy English Sheepdog you've all set your hearts on, know that the grooming and walking will be done by you, at least for the first few years. On the other hand, even a little tyke can handle some of the feeding of a gerbil or hamster, *with supervision.* Sometimes it's better to get a cage animal for little persons. That way they can't squeeze or maul by mistake. A friend of mine told me a story that illustrates this point well. Her seven-year-old dropped their pet guinea pig. The animal's leg is broken in three places. The child is sleepless with guilt and remorse. The vet's bill will be a hundred dollars.

This sort of thing happens too often not to be mentioned more than casually. Small children can't handle small, tender animals without lots of supervision. Either watch closely, establish a "hands off" rule, or get an animal that's big enough to take care of itself.

Another consideration in choosing a pet is your budget. There's very little point in breaking the bank to provide your offspring with a meaningful experience. Don't spring for the expensive and fancy breed when the creature of humble birth can give just as much pleasure. An ordinary goldfish or a mixed-breed cat or dog makes a fine and satisfactory pet. (Mixed breed dogs are sometimes better companions than pedigrees.)

A few good books on the subject will go a long way toward helping you make up your mind about what animal to choose. You and your family may want to share reading Sara Stein's *Great Pets* (Workman); *Your First Pet,* by Carla Stevens (Macmillan); or the Scholastic paperback *Favorite Pets: How to Choose and Care for Them,* by Rita Vandivert.

After you've all read the books together, you're ready for a trip to the local pet store, kennel or animal shelter. By this time you've probably decided *what.* Now all you have to decide is *which.* If the family votes are still split, here are some pros and cons on popular animal pets.

Anyone for Fish?

Fish are endlessly interesting; there seems to be something in a fish tank for everyone. They're great pets to watch, and they can be enjoyed without handling and with little mess. A well-set-up fish tank has some of the same appeal that a doll house has. It's a miniature world that a child can understand and relate to, and it's also a model of something much bigger. Kids very quickly grasp the idea that what's going on in that tank is a replica of what goes on in larger bodies of water. A fish tank can be a whole science course, with the kids doing much of the deduction. You can start with the simplest arrangement—a few guppies—and work up to an undersea world of fish, aquatic frogs, snails, and even certain crustaceans. A tank is a window on mating habits, reproduction, mating display, aggression, and feeding behavior. You won't get much affection from your scaly boarders, but you too may get hooked on watching them. Fish collecting and breeding can become a hobby that will engage the whole family—and it can be expensive, too.

Fish are easy to keep in that they can be left for a day or two unattended, if you have the proper tank setup. The only real negative about them is that they're subject to specific fish diseases, some of which can wipe out your entire population, with the attendant tears and sorrow.

There are many books especially for the fish enthusiasts. One good one is *What Do You Want to Know About Guppies?*, by Seymour Simon (Four Winds Press).

A Word about Birds

Part of the great attraction of birds is their beauty, but what I like about them is that they don't have to be walked. The care and feeding of a bird is something a child five or older can easily handle. And some birds can be finger trained. Most birds will relate to their keepers; this is especially true if the young bird fancier spends time with it, and if the bird is kept in a cage without another bird.

Canaries can't be handled but the males sing splendidly. Budgerigars (sometimes called parakeets) and cockatiels don't have gorgeous voices but they're tamer. These two species and others can often be taught to mimic human speech and to do simple tricks. Even if the bird learns only to come to a child's finger, it can be thrilling. If you enjoy seeing the bird or birds move about more freely, but don't want to allow them to fly around, you can house them in a big flight cage.

The cage must be kept clean and the bird needs fresh food and water daily. Some feathers and seed pods will sneak out onto the floor. If you allow the bird to fly around loose, you will have some mess (parakeets leave droppings and like to chew up bamboo blinds).

Canaries are priced according to looks and voice. "Budgies" are bred for color. You may like the color of the ordinary budgie (green and yellow) better than the fancier and more expensive whites and blues.

If you're in the market for a bird, don't let the pet dealer talk you into one of those rare, stunning, and expensive tropical birds. They're hard to keep, enormously fragile, and probably never should have been taken from their native habitat in the first place.

There's a lot of information in those paperbound books on bird care that are sold in good pet stores. And if you want a story about a family and birds, you might try my book, *A Bird in the Family,* available through Scholastic.

For the Cat Lovers

Those who keep cats are an evangelical group who claim cats are the best pets in the world. We personally never kept cats because one of our children is allergic to cat fur. This is a common enough problem so that you should check it out before you acquire a kitty.

Individual cats run the gamut from aloof to purringly affectionate. All felines are highly intelligent and extremely fastidious. To watch a cat cleaning itself may be the ultimate lesson in personal hygiene. The toilet habits of cats are exemplary; I once heard of a cat whose owner trained it to use the toilet. But don't depend on it—figure on cleaning out the litter box.

You can expect your cat to cuddle up, purr and even "talk" to its person. But don't expect it to fawn or grovel, the way some dogs do. Cats are more independent. Nevertheless, a kitten at play can captivate the family for hours.

You can usually persuade your cat to travel in a carrier. And they don't have to be walked. Most adult cats will sensibly avoid confrontation with a tail-grabbing toddler. However, most will scratch if they're being molested. On the other hand, kittens can be injured by overeager clutching. Here too "with supervision" applies.

If you're in the market for a cat, read *Little Cats,* by Herbert Zim (Morrow). You'll get some idea of the wide variety to choose from. On the other hand, you may want your choice to be governed by the kittens available at the local animal shelter. If you go there, be sure to take your youngster with you. It will be a rich though sobering experience for everyone. Saving a kitten's life by giving it a home will certainly deliver the message that the lives of animals are valuable. Arrange with the shelter or your own veterinarian to have a female cat spayed or a male cat altered. Explain to your children why it is the responsibility of pet owners to control the animal population, and that it is a kindness, not a cruelty, to the animal.

Small Furry Mammals

Gerbils and other small furry creatures are sometimes called "shelf pets." Each one of them has different requirements and should be investigated separately. *Shelf Pets,* by Edward Ricciuti (Harper and Row), will give you an idea of what's involved in keeping many of them. Gerbils, hamsters, guinea pigs, white rats and mice are just a few of the choices. They are all relatively inexpensive, although the cages are costly. You might want to investigate making your own housing for such a pet; it's a nice family project.

These animals vary in their ability to suffer handling; therefore their cuddle factor isn't high. Nevertheless, some youngsters will get enormous pleasure from the simple care and feeding of small furbearers, and their interesting ways of playing can be a great stimulus to written or told stories. One youngster kept a record of her pet's progress; she called it The Book of Gerbil. A fine book on gerbils is *The 17 Gerbils of Class 4A,* by William H. Hooks (Coward McCann).

Small furry mammals are more personally involving than either birds or fish, but probably not as much as a dog or cat. Be sure to get a book on the care of the particular small mammal you choose. Take a look at Randolph's *Your Pet's Complete Record Book* (Grosset & Dunlap).

Of Course, Dogs

Dogs are the most social of all animal pets. The average dog will knock itself out to please and has an elaborate set of responses to its owner. So much has been written about dogs by experts that it seems repetitive to cover that ground here, except to say that our own experience with dogs has been a source of delight to our family. We've traveled with dogs, sketched them, watched them grow from puppies, tended them when they were sick. We've even immortalized a couple of them in our books. And some of the dandiest debates between our two sons have originated over whose turn it was to walk the dog!

To get the maximum pleasure from your dog, you have to match the dog to the family. A good rule of thumb is the younger the child, the bigger the dog. Small dogs can't handle being treated carelessly. A Yorkshire terrier, for instance, has very little defense against enthusiastic squeezing except to snap. So it does. This can lead to all kinds of fears on the part of the child and a feeling in the family that the dog is mean or "no good." Better to avoid a Yorkie or other small dog until your child is older. You'll all be much happier with a patient Labrador or some other big dog known for its tolerance.

You'll probably want the dog to grow up with the family. Puppies have very specific needs and, as with children, you'll be setting a pattern by the way you treat it when it's young. Training is essential and consistency is all. Hold a powwow and decide what your plan is. Then everybody stick to it. If you don't want the dog to get on beds, no one must let the dog get on a bed. If you don't want the dog to beg from the table, never feed it from the table. Children really enjoy having a part in the making of these rules; it's part of the fun of owning a pet. But you'd better face the fact that puppies, like children, go through developmental stages, including toilet training—and, unfortunately, puppies don't wear diapers. Be prepared for accidents to happen; children will learn that most loves have their messy side too.

Another puppy need is the need to chew; it's safer to have some old socks, gloves, or toy bones handy than to let your pet choose his or her own. And even with all this forethought chances are that sometime the puppy will gnaw up a "no-no" like the sofa cushion or somebody's knitted cap. Puppies certainly help you and your family learn patience, tolerance, and sense of humor.

A good book on training is *Superpuppy: How to Choose, Raise and Train the Best Possible Dog for You,* by D. Manus and Jill Pinkwater (Seabury). You and your children will also get a kick out of Maurice Sendak's and Matthew Margolis's *Some Swell Pup* (Farrar, Straus and Giroux).

The rewards of having a gentle, loving, aware companion like a dog are so numerous that they're impossible to calculate. Whether you pay five dollars or five hundred dollars for a puppy, you're investing in a memory bank of experiences that has no price tag.

Exotic Pets

Personally I'm against them. I can't recommend monkeys, coati-mundis, Brazilian boas, or those fragile little tropical finches. A rare animal may be a status symbol but it doesn't mean much to a kid. Besides, these animals are fast disappearing from their wild habitat. Why should we help their extinction along? It's really better to stick to the species that can reproduce in captivity; they're also easier to maintain.

The same goes for taking and keeping animals from the wild on your own. I used to do it myself. But now I replace the water snake or lizard after I have a chance to watch it in action for a little while.

Getting the Most Out of Having a Pet

So here you are, a family with a pet. There are a thousand ways that the experience will be meaningful. Feeding and tending chores can be shared; they can even be the child's complete responsibility when he or she is old enough. Animals relate in a special way to the one who feeds them, and this can be pointed out to your youngster to help sweeten the task.

Just watching is a lovely way to spend time with a pet. A record of observed behavior can be kept. Often the expertise that the child develops from his pet observations forms the basis for a real hobby. It can even lead to a career choice later on.

All the major cycles of life are mirrored in the lives of pets. Take a look at a kid's face as a dog or cat gives birth to young, or when the animal has been sick and has recovered.

It's sometimes hard for a child to get the proper perspective on keeping a pet. In our society there seem to be subliminal messages that say that an animal is like a toy—bought at a store for money, exploitable, and *disposable* if you get tired or bored with it. It's important that parents don't reinforce this notion, even if having a pet isn't one hundred percent pleasure. It's important that the whole family learn to accept this live organism into their lives—to accept the work that's involved, to be aware that however "low" on the scale of life forms, this creature has needs and rights in the world. It can't be "dumped," either down a toilet or at a summer place, for the sake of convenience.

One of the things that everyone who has a pet must face is that some time the animal will die. Some people don't have pets because they don't want their children to suffer the pain of loss. But if your child can cry over the death of an animal, can go through the stages of mourning, it helps that youngster become more of a feeling, compassionate individual. And since no one can avoid death, this grief is preparation for accepting the fact that death is a part of living. In this first experience you are there to help share and ease the sorrow, and that's important too.

Pets, indeed, become members of the extended family, linking children and adults in joyous ways to the larger family of all living things.

The World of Make-Believe

SUSAN J. LEWIS

The world of make-believe is the wonderland of childhood, the vital childspace that is essential to growth.

Two-and-a-half-year-old Sam stands before the mirror with an empty shaving-cream can, "sprays" his face, and with a bladeless razor begins the shaving ritual he has seen his father go through each morning.

Three-year-old Jill slinks along the floor. "Meeow! Meeow! I'm a cat."

Two four-year-olds, Susie and Thomas, are "married" and taking care of their two sick "children." Together they comfort their dolls, take temperatures, and dole out medicine. Then Susie settles in to read the children a story, while Thomas goes to the toy stove to warm some soup for his ailing offspring.

Five-year-old Chris spends a full afternoon with his playmate, Julie, deeply absorbed in constructing a two-floor garage out of blocks. They have installed a ramp, demarcated parking spaces with masking tape, included a place to pick up a parking ticket and a place to pay. The next afternoon, with a collection of toy cars, the two friends go about using their garage. Over and over they run the cars past the ticket booth, up the ramp, into a parking space, down again, and onto the street.

Trying on Roles

In a world where children are essentially powerless, "pretending" gives them the license to be anything they wish and to create any

159

structure they choose. They can go forward in time to try on for size any number of adult roles—mommy, daddy, policeman, or doctor. They can assume extraordinary power in a fantasy realm where they take on the characteristics of their favorite superhero. They can safely vent their emotions; through the disguise of a ferocious tiger angry feelings can be played out. And when the demands of the real world become too overwhelming, a child can go back in time to the security of being a baby, with thumb in mouth and a ragged Teddy bear in hand.

Between the ages of about two-and-a-half and six, "pretending" is not only the dominant form of children's play but the way in which children learn about themselves and the world around them. It is the way children clarify and internalize their understanding of that world and how it functions.

Although older children can sustain play away from the presence of an adult, children of two and three prefer to play close by the parent. A low shelf in the kitchen containing the child's own collection of pots and pans can provide playthings to use while the parent does kitchen chores. A miniature ironing board, iron, and a few scraps of cloth are props that allow the child to work alongside the adult who is ironing the family wash. Children will also delight in having a small work bench with some tools when accompanying the woodworking parent.

In one week of play, a trio of inseparable playmates—Pete, age five, and Jenny and Adam, both four—turned an old backyard slide into several imaginary objects. One day the slide became a fire engine, with Pete as the driver and the others hanging on as firefighters. On another afternoon it was a telephone pole, with three "hard hats" climbing it to fix lines and repair wires. Finally the slide was a house, with Jenny the mother, Adam the dog, "Lassie," and the oldest, Pete, scrunched up to be the baby.

The first dramatic play of toddlers is simple imitation of characteristics that, for them, define the term grownup—shaving, putting on lipstick, answering the door, talking on the phone. As children grow older, their knowledge of the world expands along with awareness of their own and other's emotions; consequently their pretend play becomes more elaborate and complex. Entire scenes are acted out as children play mother, baby, doctor, firefighter, gas-station attendant, or librarian. Babies may be scolded or comforted and scenes between "adults" may be argumentative, loving, dictatorial, or cooperative. An activity that was initially solitary expands to incorporate another child and, later, a whole group of children.

Free from the limitations that real life imposes, pretend play allows children the opportunity to create the world as they wish it to be, to explore and experiment with ideas, to view a situation from several vantage points, to be the problem poser as well as the problem solver. Such play supports growth in many directions. It is a medium which affords children the opportunity to think creatively and develop powers of imagination. Because it gives children the chance to be in control—to plan, execute, and witness the success of their own self-determined labors—pretending builds self-confidence and self-esteem.

Enriching the World of Make-Believe

Rich and creative make-believe play requires many and varied experiences with both the animate and the inanimate world. You can't play mommy or daddy unless you've observed them in daily routines. You can't play a cat unless you're familiar with its characteristics. And you can't build a garage, gas station, supermarket, or zoo if you've never been to one.

Parents can do much to enrich children's pretend play. Simply letting them hang around you as you go about your daily work gives children the opportunity to sop up a lot of information. Activities that seem mundane to adults—setting the table, washing dishes, ironing clothes, polishing shoes, changing a light bulb—are not only fascinating to a child but provide a beginning understanding of what adults do. Letting children participate in these activities when their interest is high can increase their understanding of the task at hand; it can also be a way of initiating children into the work sharing of a household, introducing chores as a pleasurable rather than painful experience.

Accompanying a parent on errands to the supermarket, gas station, post office, or bakery increases the child's understanding of what everyday living entails. In addition, these outings give children an opportunity to witness and begin to integrate the interdependencies and interrelationships upon which society functions.

When their schedule allows, parents can build into these daily trips a child-centered time as well. Note what catches your child's eye, perhaps a truck being loaded or a sidewalk under repair, and take time to pause and watch the "happening." A neighborhood construction site can be a fascinating experience, especially when you return to the same site week after week to see the building take form. And do also allow time for short trips—to the zoo, the firehouse, a railroad yard. All these experiences are grist for the child's mill. By encouraging discussion and observing the pretend play that follows the trip, parents can recognize misconceptions and, through conversation, a return visit, or a book, can help to clarify and extend the child's knowledge.

The Role of Accessories

As children get older and their play becomes more elaborate, dress-up clothes and accessories become important for defining a character. Objects of all kinds become props that enhance their grand dramas. Chairs become cars on a railroad train, table tops are the roofs of houses, old cartons are retrieved to be used as stores or garages, and a Frisbee can function as a platter upon which to serve a sumptuous feast.

What child doesn't delight in "dressing up"? And what adult doesn't suppress a laugh upon seeing the child's inventive caricature of a grownup? Parents can have great fun collecting the dress-up clothes and accessories that are a favorite part of children's pretend play. Aside from the giveaway pile that emerges from seasonal closet cleanings, thrift shops are another source for inexpensive and sometimes wonderfully outrageous items. Outworn dresses and pants, junk jewelry, old purses and shoes, wide strips of gauze netting and satin, a worn-out brief case, neckties, belts, and a pair of old eyeglass frames are just a few of the treasures out of which a child can construct his or her own special costume. Because they stimulate the child's imagination and make pretending feel ever the more real, costumes can increase inventiveness and involvement in make-believe play.

Generally up to the age of four, children's make-believe play is concentrated upon domestic activities, the child's first and most lingering theme for pretend play. Some props that stimulate this play include:

rubber dolls, doll beds, a child-size table and chairs, miniature tableware, pots and pans, child-size broom and dustpan, a tool kit, shoeshine kit, toy telephone, toy cars, blocks, and whatever else suits a grownup's fancy (and also suits the budget and the space allotment) and the child's interests.

One need not purchase the many manufactured props that children enjoy, such as a toy refrigerator, stove, and dishwasher. A handy parent can build a wooden box with doors and place shelves inside for storage. Sturdy cardboard containers can also be used. Masking tape can denote the function of the box: circles on top can indicate the burners on a stove or a big circle in front can transform the stove into a washing machine.

Around the age of four, children become more focused on the workings of the world beyond the home. Replicas of fireman's, mechanic's, nurse's, and policeman's hats are often just the thing the child needs to establish his characters. A stethoscope, a set of handyman's tools, a policeman's badge, and a toy cash register can make pretend play seem all the more real.

One four-year-old spent months wearing "another man's hat": serious and concentrated on his own interpretation of the world, he used a variety of hats to play out his concepts. Sometimes he would come home from a friend's house to exchange one hat for another more appropriate to the group's dramatic play.

Although children can play well and lustily with whatever they have, as they grow older they will appreciate a wider variety of props and costumes. Where once a stethoscope sufficed for defining doctor, older children will enjoy a small flashlight, a plastic play thermometer, Ace bandages, Q-tips, and a white doctor's coat. Five- and six-year-olds playing store will delight in using all the empty containers that would ordinarily go in the trash—washed-out milk, cottage-cheese, and yogurt containers; cans and jars with labels, detergent boxes, and paper bags and cartons for packing. Even if they can't make change, they'll welcome some toy money to go into their cash register. The more "real" they can make it, the better.

Collecting and constructing the props for make-believe play can become a sentimental return to one's own childhood or a way to provide for your child what you never had. A collection of play accessories can grow immense and space will determine how much can be accumulated. Lucky is the parent with an attic, basement, spare room, or spare closet. Apartment dwellers may find it more difficult to keep materials on hand, but dress-up clothes and props can be stored in cartons or garment boxes with see-through windows and placed under a bed.

Sex Roles

Our increasing awareness of sex roles emphasizes the importance of pretend play in these young years. Are we influencing the roles our children choose by the materials we provide and the attitudes we project about them? Would girls automatically choose a domestic role or might they play mothers "going to work" too? Do little boys want to cook and diaper a baby? We must each decide personally what props and costumes we wish to offer our children and what taboos we associate with them. But generally speaking we should offer as full an array of adult appendages as we can—dolls; housecleaning, cooking and child-care equipment; hats and costumes depicting work roles that have traditionally been ascribed to one sex; tool kits; brief cases—and then leave our children to use them as they will.

Johnny may well shy away from cooking and doll care and continue to be a policeman, or he may do both. Some fathers, raised in a differ ent world and feeling somewhat nervous if Johnny chooses to play with dolls for a while, might feel better with these reflections

> Johnny is not establishing his adult roles yet (though who'd put down his becoming a pediatrician?).
> Such dramatic play helps Johnny to understand his world, to resolve some of his needs, to express his emotions, both positive and negative.
> Since parental anxieties can negatively affect such playful exploration, Father might consider removing himself from the scene until he can better understand, relax, and accept Johnny's activities. Everyone will be more comfortable in the long run.

Similarly, Jenny may continue dolling herself up in baubles, bangles, and beads; but Elizabeth may prefer a catcher's outfit or a doctor's kit. A wide assortment of props and costumes offers us a splendid chance not only to freshly observe our children's choices but to reassess our own hangups on sex roles and what we value. As our children learn, we learn too.

Unstructured Materials

Children use their play to pin down their understandings by creating in miniature the structures and situations that dominate their thoughts. To support this form of pretend play, parents can supply children with materials that are called "unstructured." Because they provide no blueprints for an end result, such materials allow for a wide variety of outcomes; they also serve to increase opportunities for self-expression, creativity, and problem solving. Floor blocks (also known as unit blocks) are a popular and especially fine unstructured material. With blocks, children can build whatever they wish—skyscrapers, airports, farms, houses, bridges, entire cities. Because they can be used to build either primitive or highly sophisticated structures—the outcome determined only by the child's understanding of the material, coordination, knowledge of the world, imagination, and powers of concentration—blocks are a suitable material for children from the age of two and a half through six or even older.

Additional materials such as Lego, Bristle Blocks, Tinker Toys, design cubes, toy cars, bendable rubber people and animals can be used not only to decorate block buildings, but as the tools with which children can enact their imaginary dramas and test out the functional validity of the structure they've created. Carmen and Timothy, two five-year-olds, constructed a bridge out of blocks and carefully built steps at each end. Then, when they put their toy cars to use on the bridge, they realized the steps didn't "work." In time the children figured out that they needed to build a ramp for the cars.

In addition to store-bought accessories, children can inventively use "throw-away" objects that they find themselves and that parents can collect for them—empty sewing spools, empty film containers, scraps of carpet, small pieces of fabric, corks, buttons, pieces of cellophane, cardboard, and small boxes.

After a day at the beach six-year-old Kate reconstructed the beach scene out of throw-away objects. Sandpaper served as the beach, upon which she placed small pieces of fabric for beach towels. A cardboard floor served as the cement area where the snack bar was, and large and small sewing spools sufficed for the tables and chairs. Kate then recalled some miniature paper Chinese parasols which she'd gotten on a trip to Chinatown. She pasted circles of construction paper on top of her tables, stuck her parasols through the paper, and recreated the sun umbrellas she remembered.

Extending Pretend Play

What else can parents do to participate in and enrich their child's pretend play? Observing what a child understands and then thinking of ways to extend that understanding is always a good idea. If your child is playing "restaurant," for example, you might suggest a special trip to a familiar restaurant. If you call in advance to arrange a convenient off-hour visit, the manager may have time to answer the child's questions and take him or her on a tour through the kitchen, storage room, and other usually unseen territory. A take-home present of a menu and some order forms would be received with great pleasure. Parents may discover that they too enjoy such outings, and may be surprised at how much they learn themselves. As a general rule of thumb, when you take children on such a trip, let them take the lead and ask the questions. Children are most often the best judges for determining how much new information they can absorb.

There are many other ways to participate in the child's world of make-believe. The guideline for adults should be to do what feels comfortable and natural. Some adults prefer to be the friendly but silent companion while others can have great fun pretending right along with their child—attending a tea party or shopping in a child-created store.

Don't Neglect the Ridiculous

Pretend play can also veer off into the ridiculous. Mark and Sarah, ages three and four, pay their father a daily morning visit while he's shaving. "What would you like for breakfast, Daddy?" they ask in unison. With slight variations in the menu, their father replies, "Spaghetti and ice-cream sundae!" No matter how often repeated (and this game has been going on for months), gales of laughter meet his reply and the children spin into action, using the bath stool as a stove and the hamper top as a serving counter.

Children love adults who have retained the ability to be silly, and there's room for the ridiculous in all of us. And savants say that much valuable learning often occurs in these absurdities, such as language development, selective judgment, categorizing, and comprehension of reality.

Pretending and Feelings

When her sister was born, Susannah's mother gave three-year-old Susannah a rubber doll, a doll-size bassinette, and a changing table. While her mother attended to the needs of the baby Susannah worked at her mother's side, bathing, changing, and feeding her own "baby." By providing Susannah with an absorbing activity and allowing her to be near while she cared for the newborn, this mother was able to satisfy Susannah's need for attention and diminish the feeling of exclusion that older children experience when a little brother or sister arrives. Also, given the props and the opportunity for observation, Susannah learned a great deal about the care of infants. There were moments, however, when Susannah inflicted on the doll the punishment she would have liked to give the new usurper. Some older children may, upon a sibling's birth, go back to thumbsucking and even request a bottle. When understanding adults allow a certain return to baby habits and continue to spend some time alone with the older child, this regression usually ends soon.

Another frequent stress situation for young children is parental divorce. Youngsters often respond with confusion, anxiety, sorrow, anger, or all four. While parents emphasize continuing love and support, children also need to deal with their gut-level feelings. Dramatic play can provide such cathartic relief. After her parents' divorce, four-year-old Amy began mistreating her dolls. They were beaten, yelled at, and shut in drawers. Was Amy working out her anger at her parents? Her fears that somehow she was responsible for the divorce? Not knowing the answers, her mother could only keep reassuring her of her parents' love and continuing concern. For a time Amy played only with her animal collection; then gradually the dolls came out of hiding and were no longer mistreated. Amy had vented enough of her feelings in her doll play to stop punishing her parents or herself.

Happy emotions are also recapitulated or reinforced in dramatic play. In the summer of his third birthday, Edward suddenly began recreating Christmas in his dramatic play. He made a block fireplace, a Christmas tree from a twig, and a Santa Claus from a weather-beaten doll. Totally absorbed, he would croon "Jingle Bells" endlessly. Edward evidently needed a long time to absorb the winter festival, and space and time to reenact it at his own level.

A Technique for the Self-Conscious

Finger and hand puppets are another vehicle for pretend play. If parents or children feel self-conscious about pretending, disguising one's voice and talking through the façade of a puppet can make the whole business more comfortable.

Through this medium parents can often gather a lot of information about what the child is thinking, and children are much freer to express their concerns. In identifying himself with a puppet, a child might say, "I'm Tommy the Tiger." When the parent queries, "Well, Tommy the Tiger, what did you do today?" he may discover real-life concerns woven into the child's make-believe response. Tommy using the tiger puppet growled fiercely when his father asked him this question. In a deep voice he roared, "I bited that bad Emma today! Then I put her in a garbage can. And the garbage men threw her into the garbage truck. And the truck chopper thing chopped her all up!" Gradually Tommy's father was able to discover the real problems Tommy was having with his friend Emma and help him resolve them.

Parents often find that using a puppet themselves helps. One mother became concerned at the change in her four-year-old's attitude toward bedtime. Formerly he had gone to bed happily, content to have the room dark and the door shut. Now he wanted just the opposite, and he clung to his mother anxiously at bedtime, but he couldn't put his new fears into words. Finally his mother thought of using Pinocchio, their favorite puppet. Perhaps because he could explain his fears better to the puppet's smiling but impersonal face, or because the puppet was safely removed from human emotional ties, Adam was able to explain. He was convinced that something lived in the closet that would get him if he fell asleep. Then his mother and Pinocchio were able to help Adam deal with and finally lose his terror.

Music for Fun

ELLEN PRESS MENDELSOHN

Music is a natural part of our lives from the time we are born. A crying infant is soothed by a lullaby; even if sung off-key, the love and warmth come through. Young children spontaneously and naturally make music part of their daily lives. It is typical for preschoolers to sing to themselves as they play and to dance, rather than walk, down the street.

When a family shares music, it is a highly profitable emotional and creative experience. But more important, it's a lot of fun—for everyone. If this is the case, why is it so rare for families to regularly share musical experiences? Why is musical communication so often limited to singing "Happy Birthday" once a year? One answer is simple fear, the parents' fear of failure. Many of us feel that we are unqualified to broaden our child's musical horizons or that, lacking talent ourselves, we would be the object of our children's ridicule.

As to the first fear, there is no such thing as an unqualified parent in terms of sharing musical experiences. The only qualification you need is willingness. As to the second, there's nothing to fear. The "worst" thing that can happen is that your child laughs at you because you can't carry a tune or can't dance without looking like a klutz. This isn't bad at all: educators and psychologists keep telling us how important it is for our children to see us as human beings who don't know everything and can't do everything. Not only will your children see you as more human; they will love you for making the effort. Even if you "fail," you'll succeed at something far more important.

169

A World Full of Sound

Silence. It doesn't exist, except in a vacuum. Our everyday lives are filled with sound, often subtle but always there. The modern experimental composer John Cage was aware of this when he wrote a piece called *4'33"*, which consists of a "performer" sitting at a piano with hands in lap for four minutes and thirty-three seconds. During that time the audience becomes aware of two things—the absence of music and the presence of sounds—people moving in their seats, someone coughing, a piece of candy being unwrapped, a siren somewhere in the distance.

Have you ever heard the bubbles bursting in your soda? Have you ever been aware of the rhythmic clacking of a train's wheels? Our world is full of sounds. Children know that and are fascinated by it. They love to experiment and play with sounds.

As babies discover that they can make different sounds they will play with their newfound skill endlessly, seemingly having conversations with themselves by means of their gurgles and babbles. They are fascinated with the sounds around them, shaking and banging all kinds of objects with boundless pleasure. It adds a new dimension to their lives.

Jamie, just over a year old, experiments endlessly with the pots and pans in the lowest kitchen cupboard. Tapping lids against lids, banging spatulas on pans, Jamie is a one-man band—no bought toy would have stirred his creative artistry as deeply. Lynn, at eighteen months, discovered eggbeater "music" when her mother was making eggnog for the child's lunch. Her mother watched as she slowly, unsteadily, turned around and around to the rhythmic beat.

Children use sounds in their play—the "vroom, vroom" of their imaginary car's engine, the "beep, beep" of their make-believe horn. Among the favorite songs of preschoolers are those in which they are asked to imitate the sounds of animals, machines, the wind, and a host of other things. They're really creating music on a very basic level. And they love it. Sometimes a child who is self-conscious about singing in the presence of others will feel quite comfortable imitating animal and other sounds. By encouraging children to do this you loosen up the flow of vocal production that leads to singing.

Let your children experiment with sounds. Children love to make

"silly" sounds, nonsense syllables and spontaneous parodies of familiar songs. Nursery rhymes and camp songs are filled with this kind of
illogical material.

Here are some "sound investments" that pay big dividends with
children:

1. During a quiet time ask your children to close their eyes
   and play sound detective—how many sounds can they
   discover and identify?
2. Encourage your children to imitate and make up sounds.
   They can use their mouths (clicking, popping), hands
   (clapping, rubbing, snapping), feet (tapping, sliding), as
   well as unbreakable objects
3. Let them create sound effects for stories. A cowboy story
   comes to life with sound effects—a galloping horse, the
   prairie winds. This helps children to participate actively
   in the story rather than becoming a passive or bored audience.
4. Encourage older children to experiment with sounds by
   taping them and playing back the results.

Sound, after all, is the basis of music. By just having fun with
sounds, children are experiencing and experimenting with a number
of musical concepts: loud and soft, fast and slow, different rhythm
patterns, different tone colors and textures. Small children don't
need to know the technical terms; it's the experience itself that matters.

Singing: Sounds with Special Shape and Form

The wonderful thing about singing is that your instrument is always
with you. And anyone who can talk can sing, the latter being an extension of the former. Although many people feel self-conscious about
singing, they didn't start out that way.

Singing really is inherent in our nature. I'm sure you've heard your
children chant, "*Joh*nny is a *baby*". You probably chanted it yourself
when you were a child. Musicologists have researched that little melody and found that it is universal.

Since it is a natural part of us, the best way to foster a love for singing is to create an atmosphere in which you and your children feel comfortable doing it. And the best way to create such an atmosphere is simply to allow it to happen and to sing yourself. A young mother once confessed that she considered herself tone deaf and never tried to sing until her baby was born. Then, unself-consciously wanting to please, she found herself humming and chanting easily, and finally even singing all the old nursery tunes. To her surprise she sounded pretty good to herself, and her uncritical smiling audience of one adored it.

Young children, if not stifled, spontaneously chant and sing to themselves as they play. By not interfering you are automatically supplying a great deal of encouragement. You can further encourage singing by joining in and singing with them (without criticizing or competing). You'll be surprised how much fun it is to have a conversation with your child in song rather than in plain old speech. Have you ever had trouble getting your children to get dressed or come to dinner or go to bed? If you chant these requests it can become a game rather than a contest of wills. When I was little and we had to get dressed to go somewhere and I was dawdling, my mother would play a game with me. "Are you ready?" she would sing. And I would answer, "I'm putting on my left sock." "Are you ready?" sang my mother again. "I'm putting on my right sock." Part of the fun was to see if I could have a different answer every time my mother sang her question. I felt great excitement when I could finally sing back, "Yes, I am ready!"

Here is a similar game. Ask your child a question in chant: "What's your favorite color?" or "What do you want for breakfast?" Most often your child will respond in song. If not, be patient. It may take a little while. Your child may or may not answer with the same melody that you sang. Whatever he or she does is okay. Every child develops the ability to hear and repeat a melody at a different rate. If you make children feel they are "wrong," you'll make it hard for them to be able to sing, because a big part of singing is psychological. Singing must be flowing and natural.

There is a reason why nursery rhymes and folk songs last from generation to generation. It is that they come from the people (more proof of the universality of music). And the wonderful thing about these songs is that they are just as much fun for adults as for children.

Children love to hear and sing familiar songs. There's a warmth and security in these tunes; they are like old friends.

Do you remember some of the old nursery rhymes that you sang as a child? Sing them to your children and with your children. But don't "teach" them. Just sing. Children will pick up the words and join in very quickly.

And don't worry about right and wrong versions. It's the spirit that counts. Most folk songs have many versions anyway, and you may want to make up some of your own. "Oh, do you know the muffin man who lives on Drury Lane" can become "Oh, do you know the ice-cream man who comes on down our block." Giving new lyrics to old folk songs will make them your own.

Here are some types of songs that are popular with preschoolers:

> *Songs with animal sounds.* Even if the children can't sing all the words, they can certainly make the sounds of the cow and the duck. The important thing is that they are participating. "Old MacDonald Had a Farm" is a song of this type.
>
> *Songs with finger play.* "Where is Thumbkin" and "The Teensy Weensy Spider" are examples of this type of song. Though the children may not actually sing at first, they will be able to participate by moving their fingers and hands to the song.
>
> *Singing games and action songs.* Some songs have organized actions, like "Ring Around the Rosy." Some have words that suggest actions, such as "Put Your Finger in the Air." Many other songs merely indicate movement. For example, if you sing a song about a duck, before you know it your child may be waddling around, quacking.
>
> *Simple songs with lots of repetition* (a repeated line or refrain). These are excellent for young children. One reason why the Beatles' song "The Yellow Submarine" is so popular with children is the easy, repetitive refrain. Even if they can't remember the verses they can always join in on the refrain.
>
> *Songs with funny sounds or silly lyrics.* Nursery rhymes have lots of funny sounds, like higgledy-piggledy, hey-diddle-diddle, and rub-a-dub-dub. Many folk songs have silly

lyrics. A Jamaican folk song called "Tinga Layo" is about a donkey who walks and talks and eats with a knife and fork.

Older children have their preferences too, some of which overlap those of the younger children:

Nonsense songs. Silliness is popular at any age. The Dutch folk song "Sarasponda" is made up entirely of nonsense syllables, which is what makes it so much fun to sing. There is a silly version of the old folk song "On Top of Old Smokey" called "On Top of Spaghetti," which always brings laughs.

Simple songs with lots of repetition, such as "This Old Man," are popular with children of all ages.

Echo songs (follow-the-leader type) in which each line is repeated. These are easy to pick up as well as fun to sing. If you've ever gone to camp you've probably sung these kinds of songs. One of the best known is "Oh, You Can't Get to Heaven."

Songs that invite you to make up your own rhymes. An example is "New River Train," in which you make up rhymes for the numbers one to ten.

Cumulative songs, in which more words are added with each verse. "The Twelve Days of Christmas" and "Alouette" are two well-known examples.

Action songs. When children outgrow finger play, they graduate to action songs like "John Brown's Baby Had a Cold upon Its Chest" and "My Hat, It Has Three Corners."

Rounds and partner songs. Singing in parts is exciting; even getting mixed up is fun. Everyone knows the rounds "Row, Row, Row Your Boat" and "Frère Jacques." There are many, many others. Partner songs are two songs that can be sung simultaneously, such as "Frère Jacques" and "Three Blind Mice."

In addition to all these, there are literally thousands of folk songs that are fun to sing, no matter how old you are ("I've Been Workin' on the Railroad", "Michael, Row the Boat Ashore" are only the beginning of a long list). Don't worry if you don't know all the words. "La la la" will do, or you can hum or whistle. If your child knows a song that you don't know, that's terrific. How often does a child have the wonderful opportunity to teach an adult something?

Don't be judgmental with yourself or with your children. Criticism makes people tense, and tension tightens up the vocal chords. With children there's no such thing as good singing or bad singing. There's just singing—a release, an expression, a sharing, a form of communication. Don't spoil these by-products of singing just because of a wrong note.

And don't think that you can't sing without some kind of accompaniment. Most folk songs originated in the fields, where there certainly weren't any pianos. Sometimes it's fun to add your own original accompaniment. Clapping is infectious. A lap makes a great drum. Change in the pocket makes a wonderful sound. You've got a whole rhythm band right in your own house. You can tap two pencils together to make rhythm sticks, brush a broom on the floor for the sound of brushes on a drum, jingle a bunch of keys, bang on a coffee can, scrape the teeth of a comb.

Listening to Music

Without listening, music loses its dimension. If we are not tuned in to what we hear, what results is an auditory form of color-blindness— the colors are there but we don't see them. As the kids say, "You really have to get into it." One exception may be "music to sleep by." Naptime or bedtime is a good time to softly play some classical favorites on your record or tape machine. The sweeping chords will cover up little household noises; the lovely melodies may imprint a lifelong appreciation on your tyke.

As you know, young children don't like to sit still for very long. They are doers, not listeners. Then how do we get them to listen actively? First of all, don't try. Music will be an accepted part of a child's life if it is a natural part of his or her environment. Do your children hear music on the radio? Do you play records? Do you respond to their questions about music?

Take advantage of the fact that children like to move. The only way to understand music is to feel it. And what better way to feel it than to move to it? It would be helpful to get physically involved along with your children. You may be surprised at the fun you'll have.

Here are some pointers to help encourage your child's awareness and appreciation of music:

1. The length of musical selections should coincide with children's attention span.
2. Music is more understandable to children if it has dramatic or rhythmic qualities that invite movement responses.
3. Musical subtleties and complexities are less important than strong rhythms, singable melodies, and themes that are repeated.
4. Younger children usually prefer music with faster or upbeat tempos.
5. It is not important that children identify the composer, the selection, or the category. The music itself is the message.
6. Listening doesn't have to be serious, even listening to "serious" music. Children learn best when they're having fun.

I prefer not to recommend specific listening selections for particular age groups because listening is a very personal experience with more exceptions than rules. A Bach fugue may hit a responsive chord in a five-year-old even though that kind of music is not "supposed" to be for young children. These are some of the recorded selections I have found to be of particular interest to children:

Music that uses or imitates environmental sounds
1. *An American in Paris,* George Gershwin. Uses car horns.
2. *Toy Symphony,* Josef Haydn. Uses actual toy instruments.
3. *Death Valley Suite,* Ferde Grofé. The second movement has such sounds as the scraping of wagon wheels, the shouts of the driver, and the snap of the whip.

4. *The Incredible Flutist,* Walter Piston. In the circus section, human voices portray the circus crowd.
5. *1812 Overture,* Peter Ilich Tchaikovsky. Uses a real cannon.

Stories with music and music with narration
1. *Peter and the Wolf,* Serge Prokofieff.
2. *Carnival of the Animals,* Camille Saint-Saëns.
3. *Young Person's Guide to the Orchestra,* Benjamin Britten.

Music with obvious dramatic content
1. "Circus Music" from *The Red Pony Suite,* Aaron Copland.
2. *The Sorcerer's Apprentice,* Paul Dukas.
3. "Ballet of the Unhatched Chicks" from *Pictures at an Exhibition,* Modest Moussorgsky.

Music that is infectious, encouraging physical response, such as clapping, marching, swaying
1. "Stars and Stripes Forever," John Philip Sousa.
2. *Tales from the Vienna Woods,* Johann Strauss.

Here is a listening game that encourages children to be both creative and aware. Play a short piece of music without divulging its title. Ask your children what it sounds or feels like to them. There is no wrong answer because responses to music deal with feeling rather than fact. Young children may respond with movement; older children may prefer to verbalize their responses. For a game like this select music that has obvious moods.

Spontaneity and freedom are two important elements in the learning process. With this in mind give your children access to a simple, inexpensive record player so they can play music whenever they are receptive. Children as young as three and four quickly learn how to use a phonograph. It also gives them a sense of independence and power. Include your children in decisions about record purchasing; and allow them to make some independent choices.

Don't confine your or your children's listening to "serious" music. A varied diet is not only healthier but more likely to keep them coming back for more. Tastes are individual. Don't try to impose yours on your children. Don't limit yourself to music that you feel is educationally valuable; it is likely to be a turn-off and therefore of no value at all.

What about Lessons?

Here are some guidelines to keep in mind when thinking about having your child study an instrument:

1. Physical development. A certain degree of muscular development is necessary for a child to physically manipulate various instruments. Playing the piano requires that the small muscles in the fingers be fairly well developed. The guitar requires hands large enough to reach the strings and strong enough to hold them down. Other instruments have their own physical requirements that, if ignored, will produce nothing but frustration and a sense of failure. The study of all instruments requires a degree of eye-hand coordination.

2. Educational development. The study of any instrument necessitates reading music. As a general rule, if a child doesn't read, reading music will be difficult at best and likely to cause confusion and frustration.

3. Self-discipline. The study of a musical instrument requires daily practice, and unless a child is sufficiently mature, his or her formal music education may never get off the ground.

4. Interest. There is no substitute for motivation. Children have no trouble learning to jump rope or ride a bicycle if they're motivated. Interest has to be there if it is to be encouraged and expanded upon. A child's interest in studying an instrument should be a natural outgrowth of his or her interest in music in general. If a child loves music it's likely that he or she will want to make music.

If the timing is right and the motivation is there, formal music study can be rewarding and enriching and, most of all, a lot of fun.

Music is indeed the language that the whole world speaks, and it is truly the first language that children learn. In many cases they never learn to speak it fluently, or their interest withers and dies like a flower deprived of sun and water. As a parent, you are in the unique and exciting position of being able to provide the sun and water, to make a musical investment that is both fun and highly profitable. It will pay big dividends for the rest of your children's lives. If you invest some time, effort, intelligence, and, above all, love, you will enrich your children's lives and your own.

Here are some music books I have used with great success:

Especially for younger children:

    Challis, Evelyn. *Songs for a New Generation.* New York: Oak Publications, 1974.

    Landeck, Beatrice. *Songs to Grow on: a Collection of American Folk Songs for Children.* New York: Edward B. Marks Music Corporation, 1950.

    ———. *More Songs to Grow on.* New York: Edward B. Marks Music Corporation, 1954.

    Langstaff, John and Mary. *Jim along Josie: a Collection of Folk Songs and Singing Games for Young Children.* New York: Harcourt Brace Jovanovich, 1970.

    Winn, Marie. *The Fireside Book of Children's Songs.* New York: Simon and Schuster, 1966.

For children of all ages:

    Boni, Margaret Bradford. *The Fireside Book of Folk Songs.* New York: Simon and Schuster, 1947.

    deCormier, Robert. *The Weavers' Song Book.* New York: Harper and Row, 1960.

    Leisy, James L. *The Folk Song Abecedary.* New York: Hawthorn Books, 1966.

    Silber, Irwin. *Hootenanny Song Book: Reprints from Sing Out! The Folk Magazine.* New York: Consolidated Music Publishers, 1963.

    Taylor, Mary C. *Rounds and Rounds.* New York: Hargail Music Press, 1959.

    Terri, Salli. *Rounds for Everyone from Everywhere.* New York: Lawson Gould Music Publishers, 1961.

Weavers, The. *Travelin' on with the Weavers.* New York: Harper and Row, 1966.

Winn, Marie. *The Fireside Book of Fun and Game Songs.* New York: Simon and Schuster, 1974.

Aesthetic Awareness

LOIS LORD

How do babies see? And how do babies react to what they see?

Experts tell us that a bright color is one of the things a baby first notices and reacts to physically. He or she may just watch the brightly colored object, and perhaps tremble and wiggle at the sight; but very soon the baby is reaching out toward it eagerly. Motion enhances the attraction. When a baby reaches for a bright color or a swaying mobile, appreciation of the visual world begins. When an adult shares in the delight of discovery, the pleasure is enhanced for both. This special pleasure can be developed indoors, at home; out-of-doors in nature; and in the world of art—architecture, sculpture and painting.

At Home: Colors, Objects, and Pictures

Babies learn about the world around them through all their senses. They look, feel, taste, rub, shake, sniff, and—as all parents know—throw things on the floor. While the primary purpose of this exploration is the gathering of knowledge, one concomitant result is aesthetic experience. Of course no one knows what a baby is feeling or thinking as he or she intently watches sunlight blazing from the side of a goldfish bowl; but we do know the baby is seeing and responding with many senses.

Parents hang a brightly colored mobile on the baby's crib because they know the baby will respond to it: first by watching, then by trying to grab it. When the baby can twirl it, or the bright blocks embedded in the side of the crib, he or she is actively preparing for aesthetic ex-

181

periences, and all the senses and powers are stimulated. Babies who are provided with such stimulation seem to develop more satisfactorily than those who are given little stimulation; is their aesthetic appreciation also developed more fully? One result is observable: the baby/toddler who is allowed to see more, feel more, hear more and participate more in sensory experiences becomes the child who eagerly uses and experiments with new materials and objects—the child who is the explorer and shaper

Little Jane liked to feel everything around her and early developed awareness of texture—the softness of the blanket, the smoothness of her mother's skin, the hardness of wood, the pulpiness of a banana. Her mother enjoyed her child's groping efforts and often enhanced the baby's knowledge by verbalizing her actions: "Janie pats the soft blanket, the soft, soft blanket." Janie may not have understood the words, but may have linked words and actions, and thus taken one small step on the long pathway to language facility and artistic expression. She also came to understand that her mother appreciated and supported her sensory exploration of the world; knowledge and aesthetic appreciation became authority-approved endeavors.

When Timmy was two, he showed his knowledge of the comparative size of objects in his house. "Timmy sit in little chair" or "Timmy sit in big chair" was a frequent demand, as Timmy patted the desired chair imperatively. Timmy was also a keen color discriminator; he would demand the "red pants" or the "blue coat." Even at this early age he was sharply observing and commenting on the details of his environment.

Most young children seem to possess this tendency to notice details, to finely discriminate. Some years ago Bank Street College tested a variety of pictures with youngsters in all kinds of environments, both urban and rural. To the tester's surprise, the children preferred the lively, detailed painting *Children's Games* by Pieter Brueghel to the simpler paintings of a few large objects. For years educators had been saying that children would be confused by "busyness" in art, and should be given pictures that portrayed a few objects clearly drawn. Yet here the children preferred a painting full of action and detail. The testers found that, unlike adults who tended to see the picture as a whole, and feared that the highly active contents would be too much for children to cope with, the children themselves did not look at the picture that way. Instead, they seemed to be attracted to one activity, one detail at a time; and would happily become engrossed in it, ignoring any other pictured events until they were ready to move on. A youngster's way of looking is not ours; we can only provide the raw material for his or her unique interpretation.

Even so simple an activity as a visit to the supermarket offers many opportunities for adults to enlarge a child's awareness of colors, textures, shapes, and sizes. One thoroughly bored shopper found new pleasure by joining in and verbalizing her child's growing interest in their purchases. "Yes, Billy takes one red apple, one shiny red apple. And here are three yellow bananas, smooth thick bananas. Billy wants to eat one? Wait, wait! Mommy and Billy have to pull off the yellow skin first; down comes the yellow skin on one side, on two sides, on three sides. Billy bites the soft white banana, and chews it all up!" Billy is not only connecting words with objects; he is experiencing a banana both visually and viscerally learning and appreciating "banana" with all his senses.

The very young child does not easily comprehend objects that are only partly shown, but can accommodate to unlifelike proportions. Sara, age three, would point to the tiniest elephant in a decorative motif, an elephant too small to be easily noticed by an adult eye, and pronounce firmly, "Effalunt!" though she knew that in real life elephants are enormous. However, she was very bothered by a gay little cartoon of her Aunt Ginny that showed a lively lady with a wide grin and big eyes. "But she don't got a nose!" said Sara worriedly. "Aunt Ginny don't got a nose!" She couldn't accept the cartoon concept because it didn't jibe with the reality of Aunt Ginny; she wasn't ready for an "abstract" aunt. In one study young children were confused by the same character appearing on the facing pages of a picture book. Instead of seeing one cat named Willy engaged in two activities they perceived two cats who looked alike but were separate characters.

Do we then just supply young children with book art that is accurately representational and full of busy activities, such as the popular drawings of Richard Scarry? No. We don't yet know enough about children's aesthetic appreciation to limit them to any one art experience. While Scarry deservedly has his place in children's affections, youngsters need to be exposed to all the excellent art to be found in

children's books today, from the representational to the fairly abstract
to the highly impressionistic.

There are so many children's books today with fine illustrations that
it is not difficult to avoid the stereotyped. In addition to storybooks,
even young children often enjoy looking at books of reproductions of
great art—painting and sculpture and architecture. And don't be surprised if your youngster comments on something you never even
noticed in a favorite painting.

Another way of understanding and encouraging children's aesthetic view of their world is to provide them with raw materials for
expressing that vision. The materials can range from scraps of paper,
cloth, buttons, beads, to unit blocks, paints, crayons, hammer, nails,
and wood.

Many children start drawing at two years—some earlier, some
later. But even from the beginning their special way of looking is revealed in their handling of the materials. Children all over the world,
when they begin to represent the human form in line drawings, do so
in the same way: first they use a line and a circle to represent the head
and trunk; as they develop they add eyes, mouth, and other features,
arms, legs, and finally the finer details of hands, feet, fingers and toes.

But their first pleasures in using crayons or pencils must be in experimenting with the possibilities of the tools; and often the results
they proudly show seem to adults to be just "scribbles." How is the
friendly adult to respond to these expressions? Art is not only a certain way of looking, it is also a form of communication; and with
young children we want to follow where they lead us. Attributing our
own concepts and way of perceiving the world to their early art is to
overload them with our ideas. Instead, our response is more respect-
ful of the process of their exploration if we comment only on what we
see rather than on our interpretation, as Susy's father did when she
presented him with her first "scribble."

"Why, Susy," he said. "You've made so many curved lines! And I
see jagged and straight lines too, all the way across the paper. There's
a lot to see."

Susy beamed. "Yes," she answered. "Now I make more pictures for
you."

Such comments on these early efforts satisfy the child and avoid
trying to discern a subject when there is none. Sometimes we don't

even need to comment; the fact that we take the time to look appreciatively at the work is enough. This may lead children to tell us something about the picture, especially when the child begins drawing more representationally. Then our patient restraint will bear fruit as we are privileged to have a glimpse of our child's views of the world.

Young children love to paint, and the best paints for them to experiment with are moist tempera or poster paints in white and the primary colors. They will find great satisfaction in the look and texture of the colors and in mixing them; for some time this may be all they want to do. As they are often messy, it's well to prepare ahead; a little of each primary color and white, perhaps in jar tops on a cookie tray, with a jar of water for cleaning the brushes. Lots of newspaper on the floor, an apron on the child, plenty of paper to paint on—and voilà! a happy, absorbed child. Paper bags and all kinds of used paper are happily seized for paintings, drawings, or collages. Inexpensive pads of white paper called newsprint can be bought at art stores, but brown paper and old newspapers are just as good. Like many adult modern painters, young children find artistic satisfaction in the possibilities of the materials themselves—the gushiness of the paint, the grain of the paper, the action of the brush.

Try having a "Collage Box" ready and waiting for the young child to work with. Collect scraps of many different textures and materials —shiny satins, bumpy wools, corrugated cardboard, rough burlap or sandpaper, bits of lace, soft fur or cotton, tree bark. Some materials have visual rather than tactile appeal, such as gaily patterned paper or cloth (small all-over patterns are best), or shiny transparencies. Blunt scissors and a paste stick or brush, pieces of cardboard, some gummed stars all add to the possibilities. Freedom to explore and experiment is the best support we can offer; then the young child will create his or her own aesthetic vision, not ours.

As children mature, their attempts to create representational images often become more insistent: "Show me how to draw a real horse." Having been so careful not to intrude our adult perceptions and skills on their attempts to create their own art, should we now abandon that attitude and become the master who shows the apprentice how to make a "real horse"? No, we can offer assistance without imposing our experience on their work. Helping a child to visualize a horse (if we can't study a real one together) by asking questions about the horse's proportions, head shape, length of back, and number of legs helps a child see the real animal in his mind as he guides his pencil.

Coloring books are really another attempt to impose adult skills not only on a child's developing abilities but on his or her aesthetic interpretation of the world. Children often become discouraged when they compare their pictures of animals with the usually banal sketches in a coloring book; yet their own visions and versions may in reality be more powerful. Young Herman's cat painting was questioned by a small neighbor. "Where's the cat's nose and feet?" the other child asked doubtfully.

"All curled up inside the fur," Herman replied. And indeed it was; the essence of a soft, furry kitten ball was there, almost palpable enough to touch.

Naturally, there are times when children aren't in a creative mood; they just want to relax. Then coloring in squares on graph paper or in books of squared paper can be a fascinating project and a good substitute for coloring books. Some children will spend endless time filling in and combining squares in their own special ways. Pounding, digging, and shaping clay offers another means of tactile satisfaction and emotional release, as well as artistic expression.

There are times, too, when children want to work with us, to share their creative ideas and suggestions. Making decorations and cards for parties and other festive events, or just to brighten up the house; can be a rewarding shared activity, if we accept the child's work. Adults can help in costume making too, draping and pinning old sheets or cutting out brown paper outfits, which the children can decorate as they wish.

The child who has been made overanxious by too high standards, by working only with coloring books, number painting sets, or copying patterns, finds it increasingly difficult to express his own views in any art medium. Perhaps our most important role in a child's artistic development is to allow the free exploration of a multitude of materials. Then he or she can gradually shape them into the satisfactory expression of a unique vision of the world before the urge to social conformity sets in. Ideally the child will still feel free enough to continue developing an individual "child's eye view of the world" in a variety of art forms even as social actions become more proscribed.

In Nature: Outdoors

Sharing pleasure of the visual world is valued more in some cultures than in others. In Japan it is usual, on a Sunday or holiday, to see whole families on an expedition to look at a beautiful tree, or a particular view, or the lovely shape of a special rock. From these early family expeditions children are nurtured in appreciation of natural objects.

It is not our way to be quite so direct and selective about expressing our enjoyment of nature. But our children naturally respond with delight to all the outdoor wonders of flowers, rocks, rain and snow. As they get excited about each new thing they see in a park or on a beach we can share their pleasure.

From the age of two Nancy showed an ardent appreciation of nature in all its myriad forms. "Bitty bug!" she would shriek, discovering a minute insect on a leaf. "Bitty bug walking!" as her eyes rounded in wonder. Or, in more sorrowful tones after she had poked it into permanent quiescence, "Bitty bug all asleep now!" Pussywillows were admired in all their fuzzy glory; dandelions and roses were equally beautiful in her eyes, as she eagerly snatched off their stemless blossoms. Fron ants to ocean waves, fireflies to fat raindrops that made little "merry-go-rounds" in the dust—all were enchanting. And the adult lucky enough to be Nancy's companion—or the companion of any observant child—can view the wonder and beauty around us through her morning-of-the-world vision.

What can adults add to any child's fresh perceptions of nature? Very little: as always, we learn from children as they learn from us. All we can supply is an extension of a child's experience. If a child has a persistent interest in plants, we might arrange for the child to grow one at home, and occasionally remark on the changes that occur. Or as children notice colors we can help them to become aware of differences not only in hue but in light and dark and dull and bright colors.

But we need not dim a child's aesthetic enjoyment by piling on too much factual information. As he or she demands details, offer only what is asked for rather than delivering a lecture. Young children learn from experience, observation, and research (as we all do). Our best role is that of a "research resource" and of preserver of the child's own vision.

Many city children find beauty in, as well as affection for, their pet animals. The softness of a kitten's fur, the pattern of its markings, or remarkable claw/paw relationships are closely observed by children. A city canary came in for his share of artistic appreciation when his young owner said, "When Pinny sings, it's like butterflies bobbling around "

City children also discover textures and patterns in their urban landscape. They play with pebbles, rub their hands on rough concrete walls, run a stick along the iron palings of a fence, hop up and down city steps. Touching and handling many "found" objects, they become aware of color, weight, shape and texture, and often they will share what they discover with the nearby adult.

"Hey, look!" shouts five-year-old Jonathan from his pile of stones. "A silky stone—not a bump on it!" His father, a professor, can't help responding, "A stone that smooth shows that it's been in water for a long time. Perhaps the river covered this whole park at one time." Jonathan ignores the information but picks up on the word that delights him. "Smooth, smooth," he murmurs, stroking the stone. "Smooth as noodles. Smooth as china."

But equally often Jonathan and other children play in their own private worlds, perhaps using the stones as symbols. Onlookers can only guess their thoughts as they rearrange the little rocks, gaze at the patches of sunlight and shadows and the beautiful weeds poking up between the stones, or stare at the changing shapes and colors of the moving clouds above. Then the best help we can offer is silent respect; quiet opportunities to observe, to daydream, to let our senses absorb the world around us, are to be cherished.

Art and Architecture, Painting and Sculpture

Visits to museums with young children can be rewarding with a few reasonable precautions. Such visits should be matched with a child's interests and adjusted to attention span, and probably should include only one objective. The temptation is that having finally achieved this trip, you should see as much as possible, but this is a fine way to kill all future interest in museum visits. Depart when the visit is still fun, both for your children and yourself. And don't worry about premature exposure of your children to great art; as with books, your children are entitled to the very best that humans have created in paintings, sculpture, or architecture. Your children should experience a variety of art forms from historical to modern, including those of other countries, religions, and cultures—but not everything all at once. How your children react to what they see, what they absorb or reject, how it sparks a response in them or colors their imagination is personal to each child. Your children may ask you factual or fanciful questions or say nothing at all. While you surely will be expressing some of your reactions, it's wiser not to probe for theirs. Sooner or later the quality of their silence will be revealed, either as impatience or a mulling over of what they've been viewing. If a child seems riveted to a particular scene or object, we might ask gently what intrigues him or her. Sometimes it might be the subject, a certain animal or a special scene. Sometimes it is a special color, texture, or format; or it may be some inexplicable emotion the painting arouses in the child. Whatever the attraction, we shouldn't question too much, but respect the child's privacy.

One mother sometimes takes her seven-year-old twins to see special displays in the local museum which interest her; and sometimes they initiate the trip when they want to see an exhibition that interests them. She says, "If they get restless, I know it's time to go, even if we haven't seen all we came for. That way they're willing, if not eager, to return. I love the museum now; but I hated being dragged through it for hours when I was a child. So I make an effort to share my pleasure but not to overdo each visit."

Twelve-year-old Kenneth was impatient with the notion of leisurely examining the King Tut exhibition. He wanted to rush through the displays; wisely, his father didn't insist on Kenneth's accompanying him. Instead, he suggested that Kenneth meet him at the exit to each room. While the father was still absorbed in the second room, Kenneth came up and demanded to know why he was taking so long. This gave his father a chance to explain some of the stories and the way the reliefs were made. Kenneth's interest was aroused and he began to study the exhibition for himself. Later, on a school trip, he told his friends how much more they would learn if they took a lot of time instead of racing through the exhibition.

Appreciation of architecture too can begin at a very early age, as soon as a child starts to notice his or her surroundings. When young children walk around with adults who encourage them to look at buildings, the children soon become aware of relationships in architecture, of high and low buildings, of pointed and round shapes, of curves. When they ask questions about certain buildings, information about the house style can be sought, or perhaps the house itself can be visited. Books about houses, both fiction and nonfiction, can be found in the library. Discoveries are important; even more important is sharing and supporting the child's interest, and introducing him or her to the lifelong joys of "finding out."

Children can become aware of how the differences in a building's purpose can affect its shape; we can help them discover why factories, garages, restaurants, apartment buildings, and single dwellings are differently shaped. Most children soon display their aesthetic awareness of architectural function in their unit block constructions. A house constructed by a three-year-old may consist of just four blocks in a square; the seven-year-old's "city" may have tall skyscrapers, small service stations, a mayor's house complete with pillars and pediments.

Children's paintings, drawings, and clay work also reflect their discernment of over-all proportions and styles. We can continue to enlarge their experiences as they mature by visiting various structures from an old brownstone to a model "glass house"; from a solar-heated home to an historical colonial landmark, complete with all the outbuildings necessary for maintaining an independent way of life.

The "seeing eye" is a phrase used to describe many aspects of meaningful visual examination or contemplation; most children seem to have it from birth, and it dims only when adults ignore or repress its discoveries. Adults can help children keep this "seeing eye," this special way of looking, by appreciating their unique aesthetic vision. The most helpful attitude is one of respect for the integrity of the child's vision, for his or her own special way of looking at the world.

With such respect, both adult and child will share mutual discovery and pleasure as together they explore a child's way of looking, an aesthetic awareness of our world.

Clip, Snip, and Paste

SEYMOUR V. REIT

The Fun of Making Things

Making things with children does not require elaborate or sophisticated skills and techniques. All it takes is a sense of fun, some imagination, and a willingness to explore and experiment. And don't fret if you're one of those people who are "all thumbs." Children—especially the younger ones—are not perfectionists; they don't expect precise works of art. All they want to do is have a good time—and so should you.

What, then, do you make and how do you go about it? For the less adventuresome, there are vast numbers of prefab kits and assorted hobby-craft sets on sale for various age levels. Today's toy shops are crammed with them, and many are excellent. Just keep two things in mind:

1. *The age of the child.* A kit that's too difficult will be frustrating and unsatisfying. One that's too easy will seem babyish and boring.
2. *The sharing level.* A good kit is one that you can both enjoy working on. Pick an item that you and the child can make or build together, and in a reasonable length of time.

Such items, chosen with care, can be successful. But for really spontaneous, spur-of-the moment fun and excitement, nothing equals the challenge of making something completely from scratch. Prefabricated items, no matter how ingenious, just don't allow a full range of

191

free-flowing creativity, nor the joy of turning ordinary objects into things magical. Making something without preset, prearranged rules helps to nourish other important capacities. According to psychologists, a child working at a simple craft develops concepts of size and shape, a sense of symmetry and balance, eye-hand coordination, and basic math skills such as measuring and classification.

By working with a supportive grownup the young partner also learns to communicate and exchange ideas through questions and answers. For instance, a fine activity for young children is to make play dough with them, since it involves a few simple household items and can be made in a range of colors. This claylike substance (see recipe at end of chapter), a great favorite among preschoolers, gives children tactile pleasure and allows them to create varieties of shapes and objects. It also makes conversational opportunities in which youngsters can express their ideas and feelings.

You in turn can gain insights into your child's personality. Many subtle hints are given by the way a child handles tools, how he or she tackles small problems, the kinds of questions, and the child's level of self-confidence. Naturally, you won't always find an ideal time to sit down with your child for a quiet work session. But opportunities do arise—when a sick child is convalescing in bed, or when bad weather forces a change in earlier plans.

How do you decide on a project? That depends on the interests of adult and child, the youngster's age, and the time and materials available. Very often a child will supply clues and directions. As for materials, these can be the simplest possible, basic things that are found in almost any household: newspapers, string, brown-paper bags, empty milk containers, paper clips, rubber bands, glue, toothpicks, drinking straws, buttons, and pieces of cardboard.

The food cupboard or refrigerator can also be raided. A raw carrot makes a fine rocket ship. A raw potato becomes a person's head, with raisins or small gumdrops for features. Marshmallows joined with toothpicks can become snowmen, polar bears, and other inventions. Slices of melon rind, with the fruit removed, become acceptable boats, and sugar cubes make excellent building blocks.

To all these things add a bit of playfulness, a pinch of imagination, and you're well on the way. With a few folds or snips of the scissors, a page of a newspaper can become an airplane, an admiral's hat, a telescope, or a parachute. With a little more effort—and a few more pages—you and your partner can make a tall, leafy tree or a paper coat hanger that really works (see directions at end of chapter).

The joint project can have a special meaning, if it's something the child or a family member can actually use. You may want to make simple toys or purely decorative items, and that's fine, but your object can also be something which, despite an inevitably short life span, will have a useful function. "Let's make place mats for the table." "Can we use some pot holders for the kitchen?" Goals like these give your youngster a sense of special accomplishment.

There are any number of detailed hobby and how-to books available, but at this point you may want to try some of the projects outlined at the end of the chapter. These samples of "newspaper craft" were chosen for specific reasons: because they are simple to make, original in concept, use inexpensive materials, and invite a great deal of interaction.

More than Junk

One of the best sources of learning toys for the young is the trash can. What better repository for interesting scraps of paper, string and plastic, colorful ribbons and gift wrappings, empty envelopes and fascinating cardboard boxes?

Of course older children will have more exacting needs, but the basic idea remains the same: for kids of any age, the materials they play with aren't as important as how they use them. Almost everything in our daily physical environment is grist for a child's creative mill. Even the simplest, most basic of materials can mean hours of fun and learning—and when kids and adults work on projects together, the whole process is enhanced.

Today's children are growing up in a rapid action world dominated by a kind of fast-food mentality, an environment that is built around instant gratification. Almost everything in modern society comes ready made—everything except sensitivity, growth, and learning. For this reason a balancing influence is needed—something that will help kids to learn patience and to develop their personal creative skills. Children need help in gaining ability to create things of their own which, if not "instant," can provide gratification of a richer and deeper kind.

Everyone who has ever hooked a rug, refinished a piece of battered furniture, or sewn a quilt out of scrap fabric knows how rewarding it can be to transform discarded items. Working with simple discarded objects can give children—and you, too—a chance to salvage, to rebuild, and to improvise.

A good way to begin is to set up a cardboard carton, or "scrounge corner," in your child's room, the den, or the basement. This is a family project in which your child or children can participate. Kids are natural pack rats. They notice the kinds of "valueless" odds and ends that an adult would overlook.

Naturally, you won't want to turn your scrounge corner into a garbage dump, and a degree of restraint will be needed. But you'll be surprised how quickly the carton will fill up with unexpected treasures.

Now all you and the kids have to do is to remember to keep your eyes open for suitable candidates. Among the many useful items that you might collect are:

> clothing buttons
> broken strings of beads
> egg containers
> ribbon and fabric scraps
> milk cartons (rinsed out, of course)
> wooden thread spools
> cardboard tubes from paper towels and toilet tissue
> old kitchen sponges
> empty coffee cans (*without* sharp edges)
> shirt cardboards
> soda bottle caps
> plastic containers

American packaging know-how also offers a gold mine of scrounge, now that excelsior has given way to styrofoam and plastic bubble sheets. If you live in the suburbs or the country, another dimension opens up: here, in addition to the items mentioned, your collection of found materials can include leaves, pressed flowers, pine cones, seed pods, odd-shaped stones, interesting bits of driftwood.

To supplement found materials you may also want to pay a visit to your local dime store. You'll find its counters—especially in the housewares section—crammed with usable, well-designed and relatively inexpensive objects. But try to keep such purchases to a minimum. The real fun of amassing junk creatively for your family is to do so with no extra cost.

To get you and your partner off to a good start, here are a few simple scrounge ideas to try. Though quite modest, these activites can be enjoyably shared, and will spark creative ideas for future projects.

Things that Go

Kids, especially the younger ones, love cars, trucks, trains—any and all "things that go." Three or four empty milk cartons put end to end, and hooked together with paper-clip couplings, make a very acceptable train. One enterprising father and child embellished this by unrolling several yards of paper toweling and drawing simple "tracks" with a felt-tip pen. Later the youngster added a station made from a small cardboard box. His father helped him print the name of the station (their home town) on the box.

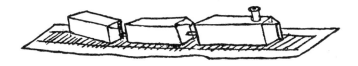

Spinning Top

Take a well-sharpened pencil stub, push it through the middle of a cardboard disc, and presto!—you have an excellent spinning top. For the disc you can use the lid of a yogurt or cottage-cheese container, and if no pencil stub is handy, substitute a short piece of plastic drinking straw. Learning to spin this new top is good hand-eye training for children.

Jewelry

Four- and five-year-olds enjoy stringing beads and buttons on a length of ribbon or twine, to make interesting necklaces and bracelets. The beads and buttons needn't match; the more variety the better. Other perforated objects, such as small thread spools, can be added to your scrounge jewelry. Bottlecaps can also be used, their centers perforated with a hammer and nail. You can also string cranberries, popcorn and dried pasta. Among teenagers a current fad is to string necklaces made of pop-top rings from soda cans.

Bouquets

Would you like a handsome bouquet of flowers for the living-room table? For stems you'll need a box of drinking straws or a package of pipe cleaners. Flower heads can be shaped from colored tissue paper or cut from colored sheets. These are then fitted into the tops of the straws or twisted around the flexible ends of the pipe cleaners. An advantage of this kind of activity is that you and your partner can each work on your own flowers, choosing your own colors and shapes to build your bouquet. (And don't forget to compliment your collaborator on his or her creations.)

Collages

Collages are a very popular form of shared activity. All you will need are some sheets of paper, glue, two pairs of scissors, and a stack of old magazines with colorful pictures. Again you and your child can collaborate in choosing your pictures, arranging them on the sheet, and pasting them in place. You may want to choose a special theme for your collage; if you do, encourage your child to make the choice. Collage themes popular with children include airplanes, TV personalities, sports, pets, costumes, and space ships. You can also tie your collage in to an activity; if you've just been to the zoo, you might make a collage of animals.

Greeting Cards

Collage techniques can also be adapted for home-made greeting cards. These are fun for kids because the results of their work can be put to practical use. The simplest greeting card consists of a heavy sheet of paper, or lightweight cardboard, folded in half. On the outside fold a colorful cut-out picture (or series of pictures) can be pasted. The inside fold is used for the written message—preferably written by both of you: a "get well" sentiment, a birthday greeting, a friendship message.

Dried Flowers

Another use for collage involves dried flowers and autumn leaves. Using a good weight cardboard sheet, mount these in a pleasing design with glue or rubber cement. As an added learning element, you and your partner can label each of your items: the names of the flowers, the tree from which your leaves came, and the locations of your finds.

Bookmarks

How about some bookmarks for the readers in the family? A short length of colored ribbon, trimmed at the bottom with pinking shears, will do the trick. The ribbon should be about one inch wide. After being cut to size, your bookmarks can be decorated by pasting small flat objects on them, such as buttons or cut-out silhouette pictures. A variation: to the same bit of ribbon add a large cardboard disc or star on one end, a safety pin on the other. Now you have a very presentable "medal" which can be pinned to a tee shirt. One pair of collaborators made medals for the whole family, with captions such as "Super Mom" and "Homework Champ."

Rubbings

Most youngsters love to make rubbings and see the results appear as if by magic. Large coins like quarters and half-dollars placed under a sheet of paper, then rubbed over carefully with a soft pencil, are perfect for this, but scrounge materials can also be used. Try making decorative rubbings from textured items such as leaves, bark, slabs of stone, window screening, or woven place mats. Try overlay effects with different-colored crayons. And don't be afraid to experiment imaginatively. One parent took her kids to a local churchyard to make rubbings of old headstones. This led to many discussions of the history of that area and opened new dimensions for everybody.

Ink Prints

For ink prints you'll need a shallow pan of water-soluble ink or poster paint, a small roller or rolling pin, and some porous sheets of paper (ordinary paper toweling, doubled over, is fine). Using the old rubber-stamp technique, and experimenting with various found materials, you can make all kinds of fascinating ink-print designs. With a small rag simply coat one surface of your object with ink, lay the paper on top of this, and go over it carefully with your roller. Usable scrounge for printing can include dry kitchen sponges, pressed flowers and leaves, flattened orange peels, cross-sectional slices of lettuce, and bits of textured rubber matting. Kids (if you don't mind the mess) also love to do ink prints of their hands and feet.

Robots

Since most kids these days are interested in sci-fi and outer space, you might try your hand at a robot. An empty coffee can will serve as the body. For a domed top, glue on a small inverted plastic bowl or a cardboard drinking cup. The tube from a toilet-tissue roll, cut in half, can become the arms and legs. For dials and gauges attach an assortment of buttons. And small colored gumdrops or glass beads are just the thing to simulate a robot's "electric lights."

You'll be surprised how many hours of pleasure these suggestions —and the ones you'll think of yourself—will provide for yourself and one or more young children. But do be prepared for the unexpected: you may have planned a marvelous project and assembled all the items carefully—only to find that your youngster has an entirely different notion of what he or she would like to create. Naturally, you'll want to keep flexible and adapt to your youngster's ideas.

At other times your youngster may not be interested at all in working with scrounge. Here too tact and patience are helpful. If you sit down and quietly begin to work, your child's interest and curiosity may be aroused, and you'll soon find yourself with a partner. If it doesn't happen, don't fuss. Remember that having fun with kids is often a question of avoiding situations that disintegrate into petty quarrels, one-upmanship, or a contest of wills. The goal is to have fun together, not to compete.

Above all, when working on a scrounge project, don't be afraid to take chances. Risk and experimentation are a part of the creative process. You may not succeed all the time—that too is part of mutual learning—but you'll never fail in achieving that all-important sense of accomplishment, shared activity, and enjoyment.

A Simple Recipe for Play Dough

In a mixing bowl, combine:

       1 cup flour

       ½ cup salt

       pinch of cream of tartar

Add food coloring (your choice) and just enough water to give the mixture a claylike consistency.

Work and knead the ingredients together with your hands, until Play Dough is formed.

Store in a covered plastic container.

Easy Newspaper Craft

Jet Plane

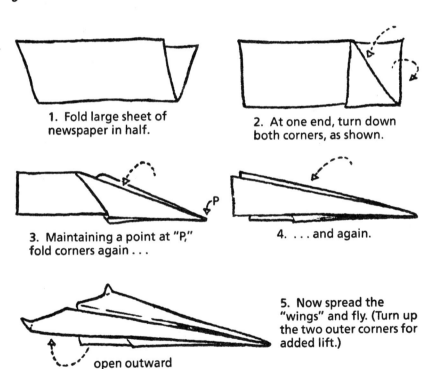

1. Fold large sheet of newspaper in half.

2. At one end, turn down both corners, as shown.

3. Maintaining a point at "P," fold corners again . . .

4. . . . and again.

open outward

5. Now spread the "wings" and fly. (Turn up the two outer corners for added lift.)

Admiral's Hat

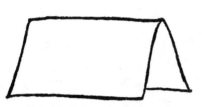

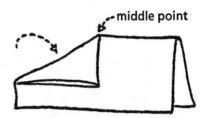

middle point

1. Fold sheet of paper, as in first diagram.

2. Now fold one corner over, as shown.

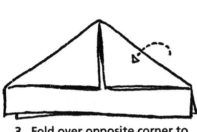

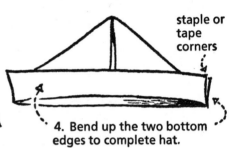

staple or tape corners

3. Fold over opposite corner to match the first.

4. Bend up the two bottom edges to complete hat.

Admiral's Telescope

Roll up a page of newspaper the long way. Insert fingers and twist, to make one end smaller. Tack down here and there with tape.

Parachute

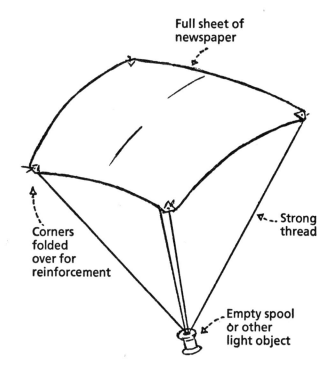

Full sheet of
newspaper

Corners
folded
over for
reinforcement

Strong
thread

Empty spool
or other
light object

Clothes Hanger

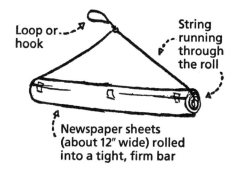

Loop or
hook

String
running
through
the roll

Newspaper sheets
(about 12" wide) rolled
into a tight, firm bar

Fancy Place Mat or Doily

1. Fold page of paper three or four times

2. Snip corners; cut out various small bits around the edges

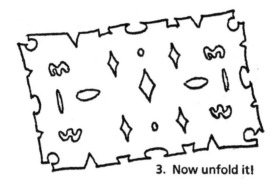

3. Now unfold it!

Magic Paper Tree

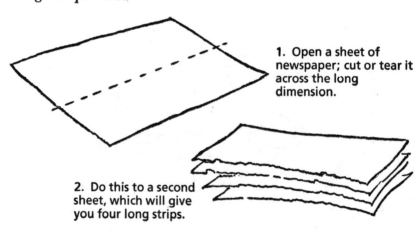

1. Open a sheet of newspaper; cut or tear it across the long dimension.

2. Do this to a second sheet, which will give you four long strips.

3. Roll up your first sheet—not too loose or too tight.

4. Near the end, slip in the next strip and continue rolling.

halfway

5. All four strips are now in one roll.

6. Next, tear or cut the roll at one end, down about halfway.

7. Now tear each of these halves, leaving four strands.

8. Reach into the middle of your tube; grasp and pull up slowly . . . and your tree will grow!

(If you add more strips to the roll, you'll have a bigger tree.)

Your Child and the Natural World

BARBARA BRENNER

How this planet works is the most important thing that a generation of youngsters can learn. Natural systems aren't simply a part of the world. They *are* the world.

There's both good and bad news from the nature front. The good news is that "Mother Nature" is still out there. The bad news is that we're losing touch with her. Many of today's children do not know that eggs are not manufactured in cartons, that milk comes from cows, and that without bees it would be almost impossible for us to grow things. This is unfortunate because, in the deepest psychological sense, a connection with the natural world is one of our connections with reality. To know nature is not only to know *where* you are but *who* you are. And to have a place in a whole scheme of things is enormously reassuring.

Who should be introduced to the natural world, then? I say everyone—and early. You don't have to lure the very young child into nature study. The interest is already there. Watch a two-year-old observe an insect. Note the absorbed attention, and also the attempt to classify, a process that would gladden the heart of Linnaeus—"Bug! That a bug. See the bug. Bug. That a bug? That no bug. That dirt." And so on.

And surely the sophisticated questions of an average four- or five-year-old give a clue to the tremendous desire in us humans to find some kind of order in our world. "Where does ice go when it melts?"

"How do birds fly?" "Why is there air?" It is a humbling experience to be on the receiving end of these challenging questions, and they certainly indicate that youngsters are paying attention to the natural world without any urging from us. It's really more a question of focusing and enlarging that interest than trying to build one.

There's no reason to feel that you have to be an expert to share nature with kids. What's the matter with a simple walk in the woods? And if you come on some interesting phenomenon you and your child will be learning about it together, through the great method of discovery. Sometimes we adults get jaded. We don't really observe with the clarity of a child. That's when it's especially nice to have a youngster along, helping us to really see again.

We often joke in our house about the fact that one of the most used phrases during our children's early years was "Let's look it up." That particular sentence may have even outranked "Whose turn is it to walk the dog?" Anyway, like most parents, we learned nature along with our kids. As a matter of fact, we wound up learning *from* them. Biologists have a nice name for the process by which two organisms live in an arrangement where each does something for the other. It's called *mutualism*. That aptly describes parents and children exploring the natural world together.

Starting to Look

One of the great things about doing something connected with nature is that it's a real *activity*. Many things these days are passive— board games, watching TV, movies—but in nature watching you have to be an active observer, if not a real participant. One of the few problems is that there's so much to do and so much to see.

One good way to start is to narrow your vision. How about taking a walk in which you set out to observe closely everything that happens on one level, say on the ground? This "under your feet" walk can be taken in a city park, on a beach, in a meadow, a desert, or a forest. Its great value is that it helps us to focus, rather than to try to see everything at one time. If you want to, you and your child together can make a list of the things you see. On the beach, you may want to collect some specimens or shells or rocks. In the woods or on the desert it's probably a better idea to look without taking. If you want to see what's under that rock, be sure you replace the rock afterward; environments are fragile.

Younger children will usually center their attention on one object: the little red salamander or the broken fragment of bird's egg will become invested with special meaning. These are the artifacts they can discover more about after they go home. A trip to the *World Book* or some other reference source can have meaning even for a very small child, especially if the information is translated as necessary for his or her age level by a helpful adult.

Another way to explore the world of nature is to concentrate on using one of the senses—your ears, for instance. What's going on in the sound department on this walk of yours? Are you hearing the roar of the ocean? What was that faint rustling in the bushes—a deer? rabbit? chipmunk? Sometimes if you focus on listening you hear things that you otherwise screen out. One nature center I know of holds a periodic silent Auditory Walk. The idea is to see how many different nature sounds you can identify and isolate when you're not distracted by traffic noises and human chatter. It's not only interesting, it's a great form of relaxation.

If your walking territory is near your home, or at a vacation site where you're going to spend some time, you might want to narrow your vision another way. Select a space perhaps ten feet square. A stretch of dunes, a rock wall in the woods, a section of an arroyo—any wild place will do. Keep a diary of the things you observe there over a period of time—say an hour—on successive days. Who moves in and out of your little piece of the universe? What kind of animal tracks do you see? Do the plants grow? Do they get eaten? Do any new ones appear? Is there more activity at certain times of the day?

My son and I are keeping just such a diary of the plants and animals in a small area behind our house. This patch of land and water is part of the shorefront of a lake. It includes a dock, the water and lake bottom, a small piece of the shore on either side of the dock, and the space under the dock (between dock and water). In the three years that we have been watching this place, sometimes in a methodical, sometimes a haphazard way, we've observed an enormous variety of species, many more than we thought was possible in such a small area. We've seen snakes, fish, freshwater clams, spiders, salamanders, frogs, crayfish, and dozens of other creatures. We even had a beaver start to build a lodge right under the dock. A Great Blue Heron landed on the dock. A gooey mass of jelly turned out to be a bryozoan colony. Many of the organisms we saw sent us to the library for more information. It has been a real learning experience.

Studying a Single Plant or Animal

Another way to enjoy nature is to study one organism. You may want to try this with an animal. Watch the metamorphosis of a caterpillar into a butterfly. Watch a tadpole become a frog, or a bird family hatch out. These activities require a certain amount of expertise and should not be taken lightly. Some responsibility for the animal goes with the process; it shouldn't be a trial-and-error game. There are many good books on these and other nature activities and it's a good idea to read up on how to do it before you start your project. In the case of birds, it's usually no favor to a parent bird to "help" hatch the offspring. A much better way is to look for a nest that is near your window or somewhere at child's eye level, so you can discreetly take a peek without frightening the family.

Where animals leave the eggs, as in the case of turtles, frogs, and some snakes, you can hatch them if you know what you're about. Again, consult a book or a knowledgeable person from your local nature center.

A tree may not be quite so dramatic as an animal, but it is one of nature's great miracles. It's a perfect example of a natural system that everyone takes for granted and few people even see, because we're so used to it. Yet with very little effort you can find a tree to concentrate on that will reward your patience and attention.

To begin with, the parts of trees are all interesting—bark, seeds, leaves, branches, blossoms. Even the roots that you can't see are amazing. A tree is a very good place to explore the concept of interdependence. There can be a whole food chain present on one tree—the insects that eat the leaves and bark, which are in turn eaten by birds, which may in turn be eaten by larger animals and birds. Some of the ecology of a tree is part of our everyday life. We see the squirrel eating the nuts from the tree and the bird nesting on its branches and the person sitting in its shade. We feel the cool as its leaves give off water. If we look hard we can see some of the small organisms at its base, creatures that eat the dead leaves at the base of the tree and turn them into soil which will nourish the tree.

Studying trees, like studying so many other natural systems, leads straight to environmental truths: things affect other things, every link in the chain is important. And out of this concept comes the caring— our common responsibility for the stewardship of the planet.

A child looking at trees so intently might want to plant one. Acorns can sometimes be coaxed into growing in a pot of soil. Maple seeds, too, can sometimes be induced to grow. Some seeds require special handling: a good book on tree seeds will tell you how to do it.

Once you have a nodding acquaintance with "your" tree, here are a few questions you might begin to ask one another:

> Are all the leaves the same? Are they different? In what way?
> Do the leaves turn color in the fall? If not, why not?
> Who lives on your tree? (Don't forget the insect population.)
> Does the tree bear fruit? What is it like?
> How do you think the tree gets its food?

These and other questions will help bring the tree alive for your children. *The Tremendous Tree Book,* by May Garelick and Barbara Brenner (Four Winds Press), will answer many questions about trees that your four- to seven-year-old may have.

If you live in a place where it's possible to plant a tree outdoors, you may want to do that. You may even want to measure it and measure your youngster at the same time, and see how much each of them grows in the space of a year. Children love this kind of real-life statistic. You may develop a family tree with as much meaning as your genealogical one.

Growing Things

I have a strong bias in favor of growing things as a way of learning about the natural world. Many American children know flowers only from a store and apples only from a plastic bag. One way they can learn just how things grow and live and reproduce is to do it themselves. A small garden can be managed by a seven-year-old who is supervised. And a family plot perhaps twenty by sixty feet can grow enough produce for a family of four, assuming shared labor.

The city dweller can grow certain edibles in containers on a balcony or in a sunny window. Some communities are now setting aside land for vegetable gardens, and I can envision elementary schools making growing a part of learning, too.

If you favor gardening as a way of introducing your child to the natural world, you may want to read *How to Make Things Grow*, by David Wickers and John Tuey (Van Nostrand-Reinhold) for five-to ten-year-olds. Ada and Frank Graham's *Dooryard Garden: Tim and Jennifer's Calendar from Planting to Harvesting* (Four Winds) is good for nine- to thirteen-year-olds.

If you like, the garden can be a tiny laboratory where you pose questions and try to find the answers. What happens if you fertilize some of the tomatoes and don't fertilize the others? What happens if you use chemical fertilizers on one crop and garden compost on the other?

Even the control of garden pests can be a lesson in ecology. Blood meal is supposed to repel rabbits. Does it? Do marigolds keep bugs away? The garden can be a mini-chemistry lesson for the middle-years child. And there are few forms of learning that work as well as demonstration.

Sky Watching

From the earth to the sky is a nice change. On a clear night in a smogless atmosphere, you can begin your acquaintance with the planets and stars. Even a newly initiated sky watcher can quickly get the hang of picking out the Big Dipper, Venus, and Jupiter. With a little more observation you will begin to identify the constellation Orion and the Seven Sisters, the Pleiades. There's no reason to rush to buy expensive viewing equipment; an ordinary pair of binoculars will show your youngster some of the craters of the moon.

Before you go much further it might be worthwhile to take a trip to a planetarium. Here, sitting in a darkened, theaterlike room, you'll get a guided trip through the universe. You and your offspring will be able to orient yourselves much better once the little arrow pointer of light has told you where we earthlings reside in that vast galaxy.

There are planetariums in many major cities. If there isn't one near you, you'll have to find your way among the stars on your own; but don't feel deprived: sky viewing is much better in the country than in the city. You have the real thing visible right above your house. And you can always go to books like *You Among the Stars,* by Nina and Herman Schneider (Addison-Wesley).

If you get into astronomy in a big way, you might enjoy using one of the star-finder charts sold by many educational toy stores. For the more serious stargazer there is everything from a miniature planetarium that will project the Milky Way on your ceiling to a telescope that will make your youngster feel like Copernicus.

Water, Water Everywhere

Most kids are more spellbound by a body of water than by any other natural phenomenon. Someone once tried to explain the near-hypnosis that sets in close to a body of water by saying that it is a biological memory calling to us, because all of our human history came from the sea. Whether you agree with this slightly mystical theory or not, we can all agree that water seems to have a certain magnetic force that isn't altogether explained by the tides.

In a brook, the small nature watcher can find water bugs, minnows, polliwogs, frogs, wild watercress, and a hundred other interesting things. In a lake he or she can observe fresh-water snails, fish, eels, dragonfly nymphs, snakes, and water lilies.

For the interested middle years (eight to twelve) one of the most fascinating explorations might be the water itself, complete with the myriad tiny organisms that live and die in a small sample of water from a local pond. A magnifying glass, a seining net, and a small aquarium tank are all splendid and inexpensive gifts for the pond watcher. For the youngest water-baby, try *Puddles and Ponds: Living Things in Watery Places,* by Phyllis Busch (Collins-World), for four- to seven-year olds.

Exploring a seashore will often give you a clue to the life of the sea. A good nature detective can stroll along a beach in the early morning and find a treasure trove. A most important warning: Keep your eye on your young companion. That old saw about more accidents happening around water than anywhere else is tragically true. A second caution is: Taking home shells is lovely; taking home remains of sea creatures (even the smallest remnant thereof) is awful! By the time you get home the smell emanating from the trunk of the car can be indescribable. If you really want to collect recently occupied crab claws or fish skeletons, be sure to process them first. Whole animals—sea anemones and the like—can sometimes be dried in the sun. Bones and shells that still have some flesh adhering to them need to be cleaned and then boiled for a few minutes in water to which a little bleach has been added.

Birding

Bird watching is a dearly loved activity for young and old. Whether you observe birds at your apartment window, in the park, or at a truly wild place, the whole family is likely to enjoy it.

There's a lot of help available to the would-be birder. Local Audubon societies will clue you into birding events in your area. Every state is different; some are more bird-conscious than others. And in many states it's more than just learning about birds; conservation groups have been instrumental in improving the survival rates of certain species. Florida Audubon, for example, is researching an enlargement of the colonies of the wood stork. Pennsylvania has an annual hawk watch that would be a memorable event for any youngster. New Jersey has been actively recruiting people to help build nesting boxes for the disappearing bluebird. Sharing any of these activities with an interested youngster would be a rich experience. Directing kids to this kind of birding may be more constructive in the long run than simply learning names or keeping a life list.

Nature Centers

If you're not a do-it-for-yourself family, then head for a nature center or local wildlife sanctuary. Such facilities usually charge only a minimal fee, if they charge at all. And they are almost always your ticket to a day's pleasure and learning. All of them have programs geared to children. Many have self-guiding trails laced with interesting tidbits of information. Young people who are graduate students in biology or ecology often serve as guides on tours through these parks and can do a great deal to spark a youngster's interest in the outdoors. If you're not sure whether there's a nature center near you, a helpful source is the Audubon Society's *Directory of Nature Centers,* available from their headquarters, 950 Third Avenue, New York 10022, for $6.95.

Living With Nature

Given the high cost of vacations, camping makes more and more sense for a family holiday, and it's a great way to nature watch without breaking the bank. State and national parks and many wilderness areas have campsites or inexpensive cabin facilities. Here you can be in touch with the natural world at any season, and there's no charge to watch the theater of the outdoors.

One expression of a fascination with the natural world is collecting. You'll know that your offspring is hooked when he or she begins to bring things home—bugs, leaves, rocks. That lucky fossil find may lead to membership in a geology club, or a summer spent digging in a likely site. Many extraordinary finds of great importance to paleontology have been made by amateurs, young people who may have been introduced to the study by a parent sharing the natural world with them.

I don't really think it's essential that you see such a direct return on your "investment" as a child who becomes a biologist because of a childhood interest in frogs, or a geologist who as a child collected rocks. What you may get as your return is simply a young person whose view of life has been enlarged along with your own.

Respect for All Life

The delight lingers and lasts; it grows and deepens as our experiences widen. We and our children become more aware of the intricacies of the lives around us; of how, as fellow earth sharers, all living things deserve their place.

When James was four years old he turned over a stone in the grass around our apartment house and discovered the ants underneath; he stood amazed as they scurried about, carrying their pupae into the ant tunnels.

"What they ants doing?" James cried. "Why they carry little eggs?"

He squatted down to watch, and he watched day after day. We discovered some of the answers he wanted from our trips to the library; but some of his questions, who could answer?

"Do ant see me?" "Why ant have skinny waist?" "Why James not ant?" The more he peered under the stone the more he marveled, as I did, at the intricacy of the kingdom under our feet. One late summer day, when we saw ants swarming over the sidewalk as the males and females set off on their mating flights, James was their stern defender.

"No step on ants," he yelled ferociously to passers-by. "Ants not for stepping on."

Ants are not for stepping on. Respect for life—all life—may be the most important result of our closer look at the world around us. We learn that we are related; and that from the midge to the eagle, from the dandelion to the redwood, from the mouse to the man, we are all not for stepping on.

In-between Times

WILLIAM H. HOOKS

"I know the party's at four o'clock, but what am I going to do until then? It's so long."

Then there is the unexpected delay. The telephone rings just as Dad finds the missing glove that completes Danny's snowy day outfit. Danny waits impatiently, looking like a colorful sausage bundled into all his winter gear. Dad finally hangs up the phone. "Your mother's going to be an hour late, Danny. Off with the mittens and cap." They look at each other and Danny says with a sigh, "What'll we do?"

These are the in-between times, the times that can become shared periods of fun or miserable stretches of waiting it out. They flow around the daily routines, the highlights and the special occasions, like the mortar that holds together the stones or bricks of a house. They are the inevitable times that no amount of preplanning or scheduling can prevent.

These situations usually fall into one of two categories: those in which the adult cannot fully participate and the child must, with minimal help from the grownup, function on his or her own; and those that can be shared. Developing a storehouse of activities, games, and routines for both independent and shared play can help change the in-between times from gray to rosy.

A grandmother once said to me, "I seemed to be the one who got stuck all the time with the kids when there was any waiting to do. I began to feel like my house was the waiting station for the kids while their parents went shopping, attended meetings, or went to the movies. Waiting at Grandma's house was a convenience for the parents, all right, but what about me and the kids?" She went on to tell me how you can serve just so many cookies without feeling guilty about

216

too much sugar, and how sitting like zombies in front of the TV set didn't seem the most appropriate solution either. "So," this spirited grandmother said, "I'm prepared now with a bunch of waiting games." She was good enough to share a few of her choice ones, such as "Treasure Hunt" and "I Packed My Grandmother's Trunk," which are included at the end of this chapter.

Often an in-between time occurs with both parent and child trapped in a small space where there is little opportunity for physical activity and a paucity of diversionary materials. Waiting in the doctor's or dentist's office where appointments are running behind schedule; waiting for buses, trains, or planes in cramped quarters; sitting in the car with one parent while the other does a two-minute errand that turns into a half-hour complication; standing in line for a seemingly endless fifteen minutes for admission to a sports event or a movie; waiting at the supermarket checkout counter when grocery carts are piled high—these settings are not conducive to fun. But even in the most restrictive circumstances there are ways to help children bear with such times.

"I Spy" is an old game that holds an endless fascination for young children. No special setting is required to play it. The adult simply says to the child something like: "I spy a thing that is round and red, and good to eat. What do I spy?" and the child who is waiting in the car searches for something of that description. In the nearby store window he quickly spies a mound of ripe red fruit and responds, "Apples!" The most effective follow-up is to give the child the next chance to play the "I Spy" role himself, with the parent guessing the answer.

Use your own judgment about how many clues you need to furnish to make the game flow along. Older children can cope with fewer and more subtle clues. Nine- and ten-year-olds are enamored with riddles and puns and often like to incorporate them into an "I Spy" game. When Tony says,"I Spy something that is black and white and red (read) all over. What do I spy?" he is referring to a newspaper and having more sophisticated fun.

Young children are still acquiring basic concepts of color, size, shape, and function, and they need many daily life experiences that use these concepts. You can tailor your "I Spy" clues to the developmental needs of your child and thereby combine the best aspects of learning and play. Remember, too, how very important it is to help your child acquire a good functioning vocabulary for "reading readiness." Word games that make language experiences enjoyable enrich your child's potential for learning.

The continuing project that extends over a fairly long period of time can not only help your child learn to sustain an interest, but can serve as an important anchor for in-between-time activities. For young children a continuing project may be the growing and care of simple window plants. Reading aloud can also become a long-term activity, with characters carried through a series of adventures. Later, when the child is able to read alone, he or she may spend many gratifying hours of in-between time with a book.

Most children are instinctive pack rats, collecting everything from bottle caps to miniature toys. These collections too can provide many hours of fun and learning. The young child who collects small family figures or animals will usually, with minimal encouragement from adults, play out many life experiences with the figures, giving them roles and dialogue and actions, mixing fantasy and reality and ordering his or her knowledge of the world.

Do in-between times always have to be chock-full of activities? Certainly not. Children of all ages need relaxed time—time to let down, do nothing, dawdle, even time to be bored. Jerry Mander, author of *Four Arguments for the Elimination of Television,* points out that a certain amount of creative energy often gets released when children are bored. Their reactions to boredom can be a driving force to inventiveness and imaginative play.

Children need time to reflect, daydream, and quietly organize their experiences. In-between times can be good times for ideas to incubate, for making connections. A friend of mine had worried about the time her young child spent "aimlessly daydreaming." One rainy day he stood a long time staring out the window. When his mother asked him what he was looking at so intently, he replied, "See how the rain drops make little merry-go-rounds in the dust!" His mother then realized that his daydreaming was rich in creative connections.

Knowing how to balance relaxed time with more structured activities isn't always easy, and there is no single prescription that applies. Each child will need different amounts of planned play juxtaposed with relaxed time. Perhaps the best clues for the right mixture are the clues that children themselves provide. Usually they give clear signals ranging from mild lack of interest to obvious irritation when they have reached their limits. Picking up on these signals and helping the child shift from frenetic play to quieter activities or vice versa can help keep the in-between times from becoming the wastelands of childhood.

Treasure Hunt

Keep a stack of old magazines handy, especially those that contain lots of illustrations.

Prepare ahead of time a list of "treasures" to be found in the magazines. Little three-by-five cards or slips of paper are fine for jotting down the list. Keep the list simple so that things can be easily read and found.

A sample card might read as follows:

TREASURE HUNT
Find these pictures!

1. CAT   2. BABY   3. HORSE   4. CAR

5. HOUSE   6. TREE   7. BICYCLE

The object of the game is to pore through the magazines and find and cut out all the things on the list. Use your own judgment of the child's capacity to adjust the list to more or less difficult objects to be found.

With younger children the game works very well if you say, "Let's see how many cats we can find"—or how many babies, cars, and so on. You may also have to help the youngest turn the pages. And remember to give the children the chance to say the names of things aloud.

In a pinch, the game can be enjoyed if you simply give directions and supply the magazines. For a variation have the older kids make out their own Treasure Lists and then proceed to find the items.

I Packed My Grandmother's Trunk

Here are two versions of an old favorite.* In its original version it can be played by two or more people.

---

* William H. Hooks and Betty D. Boegehold, "I Packed My Grandmother's Trunk," in *3 to Get Ready* (New York: Bank Street College, 1978).

The object of the game is to name articles to be put in Grandmother's trunk in alphabetical order. The first player says, "I packed my grandmother's trunk with an *Ape*" (or any other article beginning with the letter A—the zanier the better). The second player must repeat the first player's article and add something beginning with B such as *Baloney*. Each succeeding player must repeat all the articles already placed in the trunk in alphabetical order, and then must add another article beginning with the next letter of the alphabet. For instance the fifth player might say: "I packed my grandmother's trunk with an Ape, a Baloney, a Camel, a Dracula, and an Elephant."

If any player can't remember all of the articles already in the trunk, he or she has to drop out.

When the game reaches the letter Z, everybody still in the game gets a chance to add an article starting with Z and all of these are winners.

This version works best for older children but can be simplified for younger children who are just learning the alphabet and its sounds. These children should not be asked to repeat all the articles placed in the trunk. They merely add the next letter of the alphabet and an article that begins with the sound of that letter. For instance the first child might say: "I packed my grandmother's trunk with an A—Ant," and the second child goes on to say "I packed my grandmother's trunk with something starting with a B—Bear." If a young child forgets a letter of the alphabet, he or she should be given help.

For special occasions such as Halloween you might play a variation called "Dracula packed his trunk with . . ." and see how many strange and hilarious items end up in Grandmother's trunk. Try it also for Santa Claus's bag and the Easter Bunny's basket.

Pencil Tips

These pencil tips usually work best with one adult and one child, and they can help pass the time together while riding a bus or waiting in a doctor's office. Any paper will do—the margins of a newspaper or magazine, a paper bag, or the back of an envelope. Games of this kind are pleasant ways to help youngsters develop eye-hand coordination, writing and spelling ability, visual discrimination, and other valuable skills.

These games may seem overly simple to you, but for younger children they can be absorbing fun. With a bit of thought, you and your young partner can also think up good pencil tips of your own.

Magic Letters

Here's a simple alphabet game for six-year-olds that helps them with visual discrimination. Print a letter of the alphabet (block letters work best), then ask your partner to change it into a different letter by adding *one stroke*. This will work only with certain letters:

Magic Pictures

Start with a simple form—an oval, a square, and so on. Then each of you in turn must add another line or shape to create a picture. (It isn't necessary to make a specific picture every time. Abstract designs are fun too.)

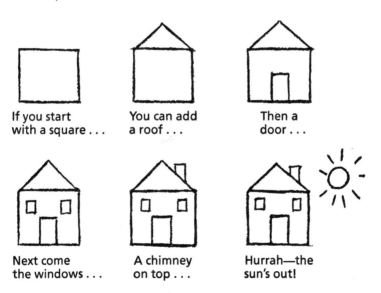

If you start with a square . . .

You can add a roof . . .

Then a door . . .

Next come the windows . . .

A chimney on top . . .

Hurrah—the sun's out!

Unfinished Letters

A simple little game just right for children learning the alphabet. First draw a number of letters in which *one line* in each has been left out. The child's goal is to draw in the missing line and complete the letter. The same game can be used to spell out simple three-letter words.

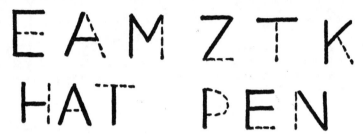

Hidden Words

This is an entertaining game for youngsters eight years old or more, and one that helps sharpen spelling skills. First, choose a long-ish word, one with a number of vowels, and print it at the top of your paper. Now use the letters to make as many three- and four-letter words as possible. Try doing this as a team. For instance, with the word *breakfast,* you can make words such as bat, rat, and bar. (Try it— there are a lot more hidden words in *Breakfast!*)

BREAKFAST

BAT	BAKE	TEAR
RAT	RAKE	BEAR
BAR	TAKE	BET
STAR		

Coin Faces

Kids love to draw funny faces but are often frustrated when they try to make the round outlines. Here's a simple solution: take a quarter or a nickel, place it flat on your paper, and trace around it carefully with a pencil. Now you have a face shape, ready for your details. Animal faces are easy, too. For instance, to make the face of a cat, dog, or rabbit, simply use the letter Y, as shown.

The basic face

Turn the curve around for Mr. Grumpy

Corkscrew lines make good curls

A singer

A clown

Happy Halloween

Pointy ears for a cat

Floppy ears for a dog

Carrots, anyone?

Coin Faces and Feelings

Young children are notably shy about revealing their true feelings, and even less able to verbalize them. But playing "Coin Faces" can sometimes help adults learn more about how their children really feel, and create a springboard for talking about those feelings.

You can ask your youngster, for example, to draw a face showing how he or she feels at the moment. And sometimes a child on his/her own will produce a certain expression in a drawing, which can then provide you with a good opening. For instance, if an angry kind of face should be drawn, you can say, "My, that's a very angry-looking face, isn't it? Let's talk about it. Why do you suppose that person is so grumpy?"

Your own drawings can also help lead into such discussions, turning a simple drawing game into a useful tool for sharing.

Happy   Angry   Worried

Sad   Mad

Four-plus-Five

As everyone knows, four plus five equals nine. But how can you take *four* lines, add *five* lines to them, and get TEN?

It can be done like this:

A Magic Number

1030 is an ordinary number—but when you add three lines it magically turns into an old-fashioned tramp.

Here's how it's done:

1030 becomes HOBO

The Upside-Down Word

There is one four-letter word in our language which, printed in block letters, reads exactly the same when it's turned upside down! Can you guess?

Here it is:

NOON

Alpha-Pics

First print a large alphabet letter (block capitals). Then you and your partner try to create a simple picture from that letter. Here are a few examples:

The letter A with a small circle on top and a face under it, becomes—

a CLOWN'S HAT

Draw the letter F then add one line, and you have—

a FLAG (your child can fill in the design)

The letter Q with a small circle and two pointy ears becomes—

a seated CAT

Take the letter V add a line and the letter "C" sideways, and you have— an ICE CREAM CONE

The letter I is easy—just pop a small circle on top and it's— a LOLLIPOP

The letter T with four lines added will make— a KITE

Draw the letter C then add a curve inside, for— a CRESCENT MOON

Let's try the letter P add an eye, a smile, a mustache, and it's— a FRIENDLY FACE

The letters H and M with a few lines added, make— HATS

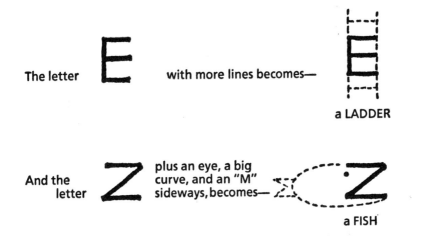

The letter E with more lines becomes—

a LADDER

And the letter Z plus an eye, a big curve, and an "M" sideways, becomes—

a FISH

(THERE ARE 14 MORE LETTERS IN THE ALPHABET. TRY YOUR LUCK!)

Code Fun

Children eight years old or older love secret codes and "spy messages." Here are two very simple codes to use with your youngster.

The Reverse Code: Print the alphabet on your paper from A to Z. Then, right under this, start at the other end and print the alphabet in reverse order, letter by letter—

A B C D E F G H I J K L M N O P Q R S T U V W X Y Z

Z Y X W V U T S R Q P O N M L K J I H G F E D C B A

To use the code all you have to do is substitute the matching letter. For F use U, for R use I, for W a D, and so on. Thus the code message

NVVG NV GLNLIILD means **MEET ME TOMORROW**

The Numbers Code: This same method can be used by substituting a number for each alphabet letter. The letter A is 1, the letter B is 2, C is 3 and so on, up to Z = 26. Again, these numbers are used as substitutes; so the message

3-15-4-5-19 1-18-5 6-21-14 means **CODES ARE FUN**

If you and your partner each keep a set of "master codes," you can exchange and decipher many secret messages, and your youngster will learn while doing so.

Tic-Tac-Toe

A perennial standby, and a great favorite with children six years old or more. First draw two sets of intersecting lines. One player picks an "X" and the other an "O." Now you take turns putting your letter in a square. The first player to fill three squares in a row is the winner.

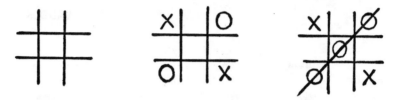

Hangman

Never mind the grisly title, kids of eight or more love this spelling game. First one person draws a "gallows," as shown below. Under it he or she draws lines representing the letters of a secret word (six or more are needed). Now the second person starts guessing. If he guesses a correct letter, it is placed on the proper line. If the guess is wrong, and the letter is *not* in the secret word, a head is added to the picture. For the next miss, the body is added, then an arm, a leg, and so on. The object is to complete the secret word before the whole body is "hanged." For older children longer words can be used. Parts are then added to the figure such as feet, hands, fingers, or perhaps a hat.

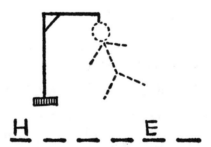

The Tic-Tac-Toe Code

Here is another excellent code with particular appeal for somewhat older kids, say the ten-to-twelve group:

First draw three tic-tac-toe structures, then add your alphabet letters in sequence, as shown. Notice that a single dot has been added in the second design, and two dots in the third:

Notice now that each letter has its own design structure, distinct from any others. Thus the letter "A" is represented by ⌡, the letter "E" by ☐ , the letter "R" by ⌐• , the letter "T" by •• , and so on.

To write this code, you simply substitute the correct pattern for the necessary letter. For example:

I   LOVE   YOU

Older children, once they master the simple design structure, find this code a great deal of ⊏ •• ⊡ !

Part 5

BIG EVENTS
AND
SPECIAL
OCCASIONS

Memories of special days are a kind of "strength insurance." Time we spend with our children while they are growing is certainly worth insuring, and special days are an affordable premium.

All of us can remember the special days of our own childhood—the holiday dinners, birthday celebrations, vacations, longed-for visits to far-away friends or relatives. Year after year these peak events were added into our memory, where they continue to give warmth and pleasure. And special memories are important in the lives of children as well as adults. Perhaps even more so. Youngsters, trapped and hemmed in by scores of dos and don'ts endlessly imposed on them by all-powerful adults, have a strong

Continued

need to break from this pattern now and then, and to enjoy their own highlights and peak experiences.

What do celebration times actually do for children? For one thing, they give a sense of meaningful ritual. They also give the priceless experience of sharing. And above all they provide a sense of security and identity, the "strength insurance" that is vital in the growing years.

Does this mean that every big occasion has to be handled like a Hollywood spectacular? Surely not. A modern art concept says that less is more, and in a similar way, when it comes to important family events, it's good to remember that "big isn't always best." Peer pressure exists on all levels, and some parents tend to be competitive, wanting to give the "biggest birthday party" or the "greatest holiday festival" ever—but the kids themselves may look at it differently. Quality is more desirable than quantity, and youngsters can be overwhelmed by the sheer size and scope of a festivity. When that happens the meaning gets drowned in the trappings, and the event becomes a jumbled montage of noise and faces with no clear, definable significance.

In the pages that follow, we'll consider some of these special occasions and how to manage them: the adult's role, the child as participant, how to maintain balance, how to arrange chores, how to keep the fun in and the hassle out. And along with the fun come the feelings, since special events have lasting value through the emotions that surround them.

Big or small, planned or spontaneous, through every major event of childhood runs a "feeling tone," which is generally set by the adults in charge. Special happenings become an affirmation of life and a restating of its values, felt through our inner selves. John Cage once wrote, "Everybody has a song which is no song at all—it is a process of singing." It is also, in many ways, a process of celebrating.

The Importance of Rituals

BETTY D. BOEGEHOLD

From the dawn of human time homo sapiens has shown a need for establishing rituals: sacrifices to unknown gods, ceremonies for the dead, the newborn, the living. The great Easter Island heads, the megaliths at Stonehenge and Avebury, the persisting Sphinx are silent monuments of the need to imprint human meaning upon impersonal forces.

Down through the years rituals have permeated not only religious observances but family life as well. Victorians not only had very strict rules for public rituals but also for everyday family living. Children were aware of their "place," not only in the social order but within the home; they knew what was allowed or forbidden. Some nineteenth-century family rites persisted well into the twentieth; but two world wars loosened many of the old obligations; and the second half of the century has seen many social structures radically altered or swept away. Some are certainly not missed—rigid codes of dress and manners; sexist conventions; big obligatory family gatherings where everybody ate too much for lack of anything else to do. But families do need rituals: pleasant, voluntary ones. Children especially, as many laymen and professionals have observed, need rituals, not only in their own games and play but in the family structure.

Daily Rituals

One of the earliest responses is to game patterns. An adult may start the game, but the child joyfully continues it, delighting in the repetition of form and content. Beginning perhaps with "Peek-a-Boo," which babies love for many important reasons, any observer can see the baby's insistence on repeating the game over and over—an insistence on the ritual.

The toddler shows the same solemn happiness in repeating again and again the game of "Ring Around a Rosy." Savants may concern themselves with the game's origin, but the youngster's delight in the repetition of form and song is obvious to anyone.

The insistence on form and repetition continues through the child's early years; as the child's own skills develop, so does the demand for "following the rules," especially in age-old outdoor games like "Red Light" (which has several other labels). Here one child is "it," and must count to a certain number, back turned to the rest of the children. While "it" is counting out loud, the others sneak up behind to try to touch him or her. Six-to-eight-year-olds severely enforce the procedures: no one may move when "it" turns around: "it" may not skip a number. In other informal but structured games like "Giant Steps" and "Still Statues," the children also insist on close adherence to the rules; tradition must be observed.

Jumping and counting chants and other street songs pass not only from generation to generation but from country to country without any visible couriers. Children pick up, reinforce, and transmit these anonymous jingles, changed only to suit the language of the particular country. In this mysterious process one element stands clear: children's need to observe and preserve these rituals.

The desire for rituals is seen also in the around-the-house daily activities of the child. Most youngsters try to establish a bedtime ritual; it may consist primarily of "one more trip to the bathroom" or "one more glass of water." Adults will most likely try to establish a more satisfactory pattern—reading a bedtime story, hearing favorite music, a heart-to-heart review of the day's events or problems, or even a simple repeated joke such as the ancient "good night, sleep tight, don't let the bedbugs bite." Whichever pattern emerges, these good-night routines soon take on ritualistic importance.

Other daily events are set off by rituals, too. Kissing goodbye in the morning, walking the dog regularly, watching TV or doing homework at established times, down to the smallest details of brushing the upper teeth first or pouring the milk on the cereal before adding sugar or honey. Establishing routine habits or performing small rites? Whatever the phraseology, the need for order and repetition seems to be strongly felt by youngsters, and upsetting or changing these daily events usually arouses anxieties, even anger. Such rituals represent a dependable degree of order in a world that is often confusing; the repetition of certain rites or rituals offers not only order but security—a safe haven from the perplexities of the day, a reassuring boundary to the chaotic ebb and flow of the stormy seas of growing up.

Parents, aunts, uncles and grandparents well know the resistance with which children meet any suggested changes of plan—especially changes in the established order: "But we can't go visiting on Wednesday. Wednesday we always go to the library." "I don't want a new story, I want the one you *always* read to me." A parent who hasn't left enough time to observe the usual bedtime routine may precipitate a stormy scene: "But you always sing me a song! You got to sing the song!"

Of course there are plenty of times when children welcome a change of plan—eating at a fast-food store instead of supper at home; or going swimming on a hot night instead of watching the usual TV show. But usually it's better if the adult explains ahead of time that a change in routine is contemplated. Children are capable of accepting such changes if they are prepared in advance, and they need to develop resiliency.

Consider this instance: Toby's and Meg's mother, Elaine, is giving a dinner party. She has decided to hire a favorite baby sitter; even though her children will be in the house, Elaine knows she won't have time to perform her usual nightly routines with them. The children will be able to meet the guests, mingle with the company long enough not to feel shut out, then depart with the sitter to share the bedtime rituals. Since Meg is only four, Elaine tells her and Toby the plan early in the morning; an earlier explanation might confuse Meg's immature time sense. When Mike, their favorite sitter, shows up, Elaine explains the plan again to Meg—Toby already has accepted it. When the guests arrive, the children are comfortable about both meeting them and leaving them. And one of the guests sighs, "What good children you have, Elaine! Mine always carry on when I haven't time for the usual bedtime business!"

From the necessity of clutching a security blanket or a sagging Teddy bear at night to insisting on regular places at the dinner table —children establish their own rituals.

Holiday Celebrations

If children tend to need rituals in their daily lives, how much more do they need and want special rituals? Most children demand certain holiday observances year after year, and protest if changes are suggested:

"We *always* open our presents on Christmas morning! We can't open any on Christmas Eve."

"Grandpa *always* comes to our house on the first night of Hannukah!"

"We can't go to Aunt Jane's on Halloween! We *always* go trick-or-treating here."

Such observances are the dependable milestones that mark off the seasons and the years in each child's life: "That was the birthday when I was three years old and got the toy store." "Remember the Fourth of July picnic when Robby was just a baby and ate all the ketchup?" "I love Valentine's Day because everyone says 'I love you.'"

Adults can make these holidays even more important milestones by emphasizing their underlying meanings rather than merely donning their trappings. In a way this seems to be what children are groping for—"Valentine's Day is when everyone says 'I love you.'" Families who observe religious holidays should ask themselves if their concern is for the spiritual as well as for the temporal; if they are placing as much importance on the meaning of the holiday as on the ritual observance.

In a world of changing values, families who have eschewed formal religious ties still must offer their children a value system upon which to base their future lives. One of the most important gifts children give us is their questioning of our standards; they force us to reevaluate our own values. If we don't stand for more than material gain, what are we saying to them? Our everyday actions probably reveal our spiritual values more than anything else we can say or do; but holidays and celebrations through the year offer a chance to reaffirm our real values, even though we may often forget them.

In *A Christmas Carol* Charles Dickens says of that holiday, "It is the only time in the long calendar of the year when men and women seem by one consent to open their shut-up hearts freely and to think of people . . . as if they really were fellow-passengers to the grave, and not another race of people bound on other journeys."

A six-year-old expressed it in her way when she said, "Sometimes Mommy yells when she's been working all day and her feet hurt; but at Christmas she says she's sorry." And preschooler Margaritta observed, "My birthday is the bestest day in the year. Then, I'm the biggest one in the family."

So we express, on these holidays or special days, the kind of joy in our children that may be lost in the everyday work world; and our children not only respond to that spiritual part of our nature with appreciation but find good models for their own future parenting.

Special Occasions

Holiday rituals are perhaps the most obvious; they depend on our culture, our heritage, and our particular place in society. Other rituals seem to be universal; we may observe them without recognizing them as important rituals, even though they come down to us through human history. These are the rituals of human beginnings and endings; the rites of "first time" and initiation; the observances of the changing seasons; the epitaphs to commemorate the end of things.

Birth

In almost every time and place, human birth is welcomed with feasting, gifts, and religious observances as celebrations of the continuance of human existence and the affirmation of the family. When large families were the norm, siblings may have accepted the new baby's arrival somewhat differently than now; for one thing they had a larger support system of brothers, sisters, and live-in or close-by relatives. But the youngest child who was losing his or her place to the newcomer may have had the same feelings of deprivation and jealousy that some children have today. In our small nuclear families, many with only one parent at the helm, such possible feelings need to be tenderly recognized and cared for. But no matter what new problems another birth may bring, the baby himself or herself is greeted with awe and joy.

Today most parents not only share the baby's birth celebration with their other children, but also share the pregnancy news and expectations. Thus even if the family unit is smaller, the children are more knowledgeable; they are helped to understand and prepare for the coming event.

Death

In the not so distant past children were often shielded from participating in, or even from knowledge of, death ceremonies. Many children were not even told that a parent was dead. Mother had "fallen asleep," or "God needed Father up in heaven, so He took him there." Small wonder some young children were afraid to go to sleep.

We are more enlightened today, but some of us still have mixed feelings about our children's involvement with death rituals. But children will inevitably experience grief as well as pleasure, and they should know that we adults can grieve deeply too. When we put on bright faces "for the children's sake," the children are well aware of our desperate tones, the contradictory body language.

Not that I would advocate a total collapse on the part of the adult; too much hysteria, too prolonged an outburst of physical demonstration could also mislead the children into thinking that real grief can be shown only by such extreme actions, when often deep grief is restrained. What I would hope is that the children will not get a mixed message, but a true understanding of our feelings. For they too must learn to release their grief; some psychologists say that if we don't release it, it will continue to eat away at us.

Most psychologists also say that there are recognizable stages of grief that we should understand, not only for ourselves but in our children. Often the first stage is that of anger: "How dare he/she die, and leave me all alone? leave me the hurt and the misery and the burden?" That reaction is hard to admit, and perhaps even harder to take if we see our children reacting similarly. But it is a very human, universal experience, and is succeeded by the time of real grieving. Young children often do not seem to grieve; they may continue their games with seeming unconcern. This too is a widespread reaction; but even if they do not express their feelings directly, they do know at least to some degree what has happened, and have observed our grief as an appropriate response.

When we feel up to it, we can begin recalling with them some of the good times and activities we shared with the dead. Some people seem to lock the dead away in silence, as if they were never an integral part of the family. Surely this confuses and distresses children—as if an ancient taboo has sealed off all mention of someone dearly loved. Talking of the dead is good therapy for adults as well as for the child.

Another need of young children is to understand what death is; it is not "sleeping" or "going away." Children who have been allowed to have pets usually have had some experience of a pet's death before they face the sometimes overwhelming loss of an adult. While we do not need to dwell on all the facets of death, we do need to answer children's questions honestly but simply.

Matthew's father died when Matthew was four. Matthew seemed to accept the fact without too much emotion and calmly went on playing with his toys. He attended the funeral but seemed restless when the mourners gathered at his house afterward. Sometime later, he asked when his father was coming home; he frowned when his mother explained that his father could not come home again, that his father was dead. Matthew recalled the time his pet hamster died. "We put him in a little box," he said. "And we putted the box in the ground."

Before bedtime that night his mother read him a sensitive book on death, intended for young children (see "Reading Aloud," page 55).

Later Matthew asked to see "where Daddy was put," and he was taken to the grave. He seemed to pay little attention to it; but wandered about picking flowers which he added to the grave's bouquet. During the year he had spells of misbehavior so unlike his even temperament that the school counselor felt they expressed Matthew's anger and emotional turmoil over the loss of his father.

Now, a year later, Matthew seems to have adjusted to the truth. He often talks of days with his father, though his mother isn't sure he really accepts his father's death yet. However, she is ready to answer any question or offer comfort if he seems to need it. An understanding, patient adult is probably the best help for a child undergoing the trauma of a loved one's death.

First Times and/or Initiation

While these rituals are as ancient as rites of birth and death, they are often less obvious. The rites of "first times" may not be seen as rites at all; the delight at the emergence of a baby's "first tooth" may be confined to the immediate family circle. But why such surprised joy at such a common occurrence? It may well be the reassurance that the baby's physical development is progressing naturally and according to expectations; a small but important milestone has been reached.

Similarly the baby's first steps and first recognizable words are greeted happily as another proof that he is making strides toward becoming an adult homo sapiens; the laws of nature are holding true. But what of the baby whose "giant steps" are not thus celebrated, perhaps not even noticed? Will he or she form the same trusting relationship with adults, or develop the same self-esteem as the more fortunate babies whose giant steps are confirmed as important by adults? All we do know is that from very early days, babies respond to adult reactions; and for most of us grownups, such joyful recognition of these important "firsts" is as natural as breathing.

Another "first rite" that has been almost universally observed in the past is the child's passage into puberty; while some of the ancient rituals were quite horrifying, they were of high importance to the participants. Today, with the exception of religious ceremonies such as Bar (or Bas) Mitzvahs and Confirmations, children's thirteenth birthdays may not be celebrated differently from previous ones, and our children may be entering puberty at a much younger age. As adults, we try to foresee coming events and prepare for them ahead of time; yet the ancient preparation for and celebrations of puberty are almost lacking. Indeed, embarrassment and careful ignoring of the physical changes often greet the event. Perhaps we might ease some preteen and teen-age problems if we honored with more ritual and celebration the bodily changes that are another "giant step" into maturity. A positive attitude of valuing puberty might give the children more ease and self-esteem at their own development.

Children themselves use initiation ceremonies when they induct peers into their own gangs or secret clubs. Since initiation has such great appeal for youngsters, might we not find ways of establishing initiation-like rituals in our own family life?

In one family the first, fifth, and tenth birthdays are celebrated in special ways; the first birthday for obvious reasons—it's another "first" ritual; the fifth because another milestone has been reached—the child has either begun or is about to begin school; and the tenth (which may be a puberty celebration) because it signifies leaving "young childhood" and entering the "middle years." And in this family the thirteenth birthday is always a special occasion, with trips to relatives, special shows, and special events the new teenager requests.

The Changing Seasons

One of the ways to form new rituals is to have family celebrations of seasonal change. This may be more difficult in some climates than others, but in most of the United States there are some observable changes. I know a single parent who began a Winter Solstice Celebration on the shortest day of the year when her youngest child was three. The children, their mother, and other families hold a winter picnic around a campfire which lasts into the dark, star-sparkling night. When the weather is bad they gather inside to read stories of the earth's journey around the sun and share special drinks and foods. Now the children themselves are making their own stories, poems and songs for the occasion.

A Midsummer's Night Festival, held on June 21, the longest day of the year, is also part of this family's calendar. The gathering is larger each year, each newcomer contributing to the celebration with food, drink, songs, or games. Stories are read and old dances tried out.

Of course the year's calendar is already sprinkled with various holidays that belong to specific cultures or religions; and the church calendar wisely marked off each Sunday, not only as a means of keeping track of religious observances but to provide a pageant of rituals.

Many of us whose lives are not closely tied to rituals could profitably rethink this lack, especially as it affects our children. Perhaps we will not want to initiate any new rituals in our everyday life but to develop those already inherent in it. And we may find that we need rituals for ourselves. For rituals are not only for special occasions, robed in the trappings of custom, traditions, and beliefs that mark our entrances and exits to life, but include as well our important commitments along the way.

Holidays without Hassle

CAROL DUNHAM

Holidays and children seem to belong together. This affinity can be the source of much pleasure when caring adults make it possible for children to find joy in active, genuine celebration. In a culture where high-pressure advertising creates unrealistic expectations and changing family patterns make it easy to lose traditions, we need to find ways to help children enjoy what is best in a holiday and survive what is worst.

The Buildup and the Letdown

Children care so much about holidays that they are vulnerable to disappointments to a degree that's difficult for adults to comprehend. They are easily caught up in a spiral of anticipation which escalates to increasingly giddy heights before the inevitable plunge.

Consider, for example, what may happen at Halloween. As children emerge from the protected early years, they begin to absorb the lore surrounding "trick-or-treat." They learn that disguises, costumes, games—all the elements which have been satisfying until now —take second place to the serious business of amassing great quantities of candy. They listen to tales of treasure as they plan their own part in the night of magic to come. Excitement builds as the fantasy grows. Finally it's time, and off they go to seek their fortunes in the mysterious night. Of course the reality can't live up to the advance billing: what seemed to be an enormous amount of time ends surprisingly soon, the older kids may be unfair competitors, and no amount of candy will really satisfy because, with additional time, there could have been more. What was expected to be a long, fun-filled evening turns out to be brief and very frustrating. The shopping bag, only half full, represents failure as these poor tired creatures return home and deal with the "Is that all there is?" phenomenon. And that feeling of a big letdown deserves some thought.

I first realized this one year when a group of parents with children seven to ten years old had an adult Haunted House Party while our children were out trick-or-treating. We had an evening of nostalgia, with peeled grapes as witches' eyeballs, cooked spaghetti as monsters' brains, the family collie as a fanged werewolf, and eerie music and flickering lights. When the children began to arrive, they seemed amused and interested to see that the grownups had been playing children's games all evening, and nearly all of them wanted to be led through the haunted house. What became very clear was the gradual change in the children's expressions and voices after they had been involved in our party for a while. They relaxed, they laughed, they began to compare experiences and swap stories, and they were able to focus on aspects of the holiday other than their loot. They were not the same anxious, cranky, disappointed-looking youngsters who had straggled in earlier. As they sat talking to one another and to their parents, they looked tired but happy.

I learned something important that night: Children need time and opportunity to wind down after a big event, just as adults do. We get together after the big game, after a family wedding, after all kinds of special events, to talk it over, to share reactions, to be in touch before we separate again. As natural as it may be for parents to start cleaning up and getting everybody ready for bed, it's probably worth a delay to let some kind of gathering take place. Hot or cool drinks, some real food, and sharing the experiences of the holiday will ease the transition back into the family circle.

Other holidays, of course, generate different needs. Family composition, local customs, ethnic heritage, and religious ties are factors in determining what is celebrated and how. Still, it is possible to consider some general guidelines for enjoying holidays with children and adapt them for individual use.

The Waiting Time

First, realize how difficult it is for children to come to terms with the concept of time. The younger the child, the more he or she lives in the present. Next week may seem as remote as next year. With shops decorating for Christmas the day after Thanksgiving and valentines appearing on shelves as soon as New Year's hats disappear, children have trouble getting any sense of how long a wait may be. Those whose notion of standard measures of time is not well developed need some adult help. Marking days off on a calendar, mentioning that we'll bake cookies before we have the big school party, pointing out that Aunt Sally will arrive before we begin lighting the special candles are good strategies. Children can get hold of the order of events at an earlier age than they can understand how long ago or how far ahead. Holidays that involve exchanging gifts traditionally have periods of preparation that stretch the time of anticipation out for quite a long time, a time that can be made bearable for the children, manageable for the adults, and, above all, fun for both.

One woman I know seemed to have some special insight into handling long-range holiday preparations. Her children appeared relatively untouched by the usual frenzy; she seemed astonishingly calm considering that her family was large and she held a part-time job; and it was clear that the people in that house were really having a good time as they got ready for Christmas. I asked what her secret was because it seemed to me that something wonderful must be at work.

She was, in fact, following a pattern of organization her mother had used, and it seemed quite natural to her. As her family began preparing for the biggest holiday of their year, activities were grouped, or clustered, not spread out over a long time. One week was designated as "cooking week," when everyone who wanted or needed to prepare holiday goodies did so. The children worked along with the adults, making the cupcakes that had been promised for a school party, cookies to take to Cub Scouts, casseroles to be frozen and heated later for family meals, special breads and relishes for gifts and guests. Everyone pitched in, and everyone who might want a special food had to say so in time to have it done during this one week when all spare time went into food preparation and freezing. The next week was shopping week, which meant, for the children, that they had to be ready with their lists and with money earned. For the adults it meant a commitment to be available to drive, to advise, to keep secrets. Shopping week was much more tiring for the parents than cooking week, but because exchanging gifts was a part of their celebration of this holiday, it had to be planned for.

What this did for the children was help put things in perspective. Shopping was seen as one element of the holiday, but not the only or the most important one. The family wasn't wealthy, so the necessary lists tended to feature items like hand lotion, new pencils, or bags of peanuts. Emphasis was on thoughtfulness. As my friend explained, "If I can concentrate all the planning and the help with budgeting and decision making in one week, I can remain fairly good-natured about it all. If I let it drag out for four or five weeks, there would always be someone wanting me to help shop, right until the end, and I'd get really crabby." The plan calls for a third week to be devoted to decorating and wrapping and a fourth to a complete housecleaning. Cleaning week isn't anybody's favorite, but it doesn't seem so bad when everyone's doing the same thing and when everyone's had a fair share of the other weeks' doings. A final week is reserved for specials and requests, which the parents try to honor on as equitable a basis as possible. They may go into the big city to have a look at especially beautiful decorations. They may give a party. They may attend a concert or a craft fair. They once went on a winter hike and picnic.

The Need for Balance

Inherent in holiday planning is the balance children need. Shopping as recreation is an easy trap to fall into when we are all bombarded with advice to acquire. Even though we know ourselves that people are more important than things, it takes more than lip service to communicate this to our children. If the only activity we share with them seems to be shopping, what message are we sending?

For children to take in significant parts of our holiday traditions, we have to put the holiday shopping into some sensible perspective. Clustering it in one week is a possible solution. Other families may read holiday stories and poems together, write cards and letters, sing and listen to holiday music, or start a holiday scrapbook together.

Connecting Past and Present

Balance can also be the key to creating holiday observances that preserve what is valued from the past while incorporating what is important in the present. Helping children feel linked to the past is the best way to bring our cherished traditions alive for them.

When a child lights the Chanukah candles it is to commemorate a historic event that occurred hundreds of years ago. New meaning comes to the child who is helped to make the connection between the symbolic act of candle lighting and the personal commitment to spiritual values held dear by his forebears. A family that joins hands to say grace over the Thanksgiving dinner reinforces through body language a message of togetherness and of special thanks for the circle of familial ties. "Over the river and through the woods, to Grandmother's house we go . . ." is not only a catchy sing-along handed down from the past but also an affirmation of connection with other generations.

Decorating Easter eggs, hiding them, and finding them is great fun for many children. But the child who is initiated into the symbolic meaning of the egg is the proud possessor of another piece of the mystery of life. He or she knows that the egg is a symbol of life, holding all of life's ingredients, waiting to be born, just as spring is waiting to burst out of its winter shell and be reborn. The ancient mysteries stir something in the back of all our memories, and children respond to them in deep intuitive ways. To allow the true meaning of a special occasion to get lost in the trappings is to shortchange our children on the most joyous part of a holiday.

Flexibility

Flexibility becomes especially important when children are a part of two families through separation of parents or even through proximity of two sets of grandparents. Spending some holidays with one parent and some with the other, or spending alternate holidays with different grandparents, can be confusing but also enriching. Children are sometimes more flexible and open than we are to new patterns, and we give a real gift if we help them acquire attitudes like "Isn't that an interesting way to celebrate?" instead of burdening them with automatic responses of "Ugh—we don't do it that way." In all situations where young children are to divide holiday time, the primary caregiver will usually have to assume responsibility for drawing the line between the reasonably meaningful and the overwhelming. Long formal dinner parties three nights in a row are too much. The person in charge has to be alert to plans which will place superhuman demands on young children.

If, on the other hand, the family is very small or isolated from a circle of relatives, there may be a dearth of ritual and tradition, in which case it's fun to start some new ones. I know two young women whose divorced father, for no particular reason, served Chinese food from a takeout restaurant one New Year's Eve when they were quite young and spending that holiday with him. It became their special custom, and both of them have preserved that tradition in their own households.

Holiday Foods

At this point we can enlarge our opening statement to read: Holidays and children and food seem to belong together. Foods often symbolize holidays—turkey for Thanksgiving, fruitcake for Christmas, pumpkins for Halloween, *frijoles con dulce* (beans with sweets) for Easter, matzohs for Passover, Hopping John (rice and blackeyed peas) for New Year's, and cherry pie for George Washington's birthday, to name a few.

Food offers possibilities for cooperation among family members and for creative learning experiences whenever it becomes an element of the celebration. If Dad's family always had frankfurters on the Fourth of July and Mother's always celebrated with a clambake, all kinds of delicious solutions suggest themselves. Blackeyed peas with the southern branch of the family and baked beans with its Boston members are truly food for thought. More important learnings than menu planning and cooking skills can come from children's participation in preparing special holiday dishes.

Cooking with children can be truly pleasurable if you ignore all advice about keeping it simple. It's much more likely to be a successful experience if you choose something fairly complex, with lots of ingredients, and allow about twice as much time as you would need to do it yourself. Look for recipes that relate to the holiday, have lots of interesting things in them, but are not delicate.

If you choose cookies that will be cut into special shapes, for instance, work with a recipe that uses more flour and less shortening than most. This will allow you and the children to take your time with the cutting and lifting without the frustration of having dough lose its shape before getting to the oven. Cookies like these are great fun to decorate with really deep colors of frosting; children whose eye-hand coordination is advanced enough can paint in details of feather, fur, clothing, and features.

If the children are quite young, do some of the steps of assembling and preparing ingredients ahead of time, to keep their time of actual involvement reasonable. It will be much more interesting for them to do something genuinely needed in a holiday menu than to prepare an item which they sense has been included because it's simple enough for them to handle. Go beyond cookies to traditional soups, breads, and main dishes. Just have a clear plan in your own mind about the steps needed and about which ones children can be responsible for.

If the children you're cooking with are yours for only short times, you can still do food preparation. Skip the Saturday morning cartoons or the hundredth trip to the zoo—get up and make those delicious Greek meatballs Grandma used to make when you were a child. Or take a dawn trip to the fish and produce market to buy ingredients for a super supper soup which you'll share with your friends and your children's friends in honor of the Spanish Three Kings Day.

Collect recipes that have interesting ingredients and several steps, and of course it helps if they end up as dishes that the children will enjoy. Copying the recipes on large cards that can be taped or pinned up is crucial. You are not going to enjoy watching your favorite cookbook gather grease spots while a seven-year-old checks the words and numbers as often as necessary. Having needed materials available in advance is your job.

When it's realistic to do so, give the children choices about what they will cook. Food preparation offers opportunities for genuine choice making with immediate, tangible results.

Try to keep the atmosphere relaxed, pleasant, cheerful. If you can share any family or ethnic traditions, this is the time for them.

One wonderful part of my mother-in-law's contribution to the Easter season was an Italian meat and cheese pie, the recipe for which existed only in her memory. In the early spring of the first year after her death, my children asked who would make the Easter pies. Recklessly I answered that we would. The resulting adventure took us on a search through many cookbooks, conversations with some of her contemporaries, and many trials and errors. Some interesting things happened as we worked: we talked about many topics more central to life than pie ingredients, we recalled some of our best and some of our worst memories, and we shared our feelings about what a break in human family ties means. We did eventually produce acceptable pies and record our recipe. Perhaps another generation will follow it; perhaps not. It really doesn't matter whether it's the proverbial old family recipe or a Chinese takeout treat; what matters is that we make good use of the important part food plays in celebrations that put children and adults in touch with their roots.

Balance Bears Repeating

Balance, then, is a useful framework for adults planning to enjoy holidays with children.

Balance the activity you're planning against the ages of the children. For the youngest, plan things that are brief, that don't make unrealistic demands upon their ability to be still and quiet, and that let the children see something through from start to finish. For example, getting a pumpkin and making the Jack-o'-lantern immediately is very satisfying. Remember that the children need to be participants in the whole process, not just spectators. Decisions about size, shapes, and decoration belong to the children, with only those parts of the job limited by financial or safety concerns going to the adults.

Balance the holiday observance you're considering against the children's other activities if you can. Are these children who live a tightly programmed, structured life? If so, consider a genuine change of pace for the holiday they spend with you—a leisurely morning of making decorations from materials you've assembled. Are they suburban children coming for a city holiday weekend? Take a bus and visit a great temple or cathedral if the holiday has religious meaning. Go to a special play or exhibit. Walk through a neighborhood where people of one particular nationality are celebrating with music, art, food different from what the children could see at home.

Or maybe no change in location is contemplated, just the usual family unit in the usual place. You can still aim for balance by building in some contrast to the usual routine. After a Thanksgiving weekend, a fourth-grade boy wrote about it: "This was the best Thanksgiving I ever had. It started to snow right after we ate, and all the company had to go home. My mom and dad played Monopoly with me all the rest of the day." You may not wish to send your guests away early, but remember how much magic there is in sustained, uninterrupted, exclusive attention.

Balance the lighthearted, recreational dimensions of holidays with the serious, more formal dimensions. It's good for children occasionally to observe rituals they can't fully comprehend. Few of us expect children to sit silently through lengthy ceremonies on a regular basis, but occasional exposure to how thoughtful people behave during patriotic or religious observances is important. If a Memorial Day celebration includes wreath laying, music, and a brief speech, let the children experience these events as well as the games that follow. If you attend services for high holy days, include the children who are old enough. Holidays hand us opportunities to strike a balance between the recreational and the solemn.

Balance the passive with the active. When in doubt, let the balance swing in favor of the active. Choose playing the game over watching, making the costume over buying, talking with one another over viewing someone else's conversation on television.

Children bring to holidays a capacity for pleasure, a spontaneous bubbling up of delight which they gladly share with us. Their fresh approach to each one is a pleasure to everyone around them. Our best gift to children is to protect them from the shoddy and superficial and allow them to be joyous, thoughtful celebrants.

Big Birthday Parties

ELLEN GALINSKY

It's getting close to your child's birthday, and he or she says, "This year I want to invite everyone in my class" or "I want a great big birthday party—just like my friend had."

Your mind starts to tick off the pros and cons: a big birthday party takes more room, more planning, will cost more, but your child has been invited to numerous birthday parties this year and it might be nice to have all those children at your home at once; maybe it could be a wonderful celebration.

My five-year-old daughter recently attended a birthday party that could be best described as a big bash. There were thirty children present. In one room the children had pizza and apple juice for dinner, while in the other their parents had lasagne, salad, bread, and wine or coffee. After dinner a magician pulled rabbits out of hats, cotton and confetti out of the children's ears. Afterward everyone had mint-chip, coffee, or chocolate ice-cream cones decorated to look like clowns, and a slice of homemade birthday cake. The tone of the party was joyful and not wild, organized but not oppressive. All thirty children looked as if they were having a wonderful time.

And this surprised me. I was prejudiced against big bashes—even though, as I thought about it, I realized that our family has big bashes for birthdays too.

Our tradition of big birthday parties began when our son was two. The year he turned eight he opted for taking a few friends to a movie for his party, but the tradition continued because our three-year-old daughter wanted the same kind of party her brother had had. It is a summer picnic lunch—an outdoor party with sandbox and swings, some trikes and bikes and wheel toys, baseball and croquet—for the children's friends and parents. My husband and I started this tradition because we both grew up in towns where many parties included adults and children, and we wanted our children to have the same experience.

Even though I have only the pleasantest memories of our annual parties, I still had some negative feelings about large birthday parties in general. Why? As I thought about it, I remembered taking my children to some parties that were confused and chaotic and others that seemed to be a chit in a competitive game among adults, designed to outdo or impress others rather than to celebrate the anniversary of the child's birth.

Motivation and Perspective

I think the crucial difference between good and bad parties begins with the motivation. If the reasons behind the party are celebratory rather than competitive, that attitude is transmitted to both parents and children. Another important factor is planning. When there are twenty-five children, a pizza delivery that is late or a shortage of napkins or drinking cups or activities is much harder to deal with than when there are only four or five children present.

Planning begins with communication with the child. If the birthday child dissolves into tears, it is usually because of differing expectations: the six-year-old thinks that there will be party games with prizes or that the presents will be opened as each guest arrives, while the parent has other ideas which he or she has neglected to discuss. The most successful parties include or even center on the child's visions of who will be invited, what food will be served, and what activities will be enjoyed.

Children can help in every phase of a birthday party. The birthday child can decorate the invitations and, later on, write them. If there are to be booty bags or party favors, the child can select and help assemble them. The child can also participate in the cooking, making popcorn or the birthday cake.

The activities—what is going to happen, plus when—also need to be planned scrupulously. It's a good idea to take a piece of paper and divide it into two columns, one for the time and the other for what is supposed to happen. Be sure to list alternative plans, in case the children finish their cake and ice cream in ten minutes instead of the twenty you had allotted, or in case most of them dislike one game or another. Then take a second piece of paper and list all the supplies you will need. Let the children help you with the list. Ask them if you've left out anything important, and ask their opinion about the kind of games their friends like to play.

Big parties do not have to be expensive or elaborate. The magician in the party my daughter attended was a teacher in the children's school who would perform at children's parties for ten dollars. My son, who is ten, has himself worked the neighborhood party circuit. Once he and a friend did magic tricks (they had taken one after-school magic course). Another time, for a dollar, he and some friends played their guitars and drums and sang to the children, and once they put on a puppet show.

Beside entrepreneurial older children, there are many adults who can help at birthday parties. One of the most successful large parties in my community involved a mother who is a potter bringing her clay to the party for the children to work with. A young man who plays the guitar and sings comes to his niece's parties every year. And a woman who does puppet shows for the library will perform at birthday parties for a very nominal cost. Most libraries have films to lend, and friends and neighbors, as well as nearby schools and colleges, may also have some. An old kinescope of Mary Martin in *Peter Pan* was a recent hit at one big party. Knowing the resources in your neighborhood can be a valuable asset, and a way of connecting to the larger community of parents and children.

It is not always necessary to bring in outside entertainment. Such games as scavenger and treasure hunts are eternally popular. In a scavenger hunt the kids can divide into two teams, each with a list of things to collect in the neighborhood (you'd have to live among cooperative, friendly people for this to work). The lists can include such items as an egg carton, a shopping bag from a nearby store, and the front page from last week's Sunday newspaper. The winning team members choose first from among the prizes, but there ought to be enough prizes for every child present. That's important. Losing and winning takes second place to having fun, and no child leaves the party feeling gypped.

Our family had a treasure hunt one year, and a friend wrote out the clues for the two teams of children. One team was handed this first clue:

> TURN THREE TIMES
> THEN SKIP, THEN JUMP
> TO THE TOP OF THE DRIVEWAY, HURRY
> TO THE BIG TREE STUMP.

The other team had this one:

> YOUR SPECIAL TREASURE
> IS NEAR, NOT FAR.
> IT'S ON THE SEAT
> OF THE ORANGE CAR.

At the tree stump and on the seat of the orange car, the children found clues which led them to twelve more places, ending, for Team 1, with:

> ON THE SIDE OF THE HOUSE
> WHERE THE SANDBOX SITS
> HANGS A NOTE THAT WILL BE
> A MATCH FOR YOUR WITS.

And Team 2 had:

> TO A ROCK YOU CAN CLIMB
> MAKE GOOD TIME
> IF A WINNER'S ROLE
> IS YOUR GOAL.

At these two sites, the children found their cache of party bags.

If the children particularly like a sport (baseball, kickball, or basketball), these games can be main events at a birthday party. In the winter, ice skating is a good idea. One mother, for her daughter's late October birthday, rents her college's swimming pool (inexpensively), and after the swimming party there is cake and ice cream in the adjoining cafeteria.

Party games are the most universal activity. Many children look forward to playing these traditional games almost as a rite, a predictable feature of their childhood. Favorite games among preschool children include Duck, Duck, Goose, Pin the Tale on the Donkey, Simon Says, Hot Potato, and Musical Chairs (see the following sections). Not every child likes to play games, and those who want to watch should be respected. And again, make sure every child is a winner at least once. It is crucial to plan more than enough games. Lulls in the activities invite chaos and frenzy, and children almost always finish a game sooner than the adult had hoped. Bingo is one good time filler; it can be stretched out, or even used in the waiting time when parents are arriving at the end of the party.

Adequate planning also means having adequate help, and that doesn't mean counting on the largesse of the other parents. Line up your helpers, adults or older children, in advance, and make sure they know what is expected of them. There is nothing more frustrating than to be in the middle of passing out the birthday cake and having to stop to comfort a child who is allergic to chocolate or who didn't get a seat next to his or her best friend—and the other helpers don't know what to do without you in the lead. These two problems, incidentally, are partly avoidable. Many parents ask, on the invitation, to be informed of pertinent allergies. Place cards, seating friends with friends, help cut down on the mad rush for seats at the birthday table.

The children at the party can participate in its running, too. At one successful party the children had a party favor hunt (like an Easter Egg hunt) through the birthday child's lawn. Since the gathering was very large, the parents of the birthday child asked half the children to hide the party favors, and the other half became the hunters. Then roles were reversed, which gave everyone a chance to both hide and hunt. What made the party even better was the food in the party favors: bags of popcorn tied with bright ribbons, peanuts, and dried fruit and nut mixtures. Sweets are traditional at birthday parties, but when the sweets are balanced with other foods (pizza, cheese and crackers, carrot sticks, nuts and raisins and popcorn), the children leave the birthday party in a less frenetic state and have fewer stomach-aches later on.

Birthday parties stand out as vivid memories to most adults, and these memories are highly charged with feeling. We remember the party that we loved or hated. And we remember the feeling of being more grownup, of being singled out for celebration with family and friends. Whether the birthday celebration is large or small, we as adults are giving our children not only a party but a statement of how we feel about them. Birthday parties are rarely without some tears and upsets, but in an atmosphere of celebration these events can seem minor. By giving children a birthday party that everyone enjoys, we are giving them a sustaining memory.

Games

Duck, Duck, Goose

The children sit in a circle. One child is "It." He or she walks on the outside of the circle, touching every child's head, saying "Duck" each time, until he or she touches a child and says "Goose." The child who has been called "Goose" chases the child who is "It" around the circle, back to the vacated space. If "It" is tagged before getting back to the empty space, "It" remains "It." If "It" is not tagged before sitting down, the other child becomes "It" and the game continues. "Duck, Duck, Goose" is a game without a winner

Pin the Tail on the Donkey

A picture of a tail-less donkey is attached to the wall at the children's eye level. Each child in turn is blindfolded, spun around (this is optional), and pointed in the direction of the donkey with a tail in hand. The child then tries to pin the tail on the donkey. If the children are younger, you may want to use tape, rather than pins. The tails are marked with the child's name. The child who gets closest to putting the tail in the right place wins.

Variations: Your children can draw the donkey and make the tails. You can also use any number of other creatures: "Pin the Nose on the Troll" or "Pin the Hat on the Gnome," for example.

Simon Says

One person (parent or child) is chosen leader. This person stands in front of the group and says "Simon says touch your nose," quickly touching his or her own nose. The players follow the leader's directions: "Simon says touch your toes," "Simon says touch your ears," etc. The leader then drops the phrase "Simon says," saying only "Touch your hips." All those players who do so are dropped from the competition, which continues until one child, the winner, remains.

Hot Potato

The children sit in a circle. One child is given something (in olden times, undoubtedly a hot potato, but now usually the prize, gift-wrapped). When the music (a record or singing) starts, the children pass this object as fast as they can. When the music stops, the child who is holding this object has to leave the game. The game continues, until one child is left and he or she can open the prize.

With small children it's a good idea to have the prize contain lots of shareable items, enough for all participants.

Musical Chairs

Two rows of chairs are set up, back to back. There are enough chairs for every player to sit down. When the music (a record, usually) begins, the children stand and march in a circle around the group of chairs. During this time the adult removes one of the chairs. When the music stops, all the children run for a place to sit down. The child who doesn't get a chair is disqualified. The game goes on until all the children but one are disqualified. This child is the winner.

Small Birthday Parties

DONOVAN DOYLE

Anyone who has been around young children knows how exciting birthdays are for them. And rightly so, for birthdays are the celebration of the individual, a time for the outward expression of familial love, and a time for self-identification—"I'm ME! Important and Unique Me!" On this day of days, family criticisms and squabbles are forgotten, many rules are suspended, and the birthday child is treated with special consideration and attention. Most magical of all, the child sees tangible evidence of growth; at last he or she is a whole year older and has attained a new identification number—say, a six instead of a five. For one day in the long year a child is a definite age; the rest of the time he or she may be "going-on" to the next birthday number.

How do we celebrate this important occasion so that the fulfillment is as satisfactory as the anticipation?

For the Youngest

For nursery-school and day-care-age children one solution is to hold the celebration in the group setting. This arrangement is particularly helpful to working parents. On the birthday morning the adult brings in special birthday treats, one for each child in the group: a cupcake and fruit for everyone, perhaps some milk or fruit drinks, and some small favors. Such foods appeal to most children and avoid overconsumption of sweets, especially if the cupcakes are made from such ingredients as whole grains, raisins, nuts, or coconut. Frostings can be left off—some youngsters may not be able to eat them.

In beforehand consultation with the group caregivers, some special recognition of the birthday child can be arranged. They may suggest letting the child choose the daily story, or bring a favorite book for reading time, or letting the child lead a march, choose a game or record. While not small in the numbers participating, the celebration itself is simple—but your child's joy will be large. After such a day, a child needs only a small family recognition at home to insure a happy ending.

For the very young child at home, the traditional way is to have a birthday party, but one that overwhelms neither the celebrant nor the hosts. Here are some rules of thumb to help insure this happy result:

> Keep the number of guests the same as the number of years being celebrated—five guests for a five-year-old.
> Keep decorations, food, and favors simple. Substitute physical and creative activities for competitive games.
> Keep the whole affair short—two hours is usually enough.
> Let the birthday child help plan and prepare for the party.
> Be prepared to play it by ear, to accept last-minute changes and to simplify any of the above.

For a one-year-old's birthday, surely "small is beautiful," like the celebrant. One birthday candle, one cake, one guest baby (there is usually also a small group of adoring adults), and one present for the birthday child to play with. After nap or rest time is an ideal party time for the one-year-old, and only tea and cake need be offered to the adults who drop in. If Grandma and Grandpa can stop by the day before, and Aunt Jane the day after, not only will the party be less crowded but the birthday child will be less overwhelmed. However, if that would cause hurt feelings, at least try to keep the relatives in an adjoining space, where they can peek in at the celebration. If there are older siblings, enlist their services in preparing and serving; this will help soothe incipient feelings of being left out and enhance feelings of importance.

For the next three birthdays the same pattern can be followed: a few young guests; a simple repast, with ice cream or frozen yogurt added to the birthday cake; a few presents from the guests; and the minimum of accompanying adults. Timmy's third birthday came during an August heat wave. His three young guests were asked to wear swim suits; Timmy's mother filled a plastic wading pool with water and water toys and turned on the sprinkler. On a small table near the pool, she served popsicles, a birthday cake, popcorn and peanuts. The adults relaxed in beach chairs nearby, sipping cool drinks. At the end of the hot afternoon, everyone, even Timmy's mother, was calm, cool, and happy.

From two on, the young guests must have something to play with and take home. Of course they will also play with the birthday presents, but having gifts of their own will take away the sting of having to leave behind the birthday presents they brought. Small children don't accept or even understand the idea of competition, especially competition for one fascinating object. Adults can spend fruitless energy trying to persuade youngsters to share the large birthday Teddy bear; a simpler solution might be to have the Teddy bear go take a nap, thus removing the battle prize. (Of course sharing must be learned, but there are better settings than a birthday party.) On one memorable occasion a restaurant owner invited his friends' very young children to a restaurant party and set up a "Pin the Tail on the Donkey" game. When the prize was awarded to the winner, he was horrified to see the other guests burst into tears. Hurriedly he sent waiters flying to the nearest store to get small gifts for the wailing guests. They were just too young to grasp the idea of "only one winner."

Giving each guest a small take-home gift is usually satisfactory— unless the guests start fighting over the gifts. Smart party givers make sure that the take-home gifts are all alike.

If the celebrant has an older brother or sister, get the sibling to help not only in the preparations and actual party, but in the leave-taking. Older children can often keep order better than adults: toddlers meekly submit to being stuffed into snowsuits or relinquishing others' possessions when an older child commands them.

Balloons and music add a special touch to the celebration. Floaty balloons and a catchy tune create a party feeling and entice youngsters to active movement. It also helps if a grownup initiates musical play without feeling too self-conscious: "Turning around and around and around with my beautiful big balloon. Throwing it high, high, high. Running and running to catch my balloon." Or just commenting on the actions of the youngsters may heighten their participation: "Roddy has a big balloon, a beautiful blue balloon. He throws it up so high, will it reach the sky?" You may feel awkward at first, but children won't object to an uneven voice or even a monotone.

Verbalizing the child's movements in a rhythmic way not only strengthens the rhythm but creates a new one from your shared experience. And you will be encouraging the development of an important element of creative imagination, the awareness of the endless possibilities that everyday objects offer. Your child also hears language used in a playful imaginative way that may stir a like response. Perhaps most important of all, your child may have a stronger self-concept because of the value and respect you show these beginning efforts at creative self-expression.

Another such shared learning experience is possible with three-, four-, and five-year-olds, a chance to use basic mathematics in real-life situations. The young child, eager to help in the party preparations, is asked to put out the necessary silverware. Instead of asking the five-year-old to "put out six spoons" (for him and his five guests), you suggest that he place one spoon at each child's plate and one at his own. He may not "count" the spoons, but in matching them to people he is acting out a numerical relationship. Then you can verbalize for him: "One spoon for Robby, one for Hildy, one for Jane, one for Matty, one for Aaron . . . one, two, three, four, five spoons for five children! And one more for you—six spoons. You have put out six spoons."

Your small helper may also want to do more; perhaps fill six little baskets with nuts and place six napkins around the table in the same way; and he might even want to dust some furniture. Sure it will take longer and be a little messier, but whose party is it? A child who's allowed to help in household chores, however messily, is learning to be an active family member.

And remember—this party isn't going to mean lots of work for you. Paper plates, spoons, and tablecloth can be discarded afterward. So you will have the luxury to allow time for the birthday child to help you, time to enjoy all the delight and wide-eyed wonder.

For Children Six to Eight

As children grow older their birthday parties often become more elaborate, usually because they have firmer ideas about what they want the parties to be. Most children now play with others their own age; they go to parties given by their friends. And, like it or not, our children often want the same for themselves. Since some parents give elaborate parties, our children are apt to desire the same fancy foods, favors, and entertainments.

You may be wondering what's wrong with the "all-out bash," if families can afford them and cope with them. Nothing, if you have the money and if you and your children can handle such supershows easily. But kids can be overwhelmed and overstimulated and end up cross and teary, and exhausted parents may have to belatedly examine their motives: "Are we competing with the Joneses in trying to put on the best party in town?"

In the "Small Is Beautiful" philosophy, such problems don't arise. The same rules of thumb still apply—keeping the number of guests equal to the number of years, simplicity in food favors and decorations, a limit to the length of the party, and letting the party child help plan and prepare for his gala day. In addition, competitive games can be introduced, such as "Musical Chairs," "Pin the Tail on the Donkey," "Peanut Hunt," or similar contests. Kids can accept a certain limited tension now, and understand the concept of "one winner"—as long as they too have something to take home just for themselves.

The biggest snag may be in convincing your youngsters that small really is beautiful. They may feel such a party would be inferior to one that has dazzled them, and may pester you to produce a similar Broadway spectacular. Six-year-old Karen came home full of her friend Toby's birthday party. "Mommy, they had an organ-grinding man with a real live little monkey. Can we have him at our party? And can we see a movie like Toby's movie? And he had a grandmother cake, an aunt cake, and his own cake. Can we have three cakes too?"

Karen's mother answered, "You really enjoyed that party, didn't you?" She didn't denigrate the variety of cakes or entertainment. Then quickly she moved to their own planning. "You're going to enjoy your party too. It won't be just like Toby's, but you'll have fun. Tomorrow you and I are going to make party hats."

For the next few days Karen was busy helping her mother prepare for the party. They went shopping to choose favors, nut baskets, paper tablecloth, napkins, and streamers in Karen's favorite color.

Karen carefully made name cards for each guest; her father let her twirl the streamers into wavy bands before he tacked them up. Not liking the empty white space in the middle of the paper cloth, Karen pasted gold and silver stars across it. And she helped make the birthday cake and frost it too.

She chose the games she wanted at the party. When the great occasion arrived, she played an important role in some of the games, such as spinning each child around before letting each try to pin up the donkey tail. At other times she became too interested in the activities or gifts to want to direct; her mother left it up to her. Karen distributed the favors and led the march to the peanut hunt in the yard. But most of the time she played with the other children.

At the day's end, Karen was happy and satisfied, proud of her contributions to the party's success. She took her six presents to bed and never referred to Toby's party at all. The personal attention given by her parents and her own personal efforts had resulted in a satisfying experience.

After the eats are gone, the presents unwrapped, and timidity has vanished, a mood of raucous frivolity frequently overtakes both the birthday child and the guests. This is a good time to provide some physical outlets for the rising energy. A peanut hunt is one way of letting off some steam. Before the party, the celebrant should hide a generous number of peanuts around the house, apartment, or preferably outdoors. This not only gets the peanuts hidden but gives the excited child a time-absorbing job.

Other outdoor games for releasing energy are Red Light (see page 266), Red Rover, and Hide and Seek. Indoors, children love Musical Chairs, or, if space is small, Punchinello (see page 267) works well. (Punchinello has the added benefit of being noncompetitive; it can also be used with younger children.) Then there are the less active games, such as Dog's Bone and Where's the Stone? (see page 267), which also absorb restlessness and focus the children's attention. Another possibility that allows for creative participation—as Punchinello does—needs musical accompaniment. Use records, carefully chosen ahead of time or find someone who can play an instrument. The idea is that you ask the children to show without words what kind of creature or character the music is telling about; then you play scary music, marching music, thunderous music, very dreamy tunes, etc. This game appeals to younger, less inhibited children, but even eight-year-olds often succumb to the tantalizing music.

At one party a few excitable guests began a rumpus, jumping up and down on their overturned chairs. Tony, the seven-year-old birthday child, feverishly began to imitate them. "What a wild rumpus!" Uncle Joe, the party giver, said, "Let's have some wild rumpus music while Jenny picks up the chairs. He banged out a series of dramatic chords on the piano while Jenny, Tony's ten-year-old sister, restored order. The fascinated guests grimaced, jigged, and leaped to the music.

"Now let's have a real rumpus *march*," shouted Uncle Joe, swinging into "Stars and Stripes Forever." The children fell into an orderly procession, marching with lively strides, saluting Uncle Joe as they passed by. Then he played more and more softly, saying, "Now Tony, the Rumpus Sandman, is coming to sprinkle sleepy dust into every Rumpus eye. They waver, they stagger, then they fall in a heap, sound asleep!" Tony tiptoed importantly around, blowing his imaginary dust at everyone. The children faltered, swayed back and forth, then, one by one, sank into silent heaps on the floor.

Voilà! From a disorderly mob scene to a peaceful rest time!

Of course we can't all be as perceptive as Uncle Joe, with his understanding of children's moods and ways to ease them into other less hectic ones. But we can pick up some pointers from his example:

> Don't be upset by upsetting behavior.
> Don't scold—"Easy does it."
> Try to lead the children into other activities.
> Assign roles to the ringleaders (as Tony was appointed to be "rumpus sandman").

Another helpful suggestion, which Uncle Joe didn't have to use, is how to help the one child who is so hyped up he can't calm down, or who may even burst into tears. Ask one adult, or your older offspring, to take the youngster aside. Often just holding the child close until he or she regains equanimity will do it—but it must be a loving, not a punitive gesture. Usually the child welcomes help in handling uncontrollable emotions or actions; this is a safeguard needed from adults in all childish behavior. The child may wish to stay apart, just watching the action with the sympathetic adult, until ready to rejoin the group. As with all interactions with children, take your lead from them.

For Older Children

Eight-, nine-, or ten-year-olds may want an entirely different kind of celebration. Instead of having guests equal to the number of years being celebrated, the older child may wish to have some best friends for supper and a sleep-over. The number of invited guests may be limited by your accommodations; obviously a small apartment can't provide for more than a few. When space is commodious, you might stick to the old rule of one child for every year; this will seem a reasonable substitute to the birthday giver who wants the whole class to come.

Now you will be serving supper rather than party food; much as you may wish to serve a well-balanced nourishing meal, you can let the food preferences of the guests dominate for once. Hot dogs, hamburgers, cheeseburgers, pizza can be the main dish; health needs can be met by adding carrot sticks, celery stuffed with cheese, or salads to the feast.

This is also one occasion when you can take the gang to a fast-food place with a clear conscience, and when we should zip up our mouths and not grumble about waste. Unfinished dinners, plates that are only picked over, milk that's spilled—on birthdays we shut our eyes and smile.

Another choice of this age group and of older children may be to take a few friends to a movie or other entertainment. Again, the exact details depend on the parents or other caregivers as well as the child. The high cost of theater tickets may preclude any guests; a local movie house, skating rink, or tennis court may be reasonable enough to allow for guests. Of course some sort of refreshments should be provided, anything from a family cookout to a raid on the local hamburger joint.

Older children's birthday celebrations tend to become more individualized. Some kids want to continue the traditional party with friends, complete with cake and fancy foods; but many have their own ideas about how to celebrate. In these years one big, longed-for gift may supplant both other gifts and celebrations with peers. This is the time when a child may get his ten-speed bike, a stereo system, a set of drums. Some older children will just want money for their own bank accounts, and some may resist any touch of the traditional, even a birthday cake at a family supper.

The "large gift celebration"—whether of materials or money—has inherent problems. There is danger of losing the meaning of the occasion, and sometimes the special request becomes a demand: "All the kids have sleep-overs, I have to have one too"; "I don't care if Mopeds cost a lot, it's my birthday, isn't it?" Or the adult may be the one to emphasize the material gain: "You don't want parties and all that kid stuff, do you? What if we give you the money and you buy what you want?"

As always, our values show in our words and actions. If we let the birthday become only an occasion for material gain, what are we saying to the kids? That such gain is the important goal? Or do we want to show our love and respect for the child in more intimate ways? Of course birthdays have meant presents since time immemorial. They are rightfully one of the highlights of every birthday celebration. But they don't supplant the joy of recognizing the advent of this child into our lives. Don't let the real focal point of the day get lost in the trappings.

Thus even as our children grow up, "small is beautiful" still applies —not "small" in love and expressions of love, but reasonable on the material side of birthday celebrations. Maintaining this position can be tough; you may be going against the mores of the community, the customs of your child's peers; sometimes you'll feel more comfortable with a compromise, if it doesn't affront your basic beliefs. As the parable says, it's not the money but the love of money that leads us astray. If your child knows you really mean this, you have given a gift of lasting value; even if your child seems to reject the gift in rebellious moments, or even for years, you have made a stand for a value system that eventually will have its effect.

Games

Red Light

One child is IT. IT stands with back turned to group, who line up at least 20 feet behind IT. IT must count from 1 to 10 aloud, then shout

"Red Light!" The group runs toward IT during counting, but must stand still at sound of "Red Light!" IT turns around quickly to try to catch someone still in motion. If successful, all runners are sent back to starting line. The game's goal is for one of the running children to touch IT and yell, "Run!" while IT is still counting. Then all race back to starting line with IT in pursuit. If IT catches someone, that person is the next IT; if not, IT must again repeat role.

Good for slightly older (6-8) group.

Where's the Stone?

One child is IT, one child is HIDER. While IT hides his/her eyes, the HIDER hides stone (or any other small object) in agreed-upon area. IT counts to 10, then starts to look for stone. Rest of children shout to guide IT; "Cold!" if IT is far from stone; "Warmer" or "Luke-warm" if IT is in the correct vicinity but not near stone; "Hot," "Very Hot" as IT comes nearer and nearer. When stone is found, IT chooses someone as new IT; Hider chooses someone to be new HIDER.

Punchinello

One child is IT, or PUNCH. Children join hands around child chosen as PUNCH; then skipping around PUNCH, they chant, "Show us what to do, Punchinello, little fellow; we'll do it too, Punchinello, little dear." PUNCH then initiates some action (jumping, twirling, creeping, bowing, etc.) and rest of children imitate PUNCH. Then another child is chosen by PUNCH for center, and first PUNCH rejoins circle. Very good for youngest and/or shyest, who often invent wonderful actions.

Dog's Bone

One child as DOG, one child as STEALER, one child as CHOOSER. Group sits on floor: DOG sits on chair, back turned to group, and eyes closed. The CHOOSER points out a child to be STEALER. STEALER creeps silently up, steals bone, returns to place. Then whole group shouts, "Dog, Dog, someone stole your bone!" Turning around, DOG has 3 chances to guess identity of STEALER. If one guess is right, STEALER becomes next DOG; if not, DOG must take another turn. CHOOSER points to new STEALER and game continues.

Simple Party Decorations

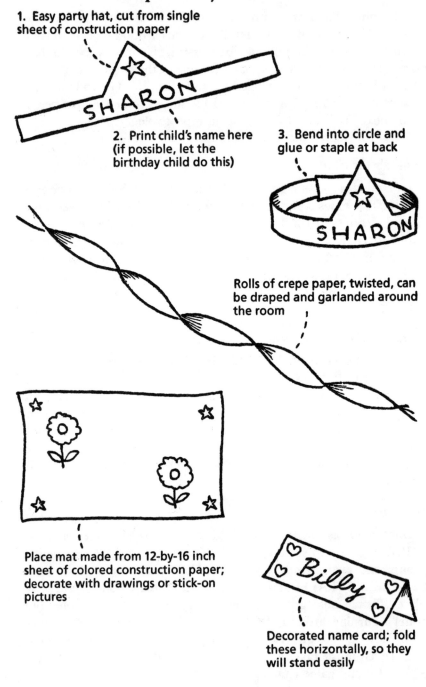

1. Easy party hat, cut from single sheet of construction paper

SHARON

2. Print child's name here (if possible, let the birthday child do this)

3. Bend into circle and glue or staple at back

SHARON

Rolls of crepe paper, twisted, can be draped and garlanded around the room

Place mat made from 12-by-16 inch sheet of colored construction paper; decorate with drawings or stick-on pictures

Billy

Decorated name card; fold these horizontally, so they will stand easily

Day Trips with Children

PEARL ZEITZ

At one time or another most of us, whether parent, grandparent, loving relative, or kindly friend, will say to a child, "Let's take a trip today, dear." But sometimes at the end of that day, as we drag our exhausted selves and cross, tired child homeward, we wonder what we did wrong—where all the fun went.

Take heart! Day trips with kids can be not only painless but enjoyable, if you hang on to these few tips:

> Fit the trip to the age and stage of the child.
> Plan ahead—but be prepared to make last-minute changes.
> Have appropriate materials for long bus, car, or train rides.
> Don't overdo—short leisurely trips are better than long chock-full ones.
> Be ready to cut the trip short if necessary.
> Be sure the trip is fun for you too.
> Take your cues and clues from the child.

The Toddler

The shorter the child, the shorter the trip—that's a good rule of thumb. Your basic toddler may be overwhelmed by museums, shows, and long trips. If you have to take a long day trip with him or her, try to go at naptime so your toddler can dream the miles away.

In exurban spots, the youngest child takes great pleasure in simplicity: exploring a field, looking for bugs, gathering flowers, digging holes, climbing up and jumping off a rock. Beaches and pools—any water activity—provide endless pleasure. Supply your child with a few kitchen tools, such as spoons, a funnel, some old pans, a colander or strainer, some plastic jugs, an egg beater; you don't need to spend money on elaborate sand or beach toys. (Caution: you really have to keep your eye on the child; toddlers can drown in even a shallow garden pool.)

In the suburbs, a toddler can show you how interesting a slow walk around the block can be; here's the "barking dog" house, where you need to hold hands; here's the "prickly hedge" that threatens unwary fingers; there is the puddle where wasps roll up mud balls; here's the big wall full of little holes to explore. Your eyes will open wider to the world of wonder that surrounds young children.

Sometimes a trip can be more specific but just as simple; for instance, to watch the commuter trains come and go—from the safety of your arms. Or to the local firehouse to admire the huge shiny engine; or to the garage to watch the fascinating work of "feeding" the cars. Store trips for a purpose in which the young child can participate are fine, such as purchasing flour and salt for home-made clay (called Play Dough—recipe on page 201). Even marketing can be fun, if you use it as an opportunity to enlarge the child's knowledge, vocabulary, and speaking skills. For instance, you might observe, "Vegetables, vegetables! So many vegetables! Let's buy a green——?" (Hold up a pepper, apple, or head of lettuce.) "Yes, a green pepper. Now what shall we get that's red?" (If the child looks blank, pick up a tomato, apple, etc.) "Here's a delicious red apple. Do you want some for lunch?"

You don't have to overdo the teaching bit, just play with as many words, colors, names, numbers as you and your companion feel comfortable with.

Such trips are fine for the city toddler too; and there are even more interesting varieties of stores to choose from. And city toddlers, like their suburban peers, may find neighborhood playgrounds enough of a trip to provide great social satisfaction. On the whole, however, city sounds and sights are so full of stimulation that we might well err on the side of less rather than more trip taking; we don't want to dull our toddler's senses with too much excitement. Even an elevator ride with a toddler button pusher is a great thrill trip. It gives an exciting sense of power.

Three- to Five-Year-Olds

Dramatic play is what life is all about to young children. Over and over they love to play out their experiences and their fantasies. In playgrounds, in nursery schools, and in their homes they dramatize their experiences of the complex world about them. They become firefighters, construction workers, mothers, fathers, doctors, pilots, shopkeepers, engineers. They are space visitors, monsters, superstars, bad witches, and other powerful beings. Their role playing of real and unreal characters helps them sort out the puzzles around them, find vicarious triumph in heroic roles, and confirm the information they are absorbing every day. Trips help to fill in the missing pieces in their fund of knowledge, extend their information, widen their horizons.

Just as the toddler loves to visit a firehouse, the lively preschooler is avid for more information about the world around him. So it behooves us to examine our trip possibilities from a youngster's point of view. Where can we find activities and people to extend the preschooler's knowledge? Is there a factory nearby that will allow us to visit? Will a firehouse or police station? A branch of the telephone company? A post office? A hospital? A local bakery? Going out for a meal at a hospital coffee shop or where local workers eat may lead to enlightening conversations. But in planning a trip to a local factory, for example, we should do our homework by getting permission and by taking the trip alone first, to get an idea of how suitable it is for the child, what events will be over his or her head, or where boredom might set in. It is imperative to confirm the exact date and time for the youngster's visit, to avoid howling disappointment.

Like the toddler, the preschooler also loves water adventures of any kind, but now they are often used for dramatic play. A local brook can be the site of dams, waterfalls, boat play, and imaginary landscapes. If fish are sighted, the little adventure reaches blissful heights.

Preschoolers can take some limited museum and zoo adventures too, depending on the place—small and intimate is usually better than big and crowded—and particular interests. A trip to see dollhouses might be very exciting for one child and a visit to a trolley museum just right for another. One child loves the children's "petting zoo" while another wants to stare at lions all day.

Longer Day Trips with Young Children

Sometimes longer trips are unavoidable; then a little planning ahead will make the trip less exhausting for adult and child. First, be sure to find out ahead if the child suffers from motion sickness and, if so, how to cope with it. Then, try to get to the bus or train station or airport well ahead of the hour of departure. This allows for exploring time: riding on the escalator, darting under the turnstiles, plus the inevitable visits to the water fountain, the refreshment bar, and, of course, the toilets. This unhurried investigation produces a tension-free atmosphere that is a good beginning for the trip ahead.

Older children can take a more active part in the travel preparations, helping to look up schedules, finding the departure gates, getting the tickets for the family. One father prepared for a bus trip with regional and long-distance maps and colored pens. His children had a wonderful time marking out the destinations of the various buses as the dispatcher kept reeling them off, and following their own journey on the maps.

Once on the trip, there will be the usual cry of "I'm hungry!" "Okay," would be the answer. "You may choose one of these bags for now," and three bags appear, one perhaps full of carrot sticks, one of nuts, and one with raisins and an apple. Knowing the child's preferences, eliminating junk foods and sweets, you can make the bags an extended surprise. An equally sensible approach is to let the child help plan and fix the food ahead of time.

Besides food, a long trip requires a favorite book to read aloud, a beloved toy or game, whatever seems homey in the strange environment. But you needn't try to be an unpaid full-time entertainer; reserve some space and rights to yourself too. When the child has plenty to occupy himself, it's all right to say, "Now I'm going to close my eyes and rest a bit. You may do the same, if you like. Or you can play or look out the window. But for a while you must amuse yourself." Young children need to learn to play alone, and also to be considerate of others.

Another essential to pack is a small plastic bag for disposal of whatever litter accumulates on the trip. It is ecologically responsible, and you will be modeling a kind of behavior that children need to observe.

One father who took his three-year-old daughter on a train trip came prepared with an adequate supply of materials for diversion but found that for the most part they weren't needed. Lisa preferred to play "pretend games," sometimes with her father, sometimes alone. Her vivid imaginings made for a lively and enlightening trip.

But whether you are drawn into dramatics or asked to read stories or play card games, remember that you're the grownup. You are the one to give your child some kind of timetable and some choices within the limits you set. "We'll play school until the next station stop," or if you are driving a car, "until the next town." Then the choice: "After that you decide whether you want to draw or look at a book, or just look out the window for a while." The child will make the decision but you give the structure and plan.

Blessed are the parents (and grandparents, relatives, or friends) whose young children fall asleep on long trips for appreciable periods of time. If you have lively ones, you can only supply appropriate materials ahead of time and, during the trip, try to pace yourself and the child. So much time for playing, for reading out loud, for trips to water cooler and toilet, for quiet independent activity, and for rest— rest for yourself as well as for the child. Children need a framework for their activities: don't hesitate to allot a goodly portion of the trip to quiet time, so that you and your child will arrive in a reasonably cheerful state.

Seven- to Nine-Year-Olds

Seven- to nine-year-olds are beginning to acquire a more refined sense of time and space. Museum exhibits such as those showing life on the African savanna, or the Dutch in New Amsterdam, may attract them. Their enlarging span of attention will allow them to more fully satisfy their curiosity, fantasy, and/or knowledge about the "olden days." And at this age your participation with challenging or informational remarks may deepen their understanding or excite their curiosity. In front of a Grasslands exhibit you might say, "I can see some tools made of stone. How many do you see?" Or in front of the African savanna you might remark, "I wonder what kids do who live in this part of Africa? What do you think you'd do if you lived here?"

But above all, don't let the child feel you are "testing" or "teaching" him or her; accept answers with respect, or if there is no response, you might answer the question yourself, then drop the subject.

Children this age love grownup terminology, so feel free to introduce your older child to scientific names of familiar objects. You can even make up games. At an aquarium, for example, you might ask "What family do you think a whale belongs to? The fish family? The mammals? Mollusks? Or echinoderms? Take a guess." If the child groans, give the answer quickly; if interest awakens, say you'll help find out; sometimes children will want to discover more about the other "families" too. But always, easy does it! This isn't a teaching trip, and making learning a chore can spoil the whole day.

Sometimes you will want to take your child to an art museum, perhaps because of a school assignment or because of a news story. Plan ahead what you will see, keeping in mind how quickly feet get tired tramping around those acres of stone floors, and save some time for refreshments and buying souvenirs. Then *stick to your plan*, no matter how tempting a side excursion to the Egyptian mummies or the Hall of Knights may be. Save those experiences for another day. On the way to and from your exhibit, of course, you will see many other pictures. You might ask, "Which picture do you think your mother would like? Your uncle? Yourself?" as you stroll by, and you may be surprised at the answers. Children have amazing sensitivities and perceptions of other people but little chance to express them.

When you go to the museum shop, remember that most children are eager to buy souvenirs and often waste money on fragile trivia. A talk about these matters before the trip is a good idea, but once there, after the pros and cons of a purchase have been discussed, the choice should be left up to the child. Good consumer practices can only be learned by experience, so bite your tongue and let your child choose.

Sometimes shopping trips with older children can cause uncomfortable dilemmas, as when an uncle took his nephew to a toy shop to choose a birthday present. In spite of his family's strong stand against guns, eight-year-old Sy had eyes only for the assortment of weapons on display. What could Uncle Len do after he had said flatly, "You may choose anything you want up to $10.00"? What he did was remind the boy of his family's feelings about gun play, then ask him to consider all the other possibilities. This would have allowed Sy to retreat with dignity—"Those dumb guns are no good, they'd fall apart anyhow"—and choose another toy. But Sy asserted his independence by choosing a triggerlike object that sent spinners whirling through the air.

Did Sy really have a free choice? What would you have done? For one thing, perhaps we should choose our words more carefully: "You can have anything under $10 that you like, provided it isn't a hurting weapon" (or whatever we abhor). If the child is spending his or her own money, what then? Perhaps all we should do is state our reasons for our moral beliefs, and then let the child choose freely—even if it doesn't seem the best choice to us.

Longer Day Trips with Seven-
To Nine-Year-Olds

Children love to go to beaches or big parks that are often far from urban or rural centers and necessitate taking a long bus, car or subway trip. Two good time fillers are playing games that are connected with the trip, and using trip boards.

Games can be simply: a version of "I Packed My Grandmother's Trunk" with anything seen outside the window; a race to see who can spot the first ten people, or who can first see someone with red clothing, a billboard, a train station, or a horse. A surefire hit with subway riders is to guess on which side the door will open before the train pulls into a station. In all these games adults are on a par with the children—their store of knowledge doesn't give them an unfair advantage.

For young readers, reading the ads in the car and matching the station stops with a list prepared ahead of time are interesting pastimes. The list will be part of the "trip board" prepared before you go on any new trip with children.

A trip board can be as elaborate or as simple as you wish; basically it is a pad of paper stapled to a piece of cardboard. Here the child may have a list of station stops, landmarks, or major intersections instead of endlessly asking, "How much farther do we have to go?" You can use the blank paper for tallies; say, from a bus window, one could tally all the weeping willows or any other distinctive tree that one sees, or perhaps the different state licenses on passing cars. Or adult and child can play "Hangman" or "Tic-Tac-Toe" (see page 228). And, of course, the child has blank paper for doodling or sketching whatever he or she wants to do.

Perhaps most important of all is to be at ease yourself with the child and the trip. Wear comfortable, appropriate clothes; keep to an adjustable timetable; be sure the kids understand your rules ahead of time; and keep a list of the Tips where you can peek at them occasionally.

Whether your trip is long or short, whether your child is a toddler or an eight-year-old, remember that trips do end, that children grow up. Keeping in mind Abraham Lincoln's remark, "Most folks are as happy as they make up their minds to be," take the opportunity to be with your children, to share their fun, and, above all, to enjoy the pleasure of their company.

Making a Trip Board

Even if you're all thumbs, a trip board is a cinch to make. All you need do is to staple some blank pages together on a piece of cardboard (about 4 by 8 inches, so it's easy to carry). A small spiral notebook or a standard clipboard will also do fine.

On the first page draw a rough map of your proposed trip. It can show:

Your starting point
Your destination
Number of stops along the way
Interesting spots or landmarks to watch for en route

Under this map, or on the next page, write a few questions that will interest your youngsters and give them something to work on during the trip. For example:

How many stops are there before we get off the bus (or train, plane, or subway)? Count them as you go along.
If traveling by bus or car, how many towns do we go through?
What direction are we going in? North, south, east or west?
Where are we now? Put your finger on the spot on the map.
Make a list of the important sights or landmarks you see.
How many sights begin with an "A" (or "B" or other letter)?

Complete your trip board by adding a few blank sheets for the kids to draw or write on.

Why a trip board? It gives your child a chance to be involved in the

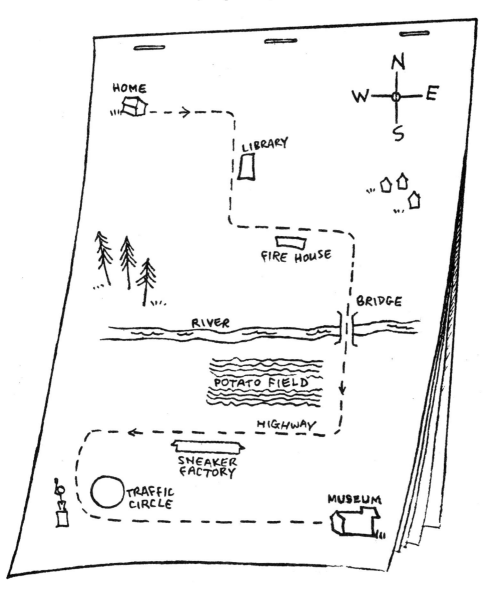

trip, to know where he or she is going, to participate rather than to be dragged passively through unknown territory. It also enriches the child's knowledge of geography, sense of direction, and general feelings of competence, control, and self-reliance.

Don't worry if you can't draw a straight line—it isn't necessary to be a Rembrandt. The important thing is to create a simple plan that shows the route and a few highlights. Let your child fill in other points of interest as you go along.

Long Trips with Children

JOANNE OPPENHEIM

There are two kinds of long-distance trips with children: trips you want to take; trips you have to take.

One woman I know had to move cross-country four times in four years with four young children. Obviously no one would choose that kind of travel on an annual basis. Yet major moves or sudden emergencies may find any of us with young travelers on a nonelective journey. Whether you're a parent, grandparent, uncle, aunt, or devoted family friend, even such no-choice trips can, with a little foresight and planning, turn out to be good adventures.

Of course there are some adults who cannot imagine any trip they'd want to take with children. They'll say, "Why don't you send them to camp?" or "Can't they stay at Grandma's?" Even Grandma may say, "Why don't you wait till they're older? What will they remember?" More than one parent has said, "I'd rather stay home than take the whole kit and kaboodle along."

Well, traveling *en famille* certainly causes some problems, but there are also many benefits, so let's look at both.

Pros and Cons

Perhaps the first and most basic benefit is that taking the children along saves the worry of leaving them behind and wondering how they are.

Summer camp may seem a reasonable alternative, but the cost of camps is rarely reasonable and may be prohibitive. With family fares, air travel at an early age may be a bargain by comparison. Don't over-look the special family rates in many luxury, as well as commercial, hotels and motel chains.

You may have family or friends willing and eager for the patter of little feet. That's fine, if you also remember that such hospitality usually needs to be repaid: the cost of your indebtedness may come to haunt you.

Staying home "until they're old enough" is a bit too open-ended and may, in fact, mean staying home indefinitely. For some of us that, too, is a nonchoice.

The fact that children may not remember everything they see should not devalue what they do see. Who remembers everything? Most of the really wonderful places in this world are not fully seeable in one visit, whether you're six or sixty. To me the real test of a place is whether it's worth going back to. Nor should we assume that the best-known landmarks will be the most memorable parts of a trip. Each of us views the world in a unique way. I recall visiting a Mayan temple with my husband and father. To Father, a rock hound, the site was a geological wonderland; while my husband, an armchair archeologist, spent his day walking through time and history as he climbed up and down the steep stone steps.

Children, too, bring their own curiosity and fantasies to new sights. Part of the pleasure of family travel is in sharing the fresh excitement of their discoveries. Many people send their young teenagers off on teen tours, but why let someone else enjoy taking your kids for a first look at the Grand Canyon or London Bridge?

There's no doubt that having some time alone, without the kids, is desirable. But taking them along does not mean you must spend every moment of the night and day together. What you save on long-distance calls home can cover the cost of bonded baby sitters in most major resorts and cities of the world.

Perhaps at the heart of the matter it's a question of philosophy—the family that lives together can travel together. If that sounds com-fortable to you, then there are concrete things you can do to make a good idea work well:

> Plan ahead—not only itinerary, luggage, reservations, and
>   such, but mental and emotional preparation—reading
>   and talking about the places you'll go.

Help children to view the trip as an "adventure" wherein they may live a little differently, experience new customs and meet different people.

Help children to accept the idea that usual routines of sleeping, eating, and dressing may be different.

Help them accept the probability of change of plans, probable delays—even unexpected adventure.

Prepare yourself too.

Plans, Schedules, and Scenic Routes

One of our family's first long journeys with children required connecting flights. Thinking how clever we were, we scheduled flight one to deliver us from a winter morning to a tropical afternoon at the beach. Our second departure was to be a dinner flight to our destination.

Nothing went as scheduled. It was overcast and too cold for the beach. Our dinner flight was delayed a half-hour. At ten that night the airline offered to feed us on the ground; of course we had eaten by then. At midnight the flight was finally canceled and at one in the morning we were settled into a hotel, after insisting that the airline locate our luggage in the hold. After all, the children needed their pajamas and toothbrushes.

Thinking back on that trip, especially that first night out, we still laugh at the importance we placed on pajamas and toothbrushes. We learned early that long-distance travel, with or without children, requires a relaxed attitude about things that are almost ritualized "musts" at home. That's one thing that sets vacation time apart from other times. In retrospect, I think the unscheduled events are often the most memorable parts of a journey, even to the young traveler.

Travel demands a sense of humor and a suspension of life as usual. Sure, the kids have to eat, sleep, and brush their teeth, but trying to live like you're at home can ruin the fun for everyone.

Children may need some help in adapting to the "adventure" of travel. Since young children, especially, enjoy predictable routines, some may view broken schedules as an unwelcomed interruption to their usual day-to-day activities. It may be helpful to make flexible but solid plans for the day. Children like to know what's on the agenda and, to the extent that it's practical, they should have a voice in planning the day's proceedings. Try to avoid making ironclad promises that may need to be canceled because of the vagaries of weather, late departures, or other emergencies beyond your control. Parents can also help foster flexible attitudes about changes in schedule by minimizing their own reactions to inevitable breakdowns. Before the days of thruways, turnpikes, and freeways, my dad often took us on long-distance trips by car. More than once, at a fork in a rural road, he'd jokingly say, "Which way shall we go?" For the next ten miles my mom would say, "This can't be right, we're lost, aren't we?" "No," my dad always said, chuckling, "we're not lost. This is the scenic route."

A willingness to chance the scenic route, to accept and even enjoy changes, is part of the sense of adventure parents can convey to children. Such attitudes have learning potential well beyond any single trip.

Luggage—Survival Kits, Security Blankets, and Light Loads

Too much luggage on a long trip can be more trouble than two children and one window seat. One can take turns with a window seat, but too much luggage just gets heavier as the days pass. Small sleeping children, too few luggage carts, and the shortage of porters can provoke lower back pain and short tempers. Luggage on wheels is noisy but helpful. Multipurpose clothes that can be mixed and matched for changeable weather are basic. Knowing the average climate conditions can be of limiting, even misleading help. We once took our sons to Arizona in January and assumed their winter clothes could be left behind. The hotel manager told us at least twice a day that they hadn't had a frost like this in thirty years. We nearly froze until we bought gloves, hats, and extra sweaters for those early morning horseback rides up Camelback Mountain.

What everyone needs is a crease-resistant, sittable, strip-downable suit for all seasons. A few well-chosen changes are preferable to carting a closetful. Rubber-soled shoes or sneakers are a must for sure-footed climbing and wet pavements. Remember, too, that if you take your shoes off on a long flight, you may not be able to get them on when you land. Party clothes always need ironing and are seldom if ever worn on a trip. Use the space for a pair of warm pajamas for cold tropic nights or for air-conditioning that won't quit. Most of us have clothes in the closet that we wear infrequently; we tend to stick to the things that are comfortable. On a trip, the need for comfort is even more important. Simple is best. Once children who traveled needed a special wardrobe, but today casual styles are universal. Unless you're planning to stay at resorts with dress codes or dine in gourmet restaurants, children don't need formal dress-up clothes.

Clothes should be selected with an eye for easy care as well as comfort. Life can be simplified if clothes mix and match into coordinated outfits. This gives the child a variety of changes and allows greater independence in choosing what to wear. Vacation time shouldn't get bogged down with questions like "What should I wear today?" or "You're not going out like that, are you?"

How to pack is no less important than what to pack. In part, it will depend on how you're traveling. If you're going to have several overnight stops before settling in somewhere, it's helpful to pack a single bag for the road. That means you need carry only one bag into a motel, or if you're flying, the rest of your luggage can be checked through. That one bag will need toiletries for all, plus a change of underwear and socks, nightclothes, and a few shirts or blouses. Keep that bag light and tuck in a plastic garbage bag for soiled clothes. If your children are close in size but not interchangeable, color code underwear and socks with a dab of permanent Magic Marker (helps in sorting laundry, too). Color coding all your luggage with bright yarn tied to the handles can ease the strain as look-alike luggage comes rolling down baggage chutes at airports. Spotting and counting the pieces is sport for the younger members of the traveling party.

Whether you're going by car, plane, train, or bus, each traveler should have a carry-bag that accommodates personal treasures—a few familiar small toys, books, maybe a blank pad and crayons or water markers—and the collection of shells, stones, maps, postcards, or other souvenirs that trips fall heir to. Limiting the size of the hand luggage limits the collecting and purchasing fever of young tourists. Our rule for backpacks, beach totes, and airline carry-on bags is simple: If they can't tote it, they can't take it. These bags should have secure closing, since in transit they will have to be stored under seats or up in racks. Small toy cars and crayons have a way of taking off down aisles. Of course the younger child will find comfort with familiar huggables when bedtime comes in a strange room or along the way. A well-loved blanket or stuffed toy is bulky but light, and well worth the inconvenience in terms of contentment.

Leaving home and liking it may depend on how well you pack. Tuck in a small sewing kit, but leave the rest of the mending equipment at home. Any garments that can be worn only once without cleaning should be left behind. Being organized and selective at the start can save you energy and needless aggravation along the way. The adage to remember before you latch your luggage is "Less is Best."

Eating on the Road

Eating out for days or weeks need not become a headache. I always try to remember a study done years ago on children's eating habits, which showed that over a period of weeks, children who selected their own food ultimately ate a nutritionally balanced diet.* If a variety of nourishing choices is present, don't make war over unfinished string beans. On the other hand, do fight the battle against junk food that simply fills children up with empty calories and may leave them too tired to enjoy their adventures. It's not difficult to find fruit, cheese, or peanuts to satisfy the snacker's appetite. A crunchy apple or a wedge of cheese makes for better health than the ever present soda and candy machines in hotels and terminals.

As often as possible, find opportunities to have picnic lunches or dinners. Shopping at the local super or outdoor market puts you in touch with local people as well as good food, and eating al fresco puts less strain on both budget and behavior. Eating on board trains, planes, and assorted transports is a personal matter. My own family has eaten on everything except a submarine, and that's only because we haven't found a submarine to take us diving yet. Most youngsters seem to love the individual service, minipacks of salt and pepper, and attention they get from flight attendants. With a little planning and

---

* C. M. Davis, "Results of the Self-Selection of Diet by Young Children," *Canadian Medical Association Journal, 41* (1939), 257–261.

luck your travel arrangements can stretch the food budget. Having dinner in the clouds may not rate five stars, but the real stars and moon should not be underrated for atmosphere.

Travel Health

It's no fun to get sick anywhere, but that shouldn't keep you from traveling. But what about sore throats, temperatures, illness? There are doctors and emergency rooms everywhere we are likely to go. Just as a hedge, I carry a small arsenal—a thermometer, antiseptic, Band-Aids, aspirin, and the expectation that none of the above will be needed. Naturally, chronic conditions such as allergies will need to be treated just as they are at home. A child who suffers from motion sickness on short hauls will likely need the same treatment on long jaunts. Luckily, jet flights don't produce such motion sickness.

Basic to good health at home or in transit is the need for adequate rest and suitable exercise. Sitting in a car for thirty-six hours, nonstop, may get you from New York to Florida cheaply, but the tax on everyone's physical and mental health may come out higher than the savings. In traveling with children, it's important to be sensitive to their natural schedules. There's no point in checking out of your motel if you know your children will need a bathroom right after breakfast. Since you're paying for it anyhow, they should have the comfort of a private, rather than public bathroom.

While we're on the subject of public rest rooms, it's helpful to plan ahead for some of the less desirable but necessary pit stops. A small pack of tissues is a "must have" item, and if you're venturing to remote places you may also want to carry a few folded paper toilet-seat covers, which take up next to no space in a purse or pocket. While you're at it, you might throw in a few foil-wrapped hand wipes against the chance of empty soap dispensers. These small comforts add up on the plus side of feeling well away from home.

In a good many families there's apt to be one child (or adult) who cannot tolerate a change in drinking water. On our first trip to Mexico we cautiously used bottled water for brushing teeth until one afternoon we realized how useless our precautions were as we sipped our Cokes in glasses filled with ice cubes. I do carry medication for diarrhea, but I've stopped worrying so much. The child who needs it is as likely to need it in Cleveland as in Cuernavaca.

Get Ready, Get Set, or Plans the Travel Agent Can't Make

Quite aside from packing your suitcase, there are things to be done long before the day of departure. Among the great pleasures of travel are the delights of anticipation. Children, both young and old, should be encouraged to participate in gathering information and background about the places they're going to visit. Photographic travel books, brochures from tourist offices, maps, dictionaries, encyclopedias, and recorded folk music can whet the appetite of young travelers and build a framework for what lies ahead.

Without heavy-handed lectures, children will generally enjoy knowing about where they're going and what they'll see. Historic and factual background can often be built through works of historical fiction. From picture books to young adult novels, the world of children's literature offers an invitation to view the lives of long ago and faraway people. Books can enhance children's respect for those who have gone before and for those who are different. Books can also help them understand the commonality we share, no matter where we live.

Getting ready may also include the nicety if not the necessity of learning some polite phrases of greeting and learning to count in another language. Some fundamentals of converting dollars into pounds, lire, pesos, or marks may come in handy, too. Children don't have to be enthusiastic math students to become astute at translating prices and at bargain hunting. A bit of menu language will also make dining out more pleasurable.

In our own country there are still some regional foods that should not be overlooked. Knowing the what, where, and when shouldn't be left to chance. Do some reading yourself and share your discoveries.

Older children may want to keep a map of where they've been and where they're going. It might be coded with the means of transportation they used. My husband started his travel map as a young preteen and his atlas is now color coded with lines that show the family's growth and travel history.

Learning to read time schedules is another math-related skill that older children often enjoy. In an age of jet travel, changing time zones has become routine, but it remains fascinating to youngsters who delight in figuring out what time it is where they are, where they're going, and "back home."

What with maps, timetables, and money and language differences, older children often find that getting there is a good part of the fun, provided there's something to munch on and sip along the way. With little children, the most direct route is usually best. Settling in gives them a chance to feel secure in their home-away-from-home. The young traveler's natural habitat will be places that allow for running, climbing, digging, and exploring, rather than cars or hotel rooms. Everyone's disposition will be improved if you find places where children can be children.

Prolonged periods of physical inactivity demand more impulse control than young children can live with comfortably. Held on too tight a string, their energy is apt to spill over into misbehavior and irritability. Vacation days need to include ample opportunities to run, jump, and shout. This means you'll spend an afternoon on the beach instead of deep-sea fishing or dancing on a terrace. If you have the good fortune to go to Paris, you'll spend less time in the Louvre and more time sailing a toy boat in the Tuileries. You'll also meet people you would never otherwise meet.

On a beach in Mexico, my English-speaking sons had absolutely no problem building a sand castle with two Spanish-speaking children. It's amazing how universal the language of play and laughter is.

You've Arrived—Now What?

There's no doubt that traveling with youngsters shapes what you do with your days once you get where you're going. Not long ago I was in San Francisco on a glorious summer day. Looking out at the beauty of the blue water and sky, I couldn't take my eyes off the bright-colored kites that were sailing in the wind. My teenage daughter and I were exploring turquoise rings, beads, and bracelets, that day. We are both devoted window shoppers, but I couldn't help thinking that a few years back we'd have spent a day like this flying kites over the bay.

Does that explain the joys of traveling with children? Sure, there are some things you can't do, but there are others you wouldn't do otherwise. Who's to say that flying a kite is less preferable than cock-tails at the Top of the Mark?

Getting in Touch

Perhaps the best gift of family travel is the time for small pleasures and discoveries that everyday busy-ness just doesn't allow.

I'll never forget our small sons covering their father's eyes when they spotted a Rotary Club sign as we drove into Los Angeles. Neither of us realized how much they disliked his weekly Tuesday-night din-ner out (on top of Friday-night court and Thursday-night board meetings). Their small protest gave us some insight and caused some changes when we returned home. Parents aren't the only ones who are often too busy for enough family time; older kids too are forever on the go. Family vacations can be a time to get in touch without the distractions of telephones and meetings. They can also put family members "in touch with themselves," sparking interests that don't end when the last bag is unpacked. The world of timetables and travel guides brings new meaning to numbers and print; a map becomes a tool, not an abstract mystery.

It's hard sometimes to know just what children take in. We can't al-ways know what connections they make. Some are eager journal writ-ers. Others tuck a picture or dried flower in their memory bag. Some begin collecting postmarks. The big thing isn't how many new facts they're learning or how many lines they're putting on their map. Traveling together gives you all another line in communication, a time for sharing enthusiasms and points of view—but not to turn your holiday into a history class on wheels. Your family history is also being written and will have more lasting effects than bits of exotic in-formation. Travel may be a framework for more finding out, but the framework of the family and feelings of mutual respect are at the heart of your shared adventures.

In all honesty, family vacations may provide more togetherness than anyone wants. It's not a bad idea to split the party up from time to time. An afternoon at a museum may be perfect for one parent and child while nature lovers explore the local zoo, park, or beach. Shop-ping is a giant bore to some and part of the fun to others. It spoils everybody's fun if the nonshoppers drag along and nag. Remember that there's no rule that says you have to spend all your time together or doing the same things.

My husband and I have on occasion used hotel-bonded baby sitters for an evening on the town. Of course it adds to the expense, but Mom and Dad shouldn't feel guilty about taking some time out. When you hire a sitter, especially for a young child, have the person spend some time with the family in the afternoon, giving all of you some time to get acquainted with an unfamiliar sitter. The point is, there's no reason to feel you can't pursue any adult entertainment when the family goes along. If you left the kids at home, they'd be missing you for more than an evening. For everyone's peace of mind, do leave word where you're going, just as you would at home, and for the quivering-chinned child, it may help to call in once during the evening.

Sometimes a shift of schedule works as well as baby sitters. After a full day of beach or sightseeing, try having a pick-me-up of fruit and crackers. With all but the youngest travelers, that late-afternoon break allows the family to dine a good deal later than we would at home. Chances are that a later dinner hour will drift into a later bedtime and a later rising time. Remember, you left the schedule at home, and kids, like all of us, can benefit from a change of routine.

Back to work, school, and home, they will soon return to regular bath time and bedtime. And every once in a while, a sight or story or taste will remind them: "Remember when we had dinner at . . .?" "What was the name of that place where we . . .?" and you'll all relish the memories.

Dos and Don'ts for Travel

Do plan ahead; but
    Don't plan to do everything you plan.
Do go prepared for health emergencies; but
    Don't keep watching for them.
Do learn about where you're going;
    Don't turn it into a college survey course.
Do pack lightly;
    Don't worry about what you forgot (you'll never miss it).
Do take time for rest and good nourishment;
    Don't take your home schedule along.

Do carry snacks in case of emergency;
 Don't fill up on junk food.
Do try some new foods;
 Don't force or expect children to (admit they) love it.
Do find places for running, shouting, and playing;
 Don't overtax their staying power in restaurants, museums, restorations.
Do let them know from time to time that you're enjoying their company;
 Don't be amazed at how long you'll treasure the memories.

Outings with Other People's Kids

VICTOR BUSCH

Are you planning an outing with a niece? A nephew? A friend's or neighbor's child? You and the child may be well acquainted or strangers; if the latter, your outing may become a kind of "getting to know you."

"When I was a little girl," says a woman I know, "we spent our summers at the shore. And one of the high points for my brother and me was our outings with Fred, the local carpenter and village poet. In the summer, when we kids all went for a nature walk with him, it wasn't an ordinary walk—we became frontier scouts, creeping along in single file, breaking new trails or stalking a deer. And when we hunted for bits of smooth beach glass in the sand, we were searching for precious 'pirate jewels' washed up from the sea."

Fred's approach was obvious but effective: he had a knack for turning the simplest of activities into an adventure. Whatever the environment, the kids and their beloved Fred turned it into a special treat by adding a bit of imagination. But Fred's real magic came, perhaps, from the fact that he had as much fun as the youngsters.

Does this mean it's necessary to have a mysterious patch of woods or an interesting stretch of beach to explore? Of course not. Children can find wonders anywhere—a park, a playground, a suburban setting, or an ordinary city street. But when you're with children in any of these settings, keep in mind that you're not expected to be an "entertainer." Whether you spend an hour, an afternoon, or longer with someone else's child, the point is for both you and the youngster to have a relaxed and enjoyable time.

Whatever your plan, it's a good idea to keep certain principles in mind.

Scale Outings to the Child's Age

Something that will "work" nicely with a seven- or eight-year-old may be inappropriate for a child of four or five. One young man took his neighbor's four-year-old daughter to the circus. It was a huge circus (intimidating enough to older kids) with crowds of noisy people, a blaring band, and three rings going full blast. Needless to say, Amy was soon anxious and frightened and had to be taken home. She would have been much happier visiting a new playground or the children's zoo nearby. Conversely, a child can be too old for a particular activity. Eight- or nine-year-olds, for instance, may feel self-conscious at a kiddie zoo and prefer to visit a "real" one.

I saw an interesting contrast at a showing of a classic sci-fi movie, filled with starships, "wookies," and lovable robots. A ten-year-old boy sat through the film totally spellbound, his eyes riveted to the screen for two magic hours. Next to him was a three-year-old who reacted quite differently. The film was far too long for this child, and the sounds and images were overexciting. The three-year-old squirmed, fidgeted, and made repeated trips to the bathroom and the water fountain, climbing over everyone's feet and generally having a wretched time. For that age level the space film was totally inappropriate, while for the older boy it was just right.

As to films, it's always wise to check them out ahead of time. Official ratings help, but it's a good idea to also get direct information from somebody who has seen the film—or see it yourself—before taking a youngster.

Consider the Child's Interests

This calls for flexibility. It's important, of course, to stretch a child's horizons, but it helps to take your cue from the child's own interests and enthusiasms. If your visiting youngster's hobby is building model airplanes, maybe a trip to the local airport can be arranged. If he or she is athletic, you might want to organize a game in the park, or take in a sporting event. A girl or boy who loves trains and boats would obviously enjoy a visit to a railroad station or a ride on a ferry. For most children, if their age level is appropriate, the environment of a train station, firehouse, boat yard, airport, factory, or produce market can be a rich and exciting one. It can also lead to further learning experiences.

If possible, before the day of your outing, check with an adult in the family about what the youngster might like. Better yet, consult with the child. You can ask simply, "Is there something special you'd like to see or do?" Try to draw the child out about his or her interests and wishes, and suggest options to see what kind of response you get.

Sometimes, of course, you won't pick up any clues from a child. Some kids are more passive and reticent, and look to you, the grownup, to plan the fun. But almost every area, neighborhood, or community has its points of interest. Is there a park with a pond where kids sail their boats? Or a spot where avid kite flyers gather? Perhaps there are bicycle paths, or places where you and your youngster can try some fishing.

If you live in or near a large city, the opportunities are endless. Are there museums suitable to the age of the child? Model train exhibits? Interesting displays open to the public? Street fairs, holiday concerts, or similar events? Are there special ethnic areas that might be interesting to explore? Unusual shops? You don't have to go overboard and plan something wildly elaborate. Just try asking yourself: If I were a child, what would *I* like to do?

Think about Location

How to get there is always a consideration. Will you go by car? Bus? Subway or train? Does the plan involve walking? If so, how *much* walking will there be? Will it be too tiring for small legs? If the outing involves a meal, will there be food available when you want it?

Above all, how *long* will your trip take? What about tie-ups and traffic jams? A trip that takes so long there is hardly time to do anything except turn around and start for home again is not usually what the child has in mind. Think of the child's attention span, too; long, boring trips can spoil the whole outing.

Check First

Trivial problems can take the edge off the best of outings, and it's easy to avoid most of them. Here are a few details you can check out in advance:

> Does your child have any health or diet problems?
> Are there certain foods he or she can't or shouldn't eat?
>   What are his or her food preferences?
> Does the child have any allergies you should know about?
> Can the child (if very young) go to the bathroom alone?
> Are there any family names or nicknames you should know?
> Are there certain things he or she might be afraid of?

A man I know remembers a trip to an amusement park when he was eight years old: "I was taken by my adored-but-seldom-seen Uncle Bill, and I wanted to put my best foot forward with him. Unfortunately, the first thing he suggested was a ride on the Ferris wheel, and I had a real terror of heights. I was too young and ashamed to let him know about my phobia. I shut my eyes when the wheel began to rise, but I couldn't stand it—I had to look. There was the ground so far below, and there I was swinging and swaying in the sky! I clutched Uncle Bill and began to scream. Somehow they lowered us down, and he carried me off. I was mortified, but Bill hugged me. 'Always tell me when something bothers you again,' was all he said. And now that I'm a man, I hope any kid I'm in charge of will let me know his fears; suffering in silence is for the birds."

Does this mean that everything has to be planned in advance, cut-and-dried? No, fun and flexibility go hand in hand, and every outing with children can have an easy, relaxed flexibility built in. To help gain this, a few "don'ts" can be added:

> Don't overload your schedule. It isn't necessary to cram a great number of sights, sounds, and busy events into a single trip. Depending on the age of your child, the best outings are usually built around one major activity and a meal, perhaps lunch or a midafternoon treat. And be sure to include time for resting.
> Don't overstructure your outing. It isn't necessary to stick

rigidly to a timetable. Try to flow with the tide of an outing, and be prepared for serendipity.

Don't be critical of the child's dress or appearance; that's the
responsibility of the child's family. But you certainly
can't surrender your own values or standards. While the
child is in your care, he or she should understand what
behavior is expected. Certain reasonable rules should be
mentioned—no gum chewing at meals, no loud talking
during the movies, always wait for the light before crossing the street, and so on. If you're clear, simple, and fair,
children won't object. Try to keep your rules to a minimum, but keep them.

Don't expect the child to react or respond noticeably to
what's taking place. Children often prefer to keep their
peak experiences to themselves and savor them later in
private, or to act on them nonverbally. Sometimes weeks
or months go by before a child begins to express positive
reactions to a particularly exciting experience or event.
This is quite normal, and since you're not playing the
role of entertainer, you don't have to wait for applause.

And *do* expect some interesting surprises. Adults may plan
and prepare, but kids have an unexpected and delightful way of turning those plans upside down. You may set
up an elaborate outing, carefully arranged, only to find
that some small side experience proves to be the youngster's real high point.

Ellen, age seven, was visiting her Aunt Meg for the week end in
New York City. The little girl lived in a small town in Connecticut and
had never been to New York before, so her young aunt planned an
exciting round of sightseeing. On the way to their first stop they took
the subway and happened to get into the very first car. Ellen was intrigued with the subway, and thrilled when she discovered that she
could stand right at the glass door in front and watch the tracks, the
lights, and the flashing rails.

All Ellen wanted to do after that was stand in the front of subway
cars, and the other carefully planned events became anticlimactic.
Aunt Meg reacted in just the right way. On their way home, they

bought a book for Ellen about trains and subways. They also picked up some crayons and drawing paper, so Ellen could draw and color her own subway scenes. Later, Aunt Meg arranged for them both to visit a subway dispatcher's office downtown, where child and adult could follow the tiny lights on the huge traffic board which showed the progress of the various subway lines. Ellen's visit to the city was obviously a great success; it became a good memory for both her and Aunt Meg.

Dr. Dorothy Cohen, a child development specialist, points out that with a child an imaginative adult has a chance "to become a resource in unfamiliar areas of knowledge."* This opportunity to interact with youngsters on new levels of knowledge and experience is the crux of any enjoyable outing. Know your child and know yourself. Remember that your own tastes and interests have to be considered. It's *your* outing, too, a chance to have fun and to expand your own horizons as well as your young companion's.

---

* Dorothy Cohen, *The Learning Child* (New York: Random House, 1973).

Part 6

SPECIAL
RELATIONSHIPS

In earlier parts of this book we have explored
the relationships and activities with children
that are more or less common to all parents and
those in parenting roles. In Part 6 we want to
talk about some special relationships with children, particularly those of single parents, working parents, and grandparents. We will also examine some of the new sensitivities of fathering
roles, and take a look at how children form
friendships beyond the intimate circle of the
family. And finally we will have a speculative
glimpse of what children themselves feel they
need for more pleasurable relationships with
the adults in their lives.

When Grandparents Visit

No two family configurations are the same. We could get rid of half
our guilt about what we do and don't do for our families if only we
would acknowledge that simple fact. Take the matter of being a good
grandparent, for example. Some cynics say that the only way to have a
warm, close relationship with the rest of the family is to keep the two
generations at least fifty miles apart. By that definition, grandparents
could only be occasional visitors. Yet other parents report that their
family would collapse if Grandma were not around the corner, ready
to dash over and save the soup or let the parents out for a drink or a
movie after a hectic day. Pleasurable grandparenting, as well as the
special relationships that can evolve with the grandchildren, depends
a great deal on the personalities of the participants. But there are
some useful guidelines for grandparenting, depending on proximity.
For the fun of it let's say that there are three kinds of congenial
grandparents. We'll call them the Hundred-Yard Dashers, the Day
Trippers, and the Visiting Firepersons.

The Hundred-Yard Dashers

The dashers are the lucky ones. If you are in this category you most
likely live only a few minutes away from your grandchildren and see
them often on a very informal basis. If you behave yourself you can
really have the "pleasure of their company" with both your own children and the offspring. But unless you give some thought to the special circumstances you can find life becoming unbearable for all. The

continuing popularity of hostile mother- and father-in-law jokes affirms the degree of risk. Perhaps some of the following suggestions will help keep the relationship relaxed and constructive.

Remember, You Are a Relative, not Santa Claus!

Establish from the start that it is you, not the local candy store, that is coming to visit. Most grandchildren have a bottomless appetite for candy and other goodies, but these days most parents know that the real way to spell candy is DENTIST. Similarly with a lot of other little bits and pieces of junk food that used to be found in Gramps's pocket. So start off early and right by being appreciated for *who* you are, not as a deliverer of endless little sweets. You don't need to buy your way into your grandchild's affections by always popping in with give-away trinkets. Such "Santa-Clausing" may well be saying to kids that love mainly depends on material giving.

Kid Stuff

That doesn't mean you always come empty-handed, but your contribution will have little or no conspicuous cash value. It might be an old bird nest (debugged!) or a gleaming conch shell still holding the sound of a far-off sea.

One grandparent keeps a cardboard box in her closet labeled KID STUFF. Into it she tosses the odds and ends that can be passed on to grandchildren. What goes into kid stuff? Well, it depends on ages and interests, but one box includes a stack of post cards accumulated from summer and winter jaunts, twelve old spools, an oil-company picture calendar, one red pencil, two fat yellow crayons, a remnant of furlike cloth, several shirt cardboards, half a train ticket (used), four shiny horse chestnuts, and a large clam shell. In such a collection one can always find something more valuable than anything Woolworth ever stocked—and less resented by the rest of the family.

Special Functions that Are Yours

Try to agree with your family on one or two special functions that you can perform on a continuing basis with your grandchild. This gives more purpose and steadiness to your frequent visits and reduces the number of hopeless and irritating discussions about "what should we do today." With small fry, trips to places like a local fire station, cement works, or pumping station are thrilling events. Don't be surprised if the older kids want to join you. Or you may be as interested as the older children in frequent visits to a planetarium or local museum to check out specific interests. One of the best special functions can be visiting the public library at a regular time. Visits to the library can have endless variety—this week looking for books on leaves, next week trucks, or trips to China. After all, the library *is* the whole world. Many libraries have story hours on Saturdays, which can give additional variety and inspire some grandparents to help out as readers.

Who Is the Boss?

As a hundred-yard dasher, don't ever forget that in your own child's home, he or she and spouse are the bosses. It's important for your grandchildren to see their parents as fully capable of caring for them and managing the affairs of the home. If you forget and begin to have the urge to be bossy, you are headed for trouble. Stay keyed to the idea that your child is, after all, only half the child-raising team, and that both are struggling hard to establish a coherent household. Uninvited interference will always make the struggle harder. That may sound hard to take, but if you are old enough to be a grandparent, you are old enough to take it.

Don't Be the CIA

It's very tempting to use the easy access to your grandchildren to subtly cross-question them on things that are none of your business. You don't need to know intimate family disagreements or actions. If you don't think much of your daughter-in-law's friends, or the fact that your son does the cooking, one piece of sterling advice is to Keep Your Mouth Shut.

But on the big issues, seek candor in your relationship with your grandchild's parents. Just dashing in and out doesn't necessarily give the various adults a chance to compare notes and views on how the relationship is really going. One successful intergenerational family has what they call a "Pop-and-Mom-off" a couple of times a year. Leaving the children with a nonrelative as baby sitter, the parents and the grandparents go out Dutch treat to a pleasant and unhurried meal, over which they share perceptions and plans for those priceless jewels, the children. Both generations know they will have a "pop-off" periodically, and they look forward to the occasions as times of clarifying candor.

Day Trippers

Grandparents who live in the next town or for one reason or other cannot come at the drop of a hat generally find they have a very different relationship with grandchildren. Whereas the dashers may be in and out of the house on an unscheduled basis, day-tripping grandparents should never arrive without advance warning. (And they shouldn't stay overnight unless invited.) If you are so situated, you are usually close enough to grandchildren to become an easy part of certain activities, but at the same time ready to acknowledge that you really do live elsewhere. In such circumstances, here are some of the routes to congenial grandparenting.

Special Teaching Talents

If you have a special skill such as photography or knitting or carpentry, try to work out your visit so that you can make it an occasion to do some teaching. If your grandchild is interested, and if you both know that each time you come a part of the time will be spent on your special lesson, it will be looked forward to and will be something that can extend over a long time, even a lifetime. Many children can barely wait for the next visit from grandparents, not because they will be showered with glossy gifts, but because they will get their next lesson in coin collecting (or cooking or skiing or swimming or whatever it is their lively grandparents do). Sharing a common interest provides a useful focus for visits and also a basis for interim phone conversations and notes.

And remember, sometimes no activity is best. Maybe just your presence is what is needed—a person who is nonpressuring, unconcerned with daily routine requirements, and counted on for affection and a willing ear. Your special talent may often be just that. What the children are telling you in their own way is that they value your company and personal attention far more than anything else you could bring them

Develop a Family History

Children are usually curious about their progenitors and want grandparents to tell them what they did "in olden times," as one five-year-old put it to her chic forty-six-year-old grandmother. A good grandparent project is to work with the grandchildren in compiling or extending the family history. Sometimes this can reach back many generations in America or other parts of the world. In other cases the focus will be on more recent relatives, often spread widely. Children need to know they belong to and are part of a larger family group. A feeling of belonging can bring added security and self-confidence that enriches a child's sense of personal value. (And a logical next step would be to discover that he or she also belongs to the family of humankind.)

The family search can be a continuing project, including making a family tree, field trips to court houses for old records, searching out family correspondence, and, most exciting of all, tape-recording conversations with old-timers who are relatives or who knew the relatives. One family had the thrill of discovering long-lost relatives living in the next city. Another found a real pirate captain hidden in the family woodwork.

Be the Family Fact File

If you prefer to emphasize the current activities of the family, get out those shoeboxes loaded with clippings about kids' doings and bureau drawers of undated and unnamed photos of babies, vacations, graduations, picnics, and new toys. Most mothers and fathers are too busy *raising* kids to keep up with their past accomplishments, but everyone would appreciate some order to the collection. You and the grandchildren can make this a shared venture—the kids will love to help sort out all these puzzles. When necessary, leave a "mystery photograph envelope" for your grandchildren to quiz their parents about between your visits.

Overnight Visits of Grandchildren

One of the things that help children develop independence and responsibility is the chance to gradually develop an identity apart from the home turf and parents. If you are in day-trip distance you can arrange overnight visits starting when the child is quite young. When grandparents are just next door, the notion of an overnight is not always so exciting, but if it's a little distance away, there is a sense of adventure. Long trips are likely to be more difficult and expensive, but a day tripper has a real advantage in overnights.

The Value of Continuity

With day trippers, continuity is the key. The main concept to keep in mind as a day-tripping grandparent is to look for activities that link the visits together and yet provide easy starts and stops. A shared hobby such as birdwatching is perfect. Other shared activities can be not only work on the "family file" but help in arranging children's collections. Ten-year-old Johnny may need more information to identify things in his rock collection; eight-year-old Jenny's leaf collection may need help too. Or all the kids may want to work together on a holiday scrapbook.

It's important to avoid projects that have involved details of construction or sharp time limits. One grandfather thought he had a fine idea when he brought his grandson a model airplane kit that they would assemble during his day-long visit. But the kit required more time and far more patience than Jimmy could muster, and it finally defeated Grandpa too. At departure time the unfinished plane was scattered all over the room.

Visiting Firepersons

If the children live in Peru, Indiana, and you live in Palo Alto, you're not a member of the immediate family, you're a visitor. Distant grandparents have few chances for regular visits, and when they do they know they have to act like guests. This has a lot of frustration and a note of sadness but offers some opportunities that closer grandparents don't have. For example, on the matter of gifts, if you are a visiting firefighter, you are excused from the usual rules and your once-a-year gift giving can be outlandish. Within your means you should feel free to make your visit as much fun as Christmas.

The problem for most long-distance grandparents is not how to make the most of the annual blitz, but how to maintain close and meaningful contact with the family through the year. Phone calls are great, but all too brief unless you work for the telephone company, and kids are apt to be indifferent letter writers at least until their teens. You can expect little more than a cryptic "Dear Gram, Thanks for your letter. Good luck, Sam" in response to that warm and chatty eight pages you spent half a day writing. Using your imagination and sometimes a few elements of modern technology is indicated. Some children will enjoy mystery letters with parts missing: "Guess where I went this morning. I went to ———, which is on Lake ———. Then I went into a large building with a gold dome. The building is called the state ———. If you can fill in the blanks and return this to me, I'll send you a picture of it." Mysteries can be people, places, things, qualities, ideas, common shared experiences, wishes, memories, or hopes. Often a present of a few stamped, self-addressed envelopes is appreciated. Banks, dentists, and college fund-raising offices know that they get a lot more replies if the stamp is already on the letter. One distant grandparent found her mail increasing tenfold when she used this device.

Writing isn't the only form of written communication. Many children love to draw picture stories, but hate to write out their experiences. Let your grandchildren know that their colorful communications are appreciated and shown off on your bulletin board.

Sponsor a family newspaper. Some of the closest families are kept together by a monthly newspaper edited by a grandparent. Your reporters can be grandchildren or other semidetached observers, and the activities of scattered family units can be united in one paper. Young ones can contribute their pictures, older ones stories of family doings and achievements. Photocopying and mimeo services are widely available, and the cost is modest compared to the rewards. You can paste up pictures and text and put a lot on just a page or two. If your mailing list is large, investigate the lower but slower mail rates available for unsigned material.

Using the same general idea as the family newspaper, you may want to take advantage of low-cost tape cassettes and set up a tape-exchange network on the model of a radio station. Get material from your roving and remote reporters and develop programs to be circulated by mail. Grandchildren can be the local station managers and "air" the programs for the whole family at convenient times. You might include "special gift offers," advertising, profiles of family pets, any gimmicks that will be fun for the primary audience, your grand-children.

Grandparenting can be a rewarding experience. What's needed to make it most congenial is a little forethought. When you discover that you are a prospective grandparent, it's time to plan ahead—first by yourselves, then in discussions with your own children. Your children will be mothers and fathers themselves; they will always remain to some degree your "youngsters," but you are no longer *the* authority. Your new role will be a lot less arduous in day-by-day decision making, and you will be free to enjoy the new generation. Indeed, grandparenting lets you enjoy the best of both generations.

Congenial Grandparenting

BETTY D. BOEGEHOLD

As grandparents, we rapidly learn one thing about our new role: it's a lot different from parenting. But from there on, grandparenting is largely a "learn by doing" kind of role; there aren't any manuals or models that will exactly match our own particular relationships with our own particular grandchildren. Most grandparent roles do, however, have two aspects that are worth some thought: first, being with the parents as well as the grandchildren; second, being alone with the grandchildren. In each instance we can use different approaches to achieve congenial grandparenting.

The occasions when we are part of a family group are a little trickier to handle than when we're alone with the grandchildren. Familial authority rests in the parents, but the children often try to obtain from us the kinds of permissions forbidden by their parents. Wanting to please our grandchildren, we are often caught in this trap.

Eager to be loved by the children and also helpful to their parents, grandparents need to be careful not to look as if they are taking over. A visiting grandmother, away from her own responsibilities, her offers to help with household chores turned down by her daughter-in-law, may be free to roam with the grandchildren, to read to them for long periods, to watch and discuss TV programs with them—not to mention taking them shopping for both essentials and frills. The parents are appreciative of all this—until the day when the kids begin to compare their parents unfavorably with Grandma: "Why can't *you* read to me some more? Grandma always reads me three stories!"

"How come you're always so busy? Grandma always has time to play with us!"

This can trigger angry feelings which need frank discussion, first among the adults and then with the children. Jealousy of someone free to act out the "perfect" parent role with the kids, free to play with them and indulge them, is natural for parents. Recognition and respect for this is essential for grandparents. Chances are that the children will have the least difficulty in understanding the role differences: visiting grandparents, like holidays, are full of fun and surprises; live-in parents are the predictable solid basis of daily living.

Another important consideration in successful grandparenting is to be aware of the duality of our role; we are not only the grandparent in this scene, we are also the parent of either Mom or Pop. One young father was apprehensive about having his own father visit; would Dad lay on "perfection rules" for his grandson as he had done with his son —a report card with three As and one B should have been straight As, and so on? But happily, the new role of grandfather seemed to have mellowed the older man. Grandfather enjoyed grandson's activities and creations even though they were less than perfect. Eventually the two men were able to discuss the difference and the grandfather confessed, "I felt it was all up to me to see that you did well, and I guess I overdid it. I'm more relaxed with Peter, maybe because I don't have to feel so responsible for him. I wish I'd taken the time to enjoy *you* more."

Some grandparents have more difficulty dropping the old role, and need to be warned against exerting nonexistent authority in what is perhaps the most damaging way: direct or implied criticism of a son or daughter's job as a parent. Watch out for remarks like: "You can't let Chris go out without his coat. And look—he's wearing sneakers, not warm shoes." "Johnny, we always keep our mouths closed when chewing our food. And we sit up straight at the table."

Of course when our grandchildren come to visit us, it's a whole other ballgame. Now we are in charge of the immediate rules, and we are also in charge of making the event enjoyable. We need to give some thought to what we can and cannot expect from the visitor. Some ages and stages will be more compatible with our own life style than others. Don't feel guilty if you enjoy some stages of the grandchildren's growth more than others; but remember that the kids will seem to pass on to new stages more quickly than your own children did, probably because you don't see them every day.

The amount of time spent with a grandchild is another factor in developing congenial grandparenting. Generally, the more we see each other, the easier it is to maintain a comfortable relationship. The grandparent who sees the grandchildren only on holidays or special visits may want a parental briefing on the current stage of development when the visit is being planned.

What else, then, should we consider when we have the delightful opportunity to have visiting children? Loving and caring will supersede everything else, but we should also establish some ground rules. Naturally, we won't hand out a rule book when our grandchildren enter the door; but we do want to let them know what to expect, both at home and on outings. If it's your child's first theater experience, he or she should know that "no talking out loud" is the accepted behavior.

The same beforehand knowledge helps smooth other activities such as eating in restaurants or riding on public transportation; for the younger set, some minimal rules should be well established. For instance, "not running ahead" is basic, even if it has to include "holding hands while crossing streets."

As the children grow older and perhaps make longer visits, your framework for living will be as natural to them as their own family's rules; in your house they will accept your routine easily. One young granddaughter admonished a friend before they sat down to lunch at Grandma's: "Don't make *smotching* noises when you chew! She doesn't go for that."

Okay, rules are good. But only as a basis for a pleasurable relationship. What is really important is the evidence of love, love that shows itself primarily in a concern to give pleasure. Sometimes what we plan for a grandchild's pleasure may not be what he or she really wants, but if we follow the child's lead, we aren't likely to go too far wrong. It's usually easy to prepare a child's favorite foods, share the favorite TV programs, plan the favorite recreations. And when we take the trouble to do so, we usually learn something new about our grandchild and about ourselves. Young Ronnie asked, "Why do you say you're ready, Grandpop, when you really aren't?" And Grandpop realized that in his anxiety about keeping up, he often made misleading statements, and some of the friction that followed was due to this small self-deception which didn't mislead the kids. When he gave more accurate reports, the children knew and accepted the situation.

For that kind of learning interchange, we don't need to spend money or devise elaborate programs; what we need is to take time to listen, time to work, to walk and talk with our grandchildren. Since we don't usually have them with us 365 days of the year, we surely can find that time. Even so, we don't always have to be onstage, hovering over the children or planning endless activities. We've lived long enough to appreciate the rewards of quiet time, and children can enjoy that too. They need time to "do their own thing" while we do ours.

Finally, we can share with them some of our own pleasures, perhaps in small doses at first. Theater lovers need not take young grandchildren to overwhelming Broadway musicals; that can come later. For now, an off-Broadway children's play, a puppet show, or Gilbert and Sullivan if the kids love music, will be quite sufficient. If you love art, pick one exhibition on an appropriate theme and of an absorbable size, and build from there. Such choices depend not only on the grandparents' interests but on what they know of their grandchildren's interests. And, as always, it varies with the children's ages and stages!

The more time we spend with our grandchildren, the less elaborate planning is needed; as in their own home, everyday activities predominate, with the occasional highlight of a special treat. Perhaps the most rewarding activity of all is the relationship which develops. A special bond seems to bridge the age gap between grandchild and grandparent. The child is often able to confide in and find security with this close, fairly undemanding parent-once-removed. All we need to do to cement this bond is to provide our time, concern, and love. Then perhaps our grandchild will view us in the same favorable terms with which a third-grader described her grandmother:

> A grandmother is a lady who has no children of her own.
> Grandmas don't have to do anything except be there.
> They are old so they shouldn't play hard or run. It is
> enough if they drive and have lots of dimes handy.
> Usually they are fat, but not too fat to tie your shoes.

They wear glasses and funny underwear. They can take their teeth and gums off. They don't have to be smart, only answer questions like, "Why do dogs hate cats?" or "How come God isn't married?" They don't talk baby talk like visitors do because it is hard to understand. When they read to us they don't skip, or mind if it is the same story again. Everybody should try to have one, especially if you don't have television, because grandmothers are the only grownups who have got time.

Going It Alone

MONA GOLDEMBERG

In a high-rise building in the city, a maintenance man spends some of his time changing the names on the directory and mailboxes in the lobby. A passer-by might assume that families were moving in or out, but the nameplates are just being changed from "Mr. and Mrs." to "Mr." or "Ms."

Separated or divorced families are now common in almost every community in America. Not only do we see the evidence ourselves but statistics bear us out. Never before have so many lone adults had to deal with one or more growing children without the classic balance of a two-parent family; and added to this challenge is the fact that single parents are moving in unexplored territory, without much guidance from social history and cultural experience.

Although there are similarities between two-parent and single-parent households, there are also many differences, and the differences may be more subtle. The single-parent-to-be may expect his or her life style to be radically changed but not be fully prepared for the decisions and emotions to be faced. One comforting fact is that just as their children will find friends undergoing similar experiences, so will the single parents; indeed, one of the sources of help to the new single parent can be found in the relatively new and rapidly growing single-parent groups. But most single parents have to face most of their new life's problems by themselves; perhaps if we understand some of the problems we have in common, we can resolve them more easily.

312

Structural Changes

The single parent is now the main authority figure, playing the combined roles of mother and father but usually with less time and less money. He or she is on duty twenty-four hours a day. A piece of the original structure has been lost, even if that piece was not a strong one. The pieces left in the structure must be reshaped to maintain the existing structure, or the existing structure can be allowed to collapse and a rebuilding process begun. In either case many changes will ensue.

Some of them will be evident in the small day-by-day events of life, such as household routines. One woman found the daily routines hardest for her and her children to cope with; now the first one home had to start dinner, the shopping and cleaning chores took a larger part of the children's time, Rhoda was no longer there when they returned from school. Mandy, age twelve, complained to her mother, "How come I get to do so much work now? I didn't divorce Daddy, *you* did!"

In the not-so-daily events, the absence of the former partner may be even more obvious. Joanna was walking to the station with her two children when the oldest said, "I really miss Daddy now. Remember how he always carried the heaviest bags? And kidded us so much, talking to everybody and making up wacky stories? This weekend won't be so much fun." A time planned for recreation brought back poignant memories that would be slow to fade.

Emotional Adjustments

For their own needs, after the marital breakup, single parents may find themselves spending a lot of time with married couples and their children. Sometimes it is very comforting to be with old friends. On the other hand, some children may find it very difficult to be with other children whose parents are still together. Children need to be able to talk with their parents about what kinds of activities would be most comfortable for them in this transition period.

Parents need to understand that both child and parent should express themselves honestly at this point. Children do feel different, and they need to know that it is appropriate to experience discomfort, anger or sadness.

Dana, a single mother of eight-year-old Alison, decided to spend the day with some of the friends in their old neighborhood. It was a warm Sunday and they all met at a favorite park. Within a very short time Alison became cranky; she whined and clung to her mother. Although Dana didn't want to leave, it soon became evident that the situation was upsetting Alison, and they went home. Mother and daughter were able to use this experience for discussing what it felt like to be around children with fathers when your own father was not there. Dana helped the child examine her right to feel sad, to protect herself from uncomfortable situations, and to do things that were more fun for her. Children need to know that they can still enjoy themselves despite some sadness in their lives. They need to know that both they and their parents can feel bad sometimes and enjoy themselves at other times (as happens also in two-parent homes).

The First Adjustment Stages

In the first stages of adjusting to their new status, single parents may be suffering from any combination of guilt, anger, sadness, bitterness, sense of failure, and loneliness. Others may be feeling relief, happiness, contentment and success; while still others have mixed emotions of panic, relief, fear, peace, or guilt. (Parents who are together also feel many of the same emotions in any given day or week.) The guilty feelings often push single parents into compensating for the divorce by showering children with an abundance of gifts and activities. They seem to feel that if they provide enough material things and "fun events" they will make up for the divorce.

But the process of shock, anger, acceptance, and mourning cannot be short-circuited; children and parents need to experience them and express their feelings. These stages of mourning are similar to the stages that follow a death; they take place even while parent and child are carrying on everyday activities.

Single parents are finding that the early stages of the divorce process are the most difficult for their children and for themselves. If the changes and differences in their lives are handled with sensitivity and honesty now, the later stages become much easier.

In conversations with single parents of young children, the word that comes up over and over is "time." The best gift that single parents can give to their children, especially in the early days, is personal time. For instance, a special activity for any child might be a ride on a ferry; but for a child of a single parent the ride assumes added importance by offering a chance for exclusive time with the parent. It is this exclusive time that will provide relief and security in the present situation and long-term rewards in the years to come.

The Younger Child

The kinds of things parents do with their children, as well as the relationship they develop with them after the separation, are very much influenced by the age of the children. For very young children the decision to separate comes as a great shock. Older children usually are not surprised. An eleven-year-old thinking back to age five and a half, when her parents told her of their impending separation, says, "I just could not believe it. I had heard of divorce but I didn't think it could ever happen to me." This child did not understand how it was possible to stop loving someone. She worried for a long time about when her father, who had moved out, would stop loving her. For years afterward she worried about what time her mother would be home, what time her brother would be home, whether or not she would be seeing her grandparents on a particular day. She seemed to believe that if her father could leave, then it was logical that other people she loved could also leave her.

Bedtime can be a particularly difficult part of the day for youngsters at this time. The technique used for ending the day is not so important as the fact that the parent ends the day in a way that says, "I am still here for you and I will be here tomorrow." Some parents read to their children at the end of the day, some listen to music, some keep their child company while the child bathes or washes up, and some simply lie down with the child and talk quietly. The important thing is to be there—warm, supportive, and reliable.

Single parents find that young children are likely to call them at work. By doing so the child is touching base, checking up, making sure. If possible, these children should visit their parents at work. Seeing and understanding this large part of a parent's day can calm or lessen the young child's fear of abandonment. If the parent's job makes this impossible, then perhaps she or he can take the children to visit the workplace on a Saturday or Sunday. Both parents need to convey to young children the fact that despite the changes in their lives, the love and security they expect from their parents have not and will not change.

The Middle-Years Child

Children from about eight to eleven years old often try to figure out what caused the divorce. "Who is at fault? Is it my fault? If I change my behavior will that help? My parents seem so troubled, I better be really good and not give them any more trouble."

Ten-year-old Adam questioned the need for the divorce. He said to his mother, "You and Daddy don't seem any happier separated; I want you together, so why can't you two be unhappy together and make me happy?" Three years later he agreed with his mother that not only were she and her former husband happier but that his life was also better. Jonathan, usually a harum-scarum kid, became painfully controlled and quiet after his parents' divorce. Gently questioned by his father (the custodial parent), Jonathan burst into tears. "You must have got divorced because I was bad," he cried. "I didn't listen, I didn't do my homework, I didn't get good marks. Maybe if I'm real good, you and Mom will get together again. Just give me a chance!"

Such feelings of guilt and fantasies of reconciliation are common with middle-years children; they need not only reassurance of the love of both parents but help in accepting the reality. Jonathan's father hugged him, then said, "Son, you had nothing to do with our divorce. Actually, your mother and I stayed together for a long time because we didn't want to hurt you. You know how we used to argue so much; we felt we were pulling you in two directions. Neither of us is a bad guy; we're just different guys! But we deeply love you—that's one thing we do agree on! And we do think separating will be better for you too, after a while. Hang in for a while, and remember—we love you and you were never, never the reason for our breakup!"

Of course words alone won't change Jonathan's feelings. Time and "hanging in" until fully assured of the continuing love of both parents and of the reality of the new situation is the best solution—until the child and the divorce itself have reached another stage.

Sometimes, in well-meant attempts to help the child, parents give in to pleas to "come together" for an outing or other event too soon, before their own hurts and hostilities have been resolved. The results can be disastrous and add to their child's emotional maelstrom, as happened to young Elizabeth. She worked at persuading both her parents to see the Thanksgiving Day Parade with her, as they had done in the past. The parents, wanting to keep changes at a minimum and to demonstrate their love for her, agreed to do so. Concealing their hostility, they felt they had succeeded in providing a pleasant day for Elizabeth. But when they returned to her mother's apartment, and the father declined to join them for dinner because of a previous engagement, Elizabeth began to cry unconsolably. Years later she was able to tell her father, "All that day I knew you and Mom were still mad at each other, though you both tried hard to hide it. But I had hoped desperately that if you watched the parade with us, maybe you'd come back to live with us."

The Older Child

If a marriage ends when the children are older, their reactions may seem quite different from those of the younger child. Normally, older children resent being fussed over or questioned about their emotions; this is the "rejecting your parents" stage. A divorce situation exacerbates these tendencies.

Older children are also more likely to side with one of the parents, although that doesn't seem to prevent them from finding fault with both. In one family the eleven- and twelve-year-old children bitterly resented the divorce; they also argued and fought with each other more frequently than before. In fact, the only time Heidi and Maurice seemed to agree was in their criticism of their parents. Maurice resented having to live with his mother and Heidi; he often spoke of running off to live with his father, although he knew his father was out of the country much of the time, and when he did get to visit his father, he was surly or withdrawn. Heidi flouted her mother's wishes, contradicted her, and spent most of her time alone in her room or with her friends. Their mother, Lara, often felt like screaming at the children, or running away herself. With the help of her feminist group, she was able to accept their feelings—but not their fantasies. She could say, "I understand how you feel; this situation is tough for you to accept right now. But your negative feelings are only making it harder for you to accept the way it is. I promise your father and I will help you all we can; we'll be straight with you, and try to understand how you feel. How about giving it—and us—a chance?"

In two-parent families it's hard enough to share activities with older children; single parents have to make a special effort. They usually have to catch their children on the run and create times for intimacy. During the early stages of divorce or separation, parents have to think carefully about the kinds of ways to have fun with their children; as with younger children, the needs of the child must be the determining factor.

Maria, the single parent of fourteen-year-old Pietro, says that the only time she sees her son is at dinner and breakfast; she has to make careful plans to make these occasions social as well as a time for eating. She tries hard to direct the dinner conversation to subjects that might interest her son, and encourages Pietro to communicate about his outside life. She has also taken pains to learn a little about basketball and baseball, so she can watch these games on television with him; and attends all his Junior League games. While Pietro retains the reticence of most young people, Maria feels she has kept the lines of communication open.

In the early months following divorce, most parents feel they must shift some of their own interests to stay close to their children emotionally and physically. With older children, single parents must find time and ways to keep communication as honest and open as possible.

Children of Different Ages

What of the single parent with children who are young, of middle years, and older? At first glance it would seem an impossible task for one person to handle such different ages and needs; in actuality, the job may be easier than it seems. For one thing, single parents may find they are developing more adultlike relationships with their children. They trust their children more, and, in turn, the children are able to become more independent. At the same time the children develop new relationships with each other. Sometimes they take on a helping role, giving a hand with homework or caring for the younger ones; sometimes they form new alliances among themselves or against the parent. The only child is often in a one-to-one confrontation with the parent; there is no one to support either of them if they differ. With other children in the family, the child is able to side with the mother, with another child, or with all the children; patterns of support and disagreement offer more options.

The working parent also finds that a large family can help when he or she has to be out of the home for long periods. The children are able to do a lot of the caring and tasks once denied them. Of course the working parent needs to provide caretakers and/or general overseers of the family while she or he is away, and a more organized structure may be needed, both for the parent and for the family, to carry out the essentials of family life and also to allow the parent time with each of the children. Sometimes the new framework helps parents order their time better than before, and delegating responsibilities to the children develops their feelings of independence and self-worth. The result may actually be more time with each child than the parent had before.

Most single parents talk not so much about what activities will keep their children busy and provide fun, but what activities will bring them closer to their children. Jennifer, the single parent of five children, purchased an inexpensive, large, and complicated jigsaw puzzle. As weeks went by, she noticed that whenever she sat down to work on it, some child would join her. She also noticed that while they shared the game, feelings and concerns surfaced; not everything got resolved, but many things did fall into perspective. For a long time the puzzle continued to be a challenge, an interesting activity, and an opportunity for quiet talk. Jennifer also found other intimate moments to be with each child. Ten-year-old Moira wanted to "play hairdresser" to her mother and this work gave the little girl a chance to feel close to Jennifer and to talk personally about her daily activities and problems.

Special Events

All single parents I've talked with, whether they have young or older children or a combination of both, find the emotional difficulties of the first stages of divorce the hardest to handle, for both themselves and their children. One of the recurring problems is the "special event"—birthdays, holidays, or a vacation, and less obvious events

such as open-school week and invitations to family reunions and wed-
,dings.

Some single parents stick very much to the old traditions and try
very hard not to change any of the old rites; they may even go so far
as to include the ex-spouse. Others make a clean break and use none
of the old ways to celebrate. They start forming new traditions more
in line with their new status. Many parents manage a combination of
new and old. Whatever the style, special events should be carefully
planned and carefully executed. For the children, they can be absolutely terrific or absolutely devastating occasions.

A lot of the special-events planning depends, of course, on the relationship between the mother and father. Children are very aware of
the working relationship between their separated parents; children's
antennae and parents' body language provide more knowledge than
the parents are aware of. The best advice is to include the children in
decision making, help them to talk about what they expect from any
given event. If they are excluded from decision making, one of the
devastating results can occur. One set of divorced parents still had
very hostile feelings toward each other, and avoided meeting or talking as much as possible, but they did agree on one decision. Only six
months after the divorce, and without consulting their eleven-year-
old son, they planned to attend his elementary-school graduation and
then go out for lunch together. Had the parents thought more carefully, they would have realized that they could not handle the pain of
being together for lunch in an old familiar restaurant. It ended with
the boy's mother crying at the table, the father embarrassed and
angry, and their son feeling like anything but the special celebrant.

At another luncheon events turned out quite differently. These
parents had been divorced for more than three years. During that
time they had straightened out their financial and custodial responsibilities, resolved their emotional conflicts to a reasonable degree, and
each became involved in a new friendship with another person. Now
they were lunching together with their three children as a prelude to
Jim's assuming custodial responsibility for the summer. Rita was
going to college to work toward a degree, and Jim was taking the children on a camping trip. He and Rita had planned all the details beforehand, and the children had been a part of the planning from the
beginning, so everyone was able to relax and converse amiably during

luncheon. The children, freed from parental tension, were at ease and the special event was a success.

Special events, then, depend on the situation (both financial and emotional) of the single parent; on the stage of the divorce and its familiarity to the children; on their ages; on the reasons for the gathering; and on the relationship of the parents. The single parent, with the children's help if possible, can decide whether or not to continue with old traditions, institute new ones, or make a blend of old and new. Together they can decide also whether or not the noncustodial parent should be involved.

Rethinking Priorities

When parents have finally taken the major step of ending their marriage, they are then able to rethink all the other traditional priorities in their lives. Single working parents may find it impossible to cope with all the things they were able to do in the past because of the absence of another adult in the home. The elimination of conflict becomes more important, and the most effective use of time becomes a priority. For instance, the amount of time children spend watching TV becomes less important than a parent's managing to watch some TV with them.

Because there is no mate in the house, parents find themselves developing more adultlike relationships with their children. When the "should" of getting married and living happily ever after disappears, many other "shoulds" and "should nots" quickly follow. A mother of a seven-year-old decides it's okay to take him to a 9:00 P.M. Friday night showing of a movie that they both want to see. The old "should" of strict bedtime hours can occasionally be changed. Reading at the dinner table is an old "should not" in my particular single-parent home, but sometimes even that "should not" is broken now, to everyone's delight.

Marriage in the traditional sense seems to be connected with certain kinds of structures, commitments, and obligations—dinner at a certain time and bedtime at a certain hour. This is not to say that these particular life styles do not include pleasure, and certainly there are many married people who live their lives in ways similar to those of single parents raising children. The difference is that single parents are forced to reexamine their priorities pertaining to their children. A single working mother of a teenage daughter says, "When I was married and during the early stages of my divorce, I always used Saturdays to do my shopping and errands. Last week I became aware of my daughter's need to get out of the city for a little while. I couldn't afford a weekend away so I planned a day-long Saturday trip to a pick-it-yourself apple orchard. We had a terrific time and came home with enough apples for some of her friends to share. When I was married I was less aware of the importance of that kind of activity. Now I realize that keeping the house in order, shopping, and all that are of less importance than doing things together, laughing and talking."

Betty, the single mother of three children, doesn't enjoy ice skating. Her ex-husband and children do. The children, who do not see very much of their father, missed ice skating and were too young to go alone. "I was finally forced into taking them ice skating," Betty says. "I won't say I loved it, but I was able to laugh with my children when they tried to teach me. I was able to share their pride as they showed me what they could do, and we had fun for weeks remembering how funny I looked learning to skate. At the same time I was able to get them to try something I enjoyed, a Gilbert and Sullivan operetta, on the same basis. We really are taking time to share our experiences more often."

Parental Relationships

The formal and informal custody arranged by the parents has a great influence on the time parents share with their children. It is difficult for one parent to be the only person arranging for children's activities. On the other hand, the involvement of the noncustodial parent in children's lives can be complicated.

Eight-year-old Ellen went to her father's house for the weekend. Early Saturday morning her mother got a frantic, tearful phone call. "Daddy wants to take me to the movies this afternoon. But he wants to take me to a movie that you said you would take me to on Monday. I don't know what to do." The mother assured Ellen that it was perfectly okay for her to go with her father; her mother could either pick another movie to see with Ellen or they could see that same film again if she wanted to. The mother was able to respond that way partly to reassure the child, but also because she no longer had angry feelings toward the father and didn't need to battle with him. The little girl, caught in the dilemma of giving equal time to both parents, got the answer she needed to help her realize that as parents' feelings change, so could her own.

No matter what is going on between parents, no matter how angry they are with each other, it is clearly in the best interest of the child for them not only to communicate reasonably but to include the children in plans for them. In the beginning stages of a divorce, it is sometimes very difficult for one parent not to be bitter about his or her partner in front of the children. Some parents go to the other extreme and attempt to be cheerful and positive and present an image of wonderful, loving, devoted parents, when the child knows that is not the true picture.

Although planning together is hard for most parents to accomplish, especially in the early stages of divorce, it becomes easier as time goes by. But from the beginning, when the parents do meet, and the children are present, it is important to try to manage a polite exchange, even if the children are aware that it is an effort. In most cases parents realize it is in their own best interest as well as in the children's to establish a working relationship with their former spouses. Many times children clearly benefit from the kinds of visiting arrangements made by their parents. For instance, one noncustodial father was asked to lecture at the University of Toronto on the weekend his daughter was going to spend with him. After consulting her, he decided to take her with him rather than disappoint her. Thus Jenny had her first plane trip, stayed in a hotel for the first time, ordered from room service for the first time, and heard her father lecture for the first time. If Tom had still been married to Jenny's mother, chances are Jenny would have stayed home with her mother.

Of course some custodial arrangements established legally may not work out as well in practice. Fathers often move away, remarry, and start new families, or they may break promises to the children or forget their custodial obligations. Similar disappointments can occur if the parent who left the family is the mother. For the child, such events can be traumatic, and for the primary custodian, such actions deepen responsibilities for playing the dual role of mother and father —a hard task. But both need to face the problem realistically and communicate honestly with each other. It won't help to indulge in bitter condemnation of the erstwhile spouse, although she must be honest about the situation. When nine-year-old Margaret went to spend a weekend with her father, whom she hadn't seen for a year, he drank heavily, forgot his promise to take her to a show, and spent the weekend sleeping it off. Later, Margaret's mother expressed her sorrow at the event: "He does love you, honey, but he probably got so worked up at the expectation of having fun with you, he started to drink. And then because of his alcoholic sickness he couldn't stop. He'll probably suffer terribly from remorse. I guess we're the lucky ones—we can enjoy ourselves without getting drunk." It didn't solve the situation, but this talk at least helped Margaret understand her father's actions.

One of the problems that single parents deal with more frequently than married people is "Who are my children going to love more, me or my ex-spouse?" Sometimes each parent tries to do bigger and better things with the children, or each parent may try to prevent them from joining the other parent in an activity that they may really enjoy. But generally speaking, although children do at times play one parent off against the other, they don't establish love relationships based on what kinds of material things or activities they are given. This may be quite hard for single parents to accept at first; but as time goes on they will come to understand that the time, understanding, and love given to their children are the mortar that cements lasting relationships.

The Long Stretch

As time passes and the initial stages of dealing with the breakup of the marriage are over, the single parent is likely to start developing a new way of life and a new social life. It is quite possible that the new circle of friends will be more diversified than when he or she was married. This becomes an opportunity for children to enjoy a much wider range of adults in their lives.

Pete, a single father, says: "My children relate to the children of the adults I now know. When I was married our circle of friends usually were people who were very much like us in age, marital status, and ages of the children. Now my children come into contact with many different kinds of life styles and living arrangements. They seem to enjoy these differences." Pete is quite pleased with the new life he shares with his children, but problems can occur if the children's mother or some of the relatives don't accept that particular way of living. Parents need to help their children deal with the dilemmas that may arise from the new patterns.

Single parents often find that everyday activities take on new social dimensions. They may attend large group festivals rather than small family picnics in the park. A haircut done by a single mother's friend becomes a social evening that includes the friend's children; or a teacher includes his children in a beach trip that he takes with his students in June. Georgina, a single mother, and her daughter Hilary have dinner and spend the evening with the child's teacher, Mrs. Doyle, who has become Georgina's friend. Mr. and Mrs. Doyle invite Hilary to "sleep over," a big, happy event for Hilary.

It is not just single parents who redefine and rethink their everyday existence; the people who surround them and their children see themselves playing different roles when there has been a breakup of a marriage. Because of single parents' needs, their children's lives are often enriched, and the surrounding adults and children become part of a new support system. As a result, their new roles enrich their own lives too.

Single parents need to think of themselves as ordinary parents raising children. They can plan and do many of the same kinds of things that married parents do. At the same time they need to be sensitive to the particular needs and wishes of their children that come from the reality of living with a lone parent. For instance, some children feel very comfortable having their parents visit them in camp on the same day and bring their new mates with them. Other children would prefer their parents to pick separate days to visit them in camp. If you ask, children will let you know what they want. Then it's your job to communicate as reasonably as possible with the other parent. Children are a joint responsibility deserving first priority.

Unfortunately, some parents who are trying to "find themselves" and fulfill their own needs often forget their children's needs, and the children become the victims of the separation. (I would recommend a children's book called *Go and Catch a Flying Fish,* by Mary Stoltz, Harper and Row, for all parents—but especially for single parents.)

The single parent who suddenly finds himself or herself in the major parenting role needs and should seek support, whether from single-parenting groups, formal or informal counseling, or from trusted friends; the emergence of a new kind of "extended family" in today's living patterns is certainly a benefit to the single parent.

But there are still many times when the parent will have to face situations alone; in those times it is helpful to remind oneself of the "stage" of the divorce process and the age of the child or children before making any long-term decisions. And, perhaps most of all, we should remember that time resolves many difficulties that at first seem overwhelming. Just living the new role of single parent one day at a time, not projecting too much worry into the future ("Where will I get the money for Johnny's law school?") or dwelling too much in the past ("Why did I ever marry him/her anyhow?"), but enjoying the children in the present, will help single parents reconstruct their lives.

The road of the single parent is admittedly a bumpy one, but help is available. For adults newly launched on the experience of single parenthood, several organizations offer guidance, advice, and support. In New York City the Single Parent Family Project—part of the Community Service Center—provides valuable help. Nationally there is Parents Without Partners, an organization with offices in many cities. And in most communities there are local health clinics, church groups, and family services aimed at helping single parents air and share their concerns.

"What They Need Is Nurturing"

PAUL SCHWARZ

I see my three children at least every other week, often more than that, and usually on weekends. Our vacations are shared. The kids live about sixty miles away, so there's a good bit of time spent picking them up and driving them home, but my strong feeling is that this is one of our most valuable times together.

In the car it's our chance to sit quietly and visit with one another, and if the radio isn't going, it's a time to talk—for all of us an important period. I don't think of it as a time to play games with license plates or things like that, but a time when they can really talk about what's on their minds, what school's been like, the problems they've had. I've found that our most important conversations have been during these car rides.

It's an hour-and-a-half trip, and very often one will sit in the front seat with me and the other two will go to sleep in the back. In the apartment I find that the kids are usually running around, bouncing from this to that—there are all sorts of distractions—but the drive is a good chance for the kind of conversation we often don't have with our children. Of course there's usually competition about who gets to ride in front, so they take turns. But sometimes I try to arrange it so that a child who I think wants to talk gets to sit next to me. It usually works out.

I pick the kids up late Friday afternoon. Then we have Friday night together, all day Saturday, and Saturday night, and I drive them back late Sunday afternoon. So it's a good long period for us to be with each other. I think the kids see their weekends with me in different ways. Suzy, my oldest, is thirteen, and I believe she feels it's a particularly important period for her. Rebecca, the youngest, doesn't see it quite the same as the other two do. I've been separated and divorced now for five years, so Rebecca was an infant at the time of our separation, and she never knew me as a "live at home" father. She also has a stepfather now—a very fine man—so for her our relationship is inevitably a little different.

What's the main thing I try to give my kids? I guess you could say it's a sense of continuity. It's terribly important, I believe, for them to see my house as *their* home; and they do. They have their own room with bunk beds. They have clothes at the house, and a lot of their toys. Paul Michael's stuffed dog, which he's hauled around with him for years, is right there on his bed. It's all part of the continuity. When they're with me, they're not merely "visiting"—their lives are really continuing.

Which brings me to another important point. My impression, from talking to friends, is that a single father (also a single mother) is often hard pressed to have something to "do" with the children. Suddenly they're here, and you've already been to the museum four times, and what do we do now? Well, I think this can be a trap—the goal of trying to fill their time and make every visit a Hollywood spectacular. That's impossible and unnatural, and I do feel that my kids need to take some responsibility for filling their own time. I love being with them but I don't feel constant pressure to entertain them, to make every moment like Halloween or a birthday celebration. For me, to *really* have fun with my son might be simply to sit down quietly with him and watch a football game on TV, or to go out for a walk and get a newspaper on Saturday morning with my older daughter. I also love to cook, and I enjoy cooking with my kids—not the conventional things like fudge or brownies, but things they might not know about. I love to introduce them to new foods.

Rituals and routines are vital, of course; they're part of security and continuity. For instance, I was brought up in a very religious family. Sundays were a time to go to church, and there was a whole routine built up around it. I'm not religious at this point, and my children and I don't go to church, but long ago I realized that something was missing: Sundays became just like any other day, and there was a lack. At that time I decided I would learn how to make soup or bake bread. Well, baking bread became a regular ritual with us, and every Sunday we would get up and bake bread together, all different kinds. For a long time that was something we enjoyed doing, and it became part of our weekend tradition. That tradition has stopped now because our interests changed, but it was an important part of our lives for a time. Sunday mornings are now the time for my kids to walk up the block and around the corner to a little candy store, where they get the Sunday paper and some lollipops. That's important to them. It's not really the candy or the newspaper, it's the ritual.

In a way I'm fortunate, living in the middle of a big city, because there are so many outlets and opportunities. We have libraries, museums, children's theater, parks, playgrounds, different ethnic neighborhoods to explore, and we do all that. But a lot of the time we just relax and let the day unfold naturally, with a feeling of continuity.

There are problems, of course. One of the things that's been difficult for me is that they have a whole constellation of friends at the school they go to, but when they come into the city they don't have that. It's important for me to try to give them some friends and other people whom they know and can be with in the city. Fortunately I'm a teacher, and I know a lot of children and parents and have been able to connect them with my children. So now they do have friends to visit and be with here. On some weekends Rebecca has come in with us and has had a date with a friend on Saturday afternoon; and she's called up and asked if she could stay overnight there, and that's fine with me. I think that's very nice because it means that they can enjoy a normal life pattern.

As the children get older one of the hardest things for me to deal with is the Wednesday night phone call that says, "Daddy, my Girl Scout troop is going camping this weekend. Do you mind if I don't come this time?" My answer is usually the same: "Yes, I mind because our time together is so important to me. But I realize that this birthday party"—or softball game or square dance—"is very important too, so have a good time and I'll see you soon." To say "No, I don't mind" is to imply that I don't care. So it remains a problem for us, and is sure to become an issue as the children's interests and time with their friends become more intense and time-consuming. I'm sure the

Wednesday night calls will soon include Saturday dates and other adolescent activities, but this is something all parents must face in one form or another.

We do have a lot of fun together. We enjoy the city—going out to see the sights, or to the park to throw a Frisbee around, or just shopping for food. Sometimes we make something very special for Saturday dinner, like a whole Chinese menu. At home the kids like to read, or we might play some Monopoly after dinner. My children aren't addicted to television, but we sometimes watch it together, and that can be rewarding, especially if it starts an interesting conversation. And we relish the quiet times—just being together—like a few weeks ago, when they took several bed sheets out and built a snow cave for themselves in the living room while I was reading.

This doesn't mean we ignore the festivals and special occasions. My daughter has been studying Japan in school, so this year for her birthday I took the kids out to a Japanese restaurant. It was a big success, and they talked about it a lot afterward.

In a way, they have the best of two worlds. In one community, which is really out in the country, they have deer and raccoons and skunks, and there's a lovely lake—and on the other hand they have the city with all its riches. I'm also beginning, now and then, to leave them on their own. Last time they were in, I went out to play tennis on Sunday morning and left them at home. They felt good about that; they felt I had confidence in them. And of course they did have phone numbers, and neighbors to call on in an emergency.

Another thing I've learned: it's important to share your own friends with your children. It's normal and healthy, and shows the kids that they don't have to worry—daddy has a normal life too. It's easy to arrange a party in your home on a weekend when the children aren't there, and I did that for some time; then I realized that I didn't like that. It's a little more difficult when they're with me, but it's worth it.

Of course all these things have come with time, after a certain amount of trial and error, but I guess it's the best way to learn. Now I've had five years of experience as a "noncustodial parent," and I think the transition has been made without too much difficulty. We've managed to keep a loving relationship, it's genuine and it keeps growing.

I guess I would sum it up this way: Children want a normal life. They don't want to always be "entertained." They don't want a constant diet of special surprises. This may be a function of my own personality, my teaching style, my way of being with children, but I think that what they really want is *nurturing*. And to nurture children doesn't mean that you have to entertain them. There's a world of difference between the two.

A Bigger Role for Fathers

FRANCIS ROBERTS

"If men had been expected to nurture children, they would have been designed a whole lot different," says an acquaintance who remains deeply skeptical of shifting patterns of parenthood. It is easy to dismiss such comments as old-fashioned, but they signify a fairly abrupt shift for many males. There really are differences in male and female biology, and respected researchers have long noted the importance of close attachment of infants and mothers, a truly symbiotic relationship.

New Sensitivities

Knowing all this, today's fathers are nevertheless discovering a whole new aspect of fatherhood. Culture begins when biology leaves off, and the best thing that has happened to America's beleaguered family in the past two decades is increased paternal sensitivity to the values of shared child care. Today's fathers now diaper without disgrace.

Admittedly this new consciousness did not come in the same package with the marriage vows, at least for many males. As the father of three, I'll admit that for many years I too was apt to pledge allegiance to more conventional divisions of labor. Two things helped reform me. First, my wife resumed her career. This caused new relationships all around. Our children quickly began to remind me, "Don't forget, Mom works at her job too," whenever they sensed some male chauvinism in the air. They were proud of her role as a respected professional and eager to sing her praises (though sometimes less eager to scour the bathroom and take on added chores).

The second factor came a bit later, when for the first time in many years I had the chance for about eight months to devote myself to writing and research on a full-time basis. Busier than ever in one sense, I was nonetheless working at home. Suddenly I found myself much more available to the kids, able to meet them at the end of their school day, to pick them up after Scout meetings, and to deliver the forgotten band instrument after the school bus left.

Such periods may be long or short, but they change your whole relationship with your kids. Hospitalization of a mate, job changes, even unemployment, whatever the stresses, can open the door to new perspectives on father-child relationships.

Macho Images

But what about the macho image, that brave, bold male ego? People who have never been fathers in an American cultural context are quick to dismiss such questions, but they do represent problems, even if only in the way others see your new role. Until recently brave deeds, guns, power tools, police, cars, and such were synonyms for masculinity, just as cooking, sewing, and caregiving were specific female functions. Even some of the most publicized exceptions were thinly disguised macho acts, as in the backyard sideshow created when Big Dad got out the charcoal grill. Under the watchful eyes of the neighbors the main dish was a red-blooded steak, not a French omelet.

Times do change, though. Just as soldiers and sailors today can be males or females, so is personnel changing in flight crews, operating rooms, and kitchens. Males and females are not duplicates or interchangeable parts, but around the house and in child care, there are some new, sensible arrangements.

Divide up the onerous tasks such as weeding gardens, washing and waxing floors, painting the bathroom, and mucking out the garage. Kids, too, know none of these is much fun, and will readily appreciate the implicit fairness of labor division based on equity, not tradition.

Rotate on an informal basis the neutral tasks such as picking up the kids.

Shop in bits and grabs *on each trip* to work. Families can keep shopping lists, not in "Mom's kitchen" but by the front door. The deal is, whoever goes out hauls back some grub. When there is no list, the expectation is that some items of predictable need will be brought home —paper towels, for example.

Great expectations are often fulfilled when shopping becomes fun for all. One family tried with success an experiment we might call "marketing mind reading," in which each member above age eight drew from a common cookie jar small amounts of money, with the understanding that on trips to shopping areas he or she would be expected to make purchases of things "the family absolutely needs today or soon." From such trips came a fairly steady supply of bread, perhaps a little more ice cream than the family really needed, and an occasional oversupply, as in the case of the 1000 tea bags. ("Imagine that!" said the nine-year-old purchaser. "I can't believe 1000 bags of anything could be sooo light.")

My favorite extension of the notion of advance shopping is what I call stockpiling. Whenever able or inclined, I try to make a mass purchase of one or two commodities regularly used but heavy to carry or otherwise awkward: a case of soup, several gallons of vinegar in anticipation of pickle season, or a whole winter's worth of favorite canned goods, for example. Opinions differ on the efficacy of "Dad's shopping style," but I think it saves work. Furthermore, I could never see the point of spending ten minutes comparing the price and quality of ten brands of sardines and then purchasing only two cans. A baker's dozen or none, I say, even though it means curtailing some other purchase. The only time I have noticed any shortcoming in my approach was the month before we moved to a new house. "Why," I inquired with genuine curiosity, "are we having baked beans and sardines at least one meal a day?"

"Dad's shopping style, at the bottom line," was the reply. I still think a lot of the plan.

"Everybody eats so everybody cooks," and/or washes up. All the members of our family are cooks and are forever developing new specialities. From daughter Betty's brownies-with-peanuts to Dad's duck soup à la Paris (sherry is the secret; otherwise duck soup is duck soup after the duck is gone), each member has a preferred list and the family eats tasty, nutritious, though occasionally surprising meals, none

with any sign of sex stereotypes. And the arguments about cleanup wither away when the job is shared; kids don't grouse about "fairness."

Discipline

Sharing is fine, but who in this new order of things will be the heavy? What happens to the traditional fatherly role of big bad wolf? Won't children grow up confused and undisciplined if Pop no longer warms bottoms?

Child rearing never was a matter of such simple things as a clear-cut role for "the enforcer." Nor was it ever primarily a matter of brute force, masculine power. This is the view that gets us *into* wars, not out of them, at home or in the large world. Respect and justice are what work at home and always has, regardless of parental dominance. Even in the days of traditional parenting the kids always saw through the stereotypes and early learned to negotiate their rights or stay out of the line of fire.

Today our more advanced knowledge of child rearing supports the need for strong parent figures, adults whose strength comes not from arbitrary commands but from respect for the well-being of each member.

Dad the Decision Maker?

Pop, the king of the mountain, used to be the all-wise ruler, some like to recall. Whether fathers really were always such decision makers is subject to some big doubts. Mother power in most cases was at least as strong. But if you want your children to grow up able to make decisions, they need to get some experience along the way. A good rule for today is for your kids to know that they have your trust, and that they are to grow up thinking themselves capable of making the significant decisions about their lives. This also means that when more than one person is involved, when a family faces decisions, the family should confer.

But should it be a case of one person, one vote, regardless of age? No. Children expect parental leadership and respect parental judgment. A child gets anxious if large issues for a whole family become his or her responsibility and hinge on his or her casting tie-breaking votes. But on general family matters where individual *choice* is the main criterion, your kids are as bright as you are and certainly have good sense if not experience.

Because of the value of children's opinions and the currency of shared decision-making, some households fall prey to artificial rituals in which the whole family, neatly scrubbed, sits straight-backed around the table and Makes Important Decisions. That may make a good picture, but it is not real life. By shared decisions and consulting the kids, I mean a much more informal process engaged in on a continuing basis as a family goes about daily living. "How should we spend our vacation?" can be explored better in a leisurely fashion on a long Saturday walk than as a corporate decision under the pressure of time. Decision-oriented questions for the family do not have to be those with the impact of a telegram.

Expressing Feelings

Actions are masculine and feelings are feminine, right? A big No! This surely was once the common view, and close in cause to the macho thing. Now, fathers can be especially helpful to children by saying, for example, "Jimmy, it's OK to cry," instead of "Buck up. Only girls and babies cry, son."

Children need to express both deep personal concerns and general feelings of apprehension about their world. International crises all around us generate anxiety that needs to be talked out in the reassuring context of parent support and interest. When to do this? I've made an informal and unscientific discovery along this line: When you and your kids need to talk about things serious but not of emergency nature, try doing so on days when the weather is soothing. Light snowfalls, foggy mornings, calm early-evening twilight seem to be conducive to the sensitive, feeling-based discussions that are helpful to children in their media-stimulated lives. Both children and adults need to keep in close touch with the natural world of which we are so integral a part.

When Both Parents Have Outside Jobs

Pop should take over as much as possible the role of school advocate for the kids. Schools almost never see fathers in daylight and are greatly impressed when they do. (Frankly, this is a way of using the culture's macho stereotype to do a beneficial reverse for your kids.) It is almost annoying to see how impressed a school staff is when a father shows up for a parent conference at ten in the morning. They almost apologize for interrupting the father's business day just to discuss the child's spelling. Your child will be even more impressed if you decide to take on the whole system in the name of a good cause. In one town we know, the authorities planned to close the local school because of population declines. A lively group of fathers took up the cause on behalf of the well-liked school, and although they eventually lost the battle, they really did win the war, as far as the children were concerned, by demonstrating aggressive citizen participation to the kids, and by showing how important school really is. The dads became minor heroes to the children, who then began to think of school in a new, more respected light. Similar efforts to get good teachers, reduce class size, expand the library, or get the ball fields resurfaced will be real bridge-builders with the children.

Sharing household tasks is obviously part of the bargain in two-working-parent homes, but this can be pretty dull. One way to brighten things up a bit is to divide into teams, Dad's Crew and Mom's Gang (assuming two or more children). The teams then rotate certain jobs. Thus, this week Dad's Crew does all the cooking, while Mom's Gang does the outside work like lawn care, snow shoveling, or car washing.

This leads to another idea. Fathers in our culture often do have a handle on lots of tools and maintenance skills. So if you have daughters, who will be growing up in a different, more sex-equitable world, what better favor can you give them than to teach them how to be handy with tools like saws, hammers, and wrenches? Show *all* your children how to make simple car repairs such as changing spark plugs or soldering a leaky water pipe. Sure, this isn't for four-year-olds, but start off early by encouraging all of them to be your helper when you change the faucet washer, put up drapery brackets, repair door handles, or screw up shelf brackets. And even very young children can twist in coat hooks or do some supervised painting with water-cleanup paints.

The flip side of this is that *mothers should do all they can to prepare male children for solitary parenthood.* Schools too can help; some high schools have child-care programs for both boys and girls. Both sexes share the operation of the centers that care for infants, toddlers, and other preschool children. In California I asked a husky seventeen-year-old halfback how he felt about the required child-care program. "Well," he said, "I got some heavy kidding from my teammates the first time they saw me wheeling a baby down the school corridor, but now I feel good about it and the kidding has long gone."

Fathers as Primary Child Rearers

There can be many reasons why one parent becomes mainly responsible for the children—illness, death, separation or divorce. In this relationship as in all special circumstances it's important to take cues from the study of the situation itself. The key to success is to fully recognize the pressure of such emotions as guilt, anger, and the child's and your sense of abandonment. What a child needs most at such times of stress is the extra time of a caring parent. There is sometimes a great temptation to give the child lots of extra gifts, lessons, and activities, partly to assure the child you are not leaving him or her too, and in the case of divorce partly to assuage your guilt about the split. Such compulsive rounds are seldom the answer. Better, arrange to have the time to listen to the child, to show by your physical presence a sense of continuity, especially during the transition from two-parent to one-parent household. Later, as time goes on and life stabilizes around new patterns, you can seek new directions and expand activities. Recent studies of one- and two-parent families show that the overwhelming proportion of single parents find post-marriage living far less disruptive and generally healthier for themselves and their children. Such findings help dispel the unhelpful fear that single-parent families are somehow unhappy places to rear children.

With this positive perspective, here are some ideas for single fathers (busy families of all configurations will get some help here, too):

Have each family member over five make own bed and pick up room; help the younger ones to learn the job.

Teach any child over eight to run the family laundry equipment.

All kids help in preparing meals and cleaning up.

Cook in quantity and put up meals in small packages; freeze for future use.

Take on one room a night with the vacuum cleaner, with child and parent alternating as driver.

When you have the option, pick housing that saves time as well as money. As a single parent you are often faced with a choice among time on the job, time on the bus, and time with your child. The closer you are to school and your work, the more time you have together.

Save one day or afternoon a week to do something interesting together.

Consider the possibilities of "off-cycle" jobs, so that you can spend more time with your child. For example, teaching offers a child-matching schedule on an annual basis. Other jobs may allow an early start each day, so as to finish at three-thirty, for instance. Employers who admire your competence and appreciate your situation are often willing to consider such changes or adjustments.

Shared jobs offer another possibility. Some employers are finding out that two halves exceed one whole. If you're feeling gutsy, perhaps this unexpected period in your life may be the long-sought and oft-delayed chance to paint or write part time while still keeping pizza on the table.

Another form of this is to leave the grind and, with your full-time fatherhood, pack your tote and spend a period in experimental subsistence farming, tent camping, or a similar venture that will cost little if carefully planned ahead and saved for and will give you and your child a memorable time together while you sort things out.

Perhaps a more conservative adventure at this point would be to go back to college and pick up the threads of that unfinished degree or extend your competence by pre-

paring for a new career or advanced responsibility in
your present occupation.

If you look back over the list above you will notice that it begins with
a few survival hints about laundry and food, but quickly goes on from
survival to growth and even adventure. By all reports, most newly single fathers feel pretty bad about themselves and their kids and often
turn their whole attention to the chores of daily living. But in this situation as in all of the others described in this book about life with children, our advice is to seek growth and build competence. Thus ap-
proached, fatherhood is not a trap but an opportunity.

When Both Parents Go Out to Work

MARK LUNDEEN

More families have two parents working outside the home than ever before, and the number continues to grow. The families we describe here all fit the pattern of the nuclear family, in which the two adults have full responsibility for meals, laundry, transportation, child-care arrangements and other household functions.

It Is Different

Suppose a five-year-old wakes up with a fever at six o'clock on a Monday morning. At Bob and Brenda Bailey's home, Bob must leave for work at seven and Brenda at eight-thirty. In their household the five-year-old's fever is an emergency, since the Baileys need to make a decision about child care for today.

Some families are fortunate enough to have a regular baby sitter able to care for a sick child on short notice for a day or two. Others may be able to call on relatives, neighbors, or family friends for occasional help. Unfortunately, this is not the case for most families. Few people are willing to stay with sick children, and few day-care centers have arrangements for children with minor illnesses. Most parents must stay home with a sick child, and since it is normal for young children to get sick, this problem will arise several times a year. Even when an emergency sitter is available, the parents must shift gears quickly. Before calling the surrogate parent, a number of decisions

341

must be made. Which parent will be available during the day to make and receive phone calls from the pediatrician and baby sitter? Which will pick up or arrange for delivery of any prescribed medicine? If conditions get worse, who can more easily come home? And if all other arrangements fall through, which parent can stay home?

Another typical family would meet the situation of a five-year-old awaking with a fever in a different way. Don and Mary Chapin have chosen another option for combining work and child care: he works three days a week and she works full time. In their family this Monday morning, much depends on whether today is a work day for Don. If it is not, then he is in charge. If it is, the situation is much like the emergency at the Bailey household. Often, however, even when both Chapins are expected at work the illness presents less stress on their family than on the Baileys. On some days Don's part-time job allows for last-minute changes in a weekly schedule, so he can stay home with a sick child and report for work tomorrow instead. A parent who works part time on any given day needs only relatively brief fill-in child care until he or she can return to comfort a child, visit the clinic, pick up prescriptions, and maybe catch a nap to make up for lost sleep.

There are a number of positive aspects to families in which both parents work outside the home. Family income is higher. In some cases adult career needs are more fulfilled. Additional career models are provided for children. Adults can continue to grow as individuals in settings broader than that provided by the family, in addition to growing as parents and partners. Increasing numbers of families are discovering that one or more of these "differences" meets real needs they are experiencing. As these needs are met, more nurturing, wholesome child rearing becomes possible.

On the other hand, a number of problems are highlighted when both parents work. Finding good child care and arranging care for a sick child are often difficult tasks, both emotionally and organizationally. In addition, less time is available for day-to-day household tasks such as shopping, cooking, laundry, and housecleaning as well as for ferrying children to and from parties, music lessons, and dental appointments. But all these matters can be resolved with thought, organization, and effective sharing, and with the firm determination that parental work will not be harmful to the children's best interests.

Resentment

"Don't go to work today, Mommy!" four-year-old Amy pleads through a torrent of tears. She plumps her small body in a corner of the room, refusing to move. It is eight o'clock in the morning and she must be taken to her sitter in a nearby apartment, so Mom can catch the eight-thirty bus and Dad can drive Amy's sister to school before he reports to work. How shall we deal with such a scene? We know, by report or by personal acquaintance, that children who live in Kibbutzim in Israel or communal nurseries in China during most of each week do not seem deprived; yet as parents we *feel* we are depriving young Amy when she behaves this way. But if the environment that Amy's baby sitter provides is familiar, and if it is also warm, responsive, and stimulating to her interests, Amy will soon accept and embrace this portion of her world.

If she does not soon show signs of healthy acceptance, there are a number of environmental factors to assess. For example, how secure and comfortable are both parents with leaving her in this person's care? Are they contributing to Amy's difficulties by communicating misgivings? Are these misgivings well founded? Is the environment sufficiently consistent, caring, and interesting? Are Amy's particular ways of expressing her needs, desires, and feelings properly recognized? If not, can the situation be improved? If it cannot, then it's best to immediately invest energy in finding another and better setting for her.

Children do not per se either like or dislike the fact that both parents work. What matters is the match between the child and specific, usually identifiable aspects of his or her environment, whether that environment is a day-care center, a baby sitter, or a mother's care. Good mother and father care, as well as good day care, must provide all these supports.

Scenes like the one with Amy are not uncommon. They are often disorienting and painful, especially for working mothers. Nonetheless, this is only one of many types of stress that normally occur as a family grows and develops, and it is not necessarily the most traumatic or difficult problem to resolve.

It is important for parents to talk together and with others about such problems; to review their options in a broad perspective; and that they plan their time and make their decisions for the benefit of all members. One decision easily reached is to see that the day begins as pleasantly as possible for all members of the family, even those who don't wake up until the first cup of coffee or glass of juice. Waking the children or exchanging greetings with them when they first appear each morning is a special activity that can be highly pleasurable. Parents may like to cuddle the children for a while before getting them up. Such initial loving contacts can set the tone for much of what follows each day, and this also applies to the later reunions of the day, including after-school and after-day-care greetings. Hugs, handholding, smiles and loving words convey special affection and can be meaningful ways of saying "I like you," "We belong together," "I really enjoy being with you."

Working parents may find that at more troublesome times of the day they have not been handling the situation effectively. For instance, when James and Paul Johnson were three and five, their parents found that the most quarrelsome part of each work day was the trip with the children to the day-care center. At first it had seemed a good idea for all four to go in one car, but the boys were continually competing over who was to be first out the door, first in the car, and who was to sit on Mother's lap.

The climate was transformed when the parents worked out a different schedule. On Monday, Paul went with his dad and James with his mother; on Wednesday, Mother took Paul and Dad went with James. On Tuesday and Thursday, when Father went to work early, the boys both went with Mother, and on Friday, Dad took both children. Though the schedule sounds complicated, the boys soon learned it and reacted to it well. Now they had more of the individual attention they needed, and there was less stress for the parents.

Affection

Children whose parents go out to work are likely to know a greater variety of adults than those with a parent who cares for them at home. But this widened world can give rise to a nagging thought: "By working, am I weakening the bonds of affection between myself and my child?"

The quality of a relationship is not determined by the amount of time spent in each other's company. A parent can be around a child all day every day for years and still not have a consistent, warm, or responsive relationship. On the other hand, Brenda Bailey, whose family was mentioned earlier, has just such a relationship with her daughter. They are together regularly on weekends and on weekdays between six-thirty and seven each morning and after five o'clock in the evening, when Brenda picks Melinda up at the day-care center.

We should remember too that feelings are "stretchable." Children can and do have more than one strong bond of affection; their devotion to other loving, caring adults doesn't in any way diminish the love they feel for caring, concerned parents. And being with other warm, responsive caregivers either in their own homes or in centers broadens their interpersonal skills, makes them more interesting to us and to themselves.

Parents' Needs

Growth and development occur not only in childhood but throughout our adult lives. Many parents choose to keep working after their children are born because they realize that one need not discard all important aspects of one life stage in order to grow fully into another. Others realize that there are later stages of adulthood after children are grown and that a continuing career, at least on a part-time basis, keeps future options open. Still other parents continue working only out of pressing financial need. In all these situations, awareness of the developmental stages of both childhood and adulthood can increase the pleasure we experience in the company of other family members.

Let's think of "adult needs" in two groups. First, there are the needs we can identify and talk about clearly, and for which we can plan together. Second, there are those we only dimly perceive through situations in which we find ourselves feeling frustrated.

It may be helpful to divide the first set of needs, those we can identify, into three groups: personal interests, personal ambitions or desires, and personal limits.

Personal interests, such as bowling regularly with a team or attending the ballet each season, or birdwatching, or reading bedtime stories to children, are activities that one enjoys and wants to continue doing.

Personal ambitions or desires, such as earning a university degree or developing an artistic talent, are commitments that require continued application. They are often areas that do not directly involve other family members, and are usually related to one's own strengths and talents.

Personal limits, such as irritability when mealtimes are disturbed or difficulty adjusting to unexpected shifts in schedules, need to be recognized and dealt with by the whole family. It is valuable to children to know that their parents, too, have limitations and are struggling to express them appropriately.

The second category is harder. If parents are not clear just what their needs are, but feel frustrated, they are likely to get angry with the children, the spouse, or others, whether they express their rage openly or not. Hostile daydreams in response to small frustrations, inquiries from friends about whether one is "feeling all right," or unsolicited offers of "Is there anything I can do to help you?" are warning signals. We need to become alert to our own and others' characteristic signs of frustration if we are to clarify with one another the reasons for these signs of distress, and make concrete plans to resolve or alleviate the problem.

In working families especially, two general rules are helpful. First, plan together to include in your lives as many interests, desires, and special strengths as possible in the framework of present family responsibilities. Second, explore together the areas of frustration (including your own). In one such discussion Don and Mary Chapin realized that they had each come up with plans for the family on a particular Friday afternoon and evening. Don was disappointed to learn that Mary was not interested in revising her own plans, especially since she was sure she would be too tired to do anything additional that day. After their discussion they had a complicated but rewarding Friday plan, based on Don's part-time work and allowing for the children's interests too:

> At three o'clock Friday afternoon Don picked up the two children at the preschool and day-care centers. After shopping for a birthday present and delivering one

child to a birthday party, he took the youngest home for a short nap before supper. Meanwhile, after work, Mary attended her class at the university. After class and supper in the cafeteria she went to the local swimming pool, where Don and the children would meet her. Today Don would not stay to swim, but would have a snack, visit the library, and just spend a little time alone until seven-thirty. Then he and the children would walk to the gymnastic performance he wanted to see at a nearby theater. After a busy day at work and school, followed by a swim with the children, Mary was ready to go home and relax until the others arrived later for a "bednight" snack and the family's warm, brief bedtime ritual.

Had the adult Chapins not been clear about their interests and limits, they might have simply assumed that the entire family should do each activity all together. As it was, the evening went very well, with enough but not too much activity for everyone.

Time away from the Children

Finding time away from the children, especially time spent in active pursuit of adult interests, can often help parents slow down, refuel, and refresh themselves so that they can return more fully attentive to their children's needs. Don and Mary Chapin's Friday plan shows one way to find time for each adult to be both with the children and alone.

If your working hours are long, such time for yourself may conflict with the need to be with your children. Ideally some of your interesting and absorbing time away from the children occurs during your work hours, but this is not true for boring or exhausting, but necessary jobs. In addition, some parents recognize a need for regular periods of time away from both work and family responsibilities. Once or twice each week a parent may set aside a block of time to play tennis, swim, see a movie alone or with a friend, explore nature, attend a class, or otherwise maintain personal interests and relationships. Both parents need such free time and need to plan the schedules together.

Some adults occasionally need prolonged periods in which they are relieved of child-care responsibilities while knowing that their children are still being well looked after. Sometimes it is possible for one parent to visit relatives with the children over a school vacation, while the other has several days at home alone. Children, too, can benefit from time away from their parents and siblings.

Adults also need an occasional evening at home with just each other. Sleep-overs with the children's friends are helpful solutions, and can usually be arranged with regularity in exchange for some return child care. The return favor may be quite similar, as when one "overnight" is traded for another, or if friends have picked your children up after school on several occasions, a gift of circus tickets may express your thanks to them. It's a good idea to suggest specific trade-backs when asking or thanking people for such help. Sometimes relatives will share the care of children for a few weeks in the summer, enabling the parents to travel together or enjoy other vacation plans. In such instances return favors may be superfluous, for what an uncle or aunt or grandparent may want most is the fun of having the children visit.

Most of these types of time away from children do not require a baby sitter. But often when parents want to go out without the children, baby sitting must be arranged. It adds to the expense of the occasion, but parents need some social and intellectual life together, apart from the children. Just as time with children is very important for working parents, so is time spent with one's spouse. Family unity is maintained and nourished by the careful balance of time devoted to children, to one's partner, and to one's own needs.

Time with the Children

Some working parents find themselves living a more schedule-bound pattern than they would prefer. At times this is unavoidable, but a family review of plans for a particularly busy week may reveal that people are planning for more than they can do without becoming overtired. Parents should not overlook the fact that they as well as their children are more pleasant to be with when adequately rested. When caring for children aged three and under for periods of several hours, adults often need a brief interim nap if they are to stay alert and responsive to the different pace of the children.

Adults frequently become preoccupied and let the interests and

concerns of adult life break into their quiet times with their youngsters. One clue to this preoccupied state is to hear oneself saying
something like "Well, not now, but maybe later" to the child's requests. A good way to deal with such a state is to identify the subject
of the preoccupation as clearly as possible and set a specific time later
to handle it. Then one can "rejoin" the child.

Brenda Baily has been meeting her daughter at five o'clock each
week day for three years. For the first year her child, Melinda, was
cared for by a baby sitter. Now Melinda goes to a nursery school and
an after-school program until her mother's work day is over. Mary
Chapin, on the other hand, reports for work at seven o'clock two
mornings each week. On those days she meets her two children at the
day-care center and nursery school shortly after three o'clock. Both
mothers are sometimes tired by the time they meet their children and
sometimes, if the children have not had a nap, they are tired too. But
even on such days the parents look forward to the "reunion" as much
as the children do. Mary Chapin says:

> Often, either because one of us is tired, because of the
> weather, or perhaps because there is something we
> really want to do together at home, we head directly
> home after school. Once there we may work, play, rest,
> or invite a friend or two to play until suppertime.

Don Chapin is often less tired from his part-time job when he meets
the children at three o'clock on other days:

> The experience is usually quite different from our morning
> travel. The children and I often slide into a weekend or
> vacation mood after we've been together for a few min-
> utes. We go sledding and throwing snow, scuffle
> through fallen leaves, build in the sand, run through a
> sprinkler spray, or have an ice cream or pizza. Quiet
> conversations are possible on the way home. Sometimes
> we talk about what's on for that evening, what each of us
> is looking forward to, so things go more smoothly once
> we're home.

To better enjoy the early-evening reunion, the Chapins plan only a
few activities for this time of day. For Mary, this replaces the time she

missed with the children from the time they woke up until they were delivered to day care and nursery school. If adult chores, such as grocery shopping or laundry, are part of the plan during this period, the children participate. But the Chapins prefer to think of this time together, whether one hour or perhaps three, as a time free from obligations to others beyond the family. Some families make lists of things they would like to do, and select from the list during the morning or afternoon. This is not to say that separate tasks or pleasures shouldn't occur too. Being together doesn't mean being glued together.

When we are not rushed, preoccupied, or otherwise under external pressure, we become relatively free to live in the present, which is where our children are usually found to be living. Accordingly, adequate planning must take into account the total time available. If there is not enough time to do what you want in a pleasurable way, then try either to replan the supper arrangements or select a more promising activity. Share this process with the children in a way that lets them know you are considering a number of factors, including their interests and limits, but that you are in charge and will make the final decisions.

Whether you plan a trip to the zoo, the museum, a special playground or sledding hill, a movie or a visit to a cousin, the major element of all after-school time must be the quality of your moments together. For parents who work, time is perhaps the most precious of all commodities. Shared with your children, in an atmosphere of fairness, respect, and mutuality, these important hours can be a true source of family growth and enjoyment.

Friendships and Role Models

DONOVAN DOYLE

Take a Giant Step

Sooner or later most parents hear a question like Matthew's, "Mom? Dad? Can I sleep over at Barney's house?"

If Matthew has "slept over" at Barney's house before, well and good; the only consideration before consenting may be the state of Matthew's chores, homework, or health.

But if this is the first time, be prepared for a sudden change of heart on Matthew's part. He may eagerly pack his Star Wars tote bag with pajamas, toothbrush, and clean jeans, only to slow down at the door.

"I need my Teddy bear," he may say—or his stuffed dog or a favorite blanket or game. Or he may discover he has developed a sniffle or a stomach-ache. Matthew is undergoing that familiar conflict for youngsters, to be or not to be independent.

The solution depends largely on the "age and stage" of the child. Five-year-old Matthew has slept away from home at his grandparents'; he has spent several afternoons at Barney's house and has eaten supper there. He would seem to be prepared for a sleep-over.

But going to bed is always a little traumatic for Matthew. He needs to enact certain rituals nightly. Kissing his whole family good night, having a glass of water by his bed, listening to his "sleepy record," having a night light on. How different will it be at Barney's?

Yet he fervently wishes to sleep there, and his parents decide he should try it. But they are prepared for his early return. Luckily, Barney lives next door, for at eleven o'clock Matthew comes home.

351

His mother and father don't ply him with questions but calmly tuck him in his own bed. And they let him try sleeping over at Barney's again. This time Matthew stays till seven in the morning. By the time Matthew is six he and Barney are sleeping at each other's house quite frequently.

Matthew's parents recognized his ambivalent wishes as natural for his age and were willing to let him experiment. However, when Willa, his four-year-old sister, wanted to copy his daring deed they said no. Willa was still shy in new situations with other children. Though she now went happily to nursery school, she had clung to her mother at first, wanting her presence there much longer than Matthew had. And Willa hadn't yet had supper at a friend's without her parents. In short, she hadn't reached the stage for sleeping over yet.

Most parents aren't, always aware of what good psychologists they are, how they pick up clues to guide them in everyday situations with their children. But most parents do react sensitively to children's demands for independence by recognizing this need as a positive and important step toward maturity. As one mother said, "It seems I've been working hard since Janey was born to establish a strong bond between us; she could count on me day or night. Now, when I feel we are really close, she's starting to pull away; she wants to do things her own way and by herself; she wants to be with other kids. She isn't just my little baby any more. Sometimes I have a twinge, but of course I'm glad she feels secure enough to leave me."

Toward Independence

No, Janey isn't a baby any more. She is obeying the imperative demand to become her own person, to establish her independence, both in growing self-reliance and in becoming a social being. However, this drive is not a steady forward push; many times Janey, like other youngsters, will retreat to baby ways, enjoying the close cuddling of adults; wanting to be fed instead of feeding herself; asking to be dressed instead of grappling with buttons; temporarily changing her cry of "Janey do it herself" to "Mommy do it." Two steps forward, one step back—that's the usual pace toward independence. And the step backward often accompanies the difficulties a young child encounters in trying to establish satisfactory social relationships.

Parents can help by providing situations where the young child can play with other children on a regular basis, sometimes in a play park, often in an established child center, day-care group, or nursery school. When such opportunities are scarce, parents may band together to create their own center; for most parents recognize that good day-care centers or nursery schools offer opportunities for young children to develop necessary social relations beyond the family circle.

Look before You Leap

The formation of such friendships may not always go smoothly. Janey and her peers must adjust from a me-centered world to a me-and-thee universe—an adjustment that may not ever be fully accomplished but is instead a lifelong process. Probably we don't attain a satisfactory maturity until we recognize the rights of others and our responsibilities toward them as well as seeking our own satisfactions. Experts say that one characteristic found in most adult criminal personalities is their inability to move out of the "me" world. The same inability is often observed in the mentally ill; they are trapped in the small, sad universe of self.

The young child moving into a setting of peers will inevitably clash with other "me's"; toys will be grabbed away, blows may be exchanged. The first impulse of parents is to stop the hostilities; but too much intervention may interfere with the socializing process. One answer is to have enough desired objects to lessen the need to fight over one toy or doll; the adult can then direct the aggressor to a similar object. At other times, children may need to work out their own solutions—always the best learning method.

In one children's center three-year-old Joanne suddenly snatched Huey's toy truck. For a moment a silent struggle ensued. Then Joanne suddenly ran over to the easel to paint, and Huey continued to play with the truck. Did Joanne lose interest? Or was she intimidated by the fierce resistance of Huey? The person in charge noted the incident and resolved to watch Joanne's future actions carefully. After he saw Joanne try to obtain a doll and give up in the same way, he took some positive steps to help her.

"Would you like a doll too, Joanne?" he asked. Thumb in mouth,

Joanne nodded silently, pointing to the doll in the other child's possession.

"Robert is playing with that doll," the teacher said. "But here is a doll for Joanne."

Joanne took the doll. Later the teacher observed Joanne exchanging dolls with Robert.

Constantly aggressive actions need more help, more observation and understanding. Henry tore into the park play group frequently, shouting and hitting. His mother was horrified at first; then she realized Henry was really trying to enter the group. She stopped him, saying, "Children are not for hitting, Henry! Balls are for hitting, not children!" In a fairly short time Henry was able to adopt a more acceptable technique without having to feel that he had been "bad." His mother had helped him understand the social limits he needed to know; she had rejected his action but not Henry.

Every time four-year-old Steve went next door to play with Julie, also four, sooner or later she hit him. Steve would run home crying but return later to try again. Julie's mother noted that hitting Steve left Julie crossly excited. Steve's mother told Steve to hit Julie back; Julie's parents told her to stop. But the same sequence of events happened again and again. One day the children were lunching with their mothers when Steve's father was present. For no obvious reason Julie punched Steve, then grinned nervously.

"Don't hit her back," ordered Steve's father. "Boys don't hit girls."

"Why not?" asked Steve's mother. "She hit him, didn't she?"

Steve's father looked taken aback. Then he said slowly, "That's right. You can't let her keep hitting you, can you, Stevie?"

Stevie reached out and pushed Julie off her chair. She began to yell.

Helping her up, Julie's mother said "You don't like being pushed, do you, Julie? Neither does Steve."

The meal was finished amiably, with both children relaxed and happy. Each had tested the social limits and each seemed relieved to know they had been reached. And the parents had agreed on a principle of action. Had Steve unconsciously been carrying out his father's injunctions? Had Julie needed to know the adults of her world were united in their philosophy and actions? Whatever the reason, the results were satisfactory to both parents and children.

Very often parents need to discuss their views of social misbehavior with other concerned parents and, if possible, reconcile their ideas. If Julie's mother hadn't agreed with Steve's parents, she might have, as their guest, had to accept their actions but explained to Julie later that at home things are done differently—and that different ideas are okay.

"Me" and Unsuitable "Thee"

Children keep testing the "me" against the "thee"; wise parents set helpful limits but try to understand the child's needs too. The over-shy, the very aggressive, the undemanding child have different ways of expressing their social problems but are, in different ways, asking for help. Adult guidance is needed, even if it is not overtly asked for. Supporting the child, observing and working out plans for his or her needs with other adults, setting limits on seemingly uncontrollable behavior, and, as always, being a refuge from the world's rebuffs are the adult's responsibilities.

One situation that bothers parents, especially those with school-age children, is the problem of unsuitable friendships. Usually the parent's objection is not based on superficial values of race, socieconomic status, or religion, but on behavior he or she deplores.

Six-year-old Peter formed such an attachment to his classmate, Billy, and delighted in copying Billy's habits of spitting, nose thumbing, and cursing. Visiting Peter's house, Billy got in trouble for messing up the parents' desk, and was taken home when found, with Peter, trying to shave the cat with Mr. Parker's electric razor. Attempts to discuss the matter with Billy's parents failed; the Parkers had to resolve the problem themselves. After much discussion, they decided that Billy's brash actions and speech had a natural attraction for their quiet, well-behaved son. Since Peter obviously gained some kind of relief and/or power from Billy's behavior, they didn't feel justified in preventing the friendship, but neither were they willing to depart from their own value systems, and they made plans which they discussed with Peter. On his next visits, Billy, who was allowed no pets, was asked to feed the cat and dog and help groom them under adult supervision. Mr. Parker took time to work on a project that interested both boys, and Mrs. Parker let them help her make cookies. Both parents overlooked some of Billy's crudity but refused to accept all his manners. "In this house we do it this way" was the general line they adopted. After a long while with Billy as his sole friend, Peter began asking other children to visit. While he still seemed to admire Billy, Peter ceased to need him as much as previously and, to the Parkers' relief, slowly stopped imitating Billy's language and behavior. The Parkers' consistent behavior seemed to hold fast against a conflicting set of values.

There are several ways parents can deal with such friendships. First, try to observe the children together more than one time. Perhaps the objectionable actions are not repeated; if they are, the parents face other choices. Do they feel strongly enough to forbid the friendship, or will they be content to discuss their own values with their child, explain their objections, and see what happens?

Whatever the parents decide, the best results are obtained when the child is included in all aspects of the final decision.

Parents as Models

In the long run, the values that parents show in their everyday actions, philosophy, and treatment of their own children, are the most positive help they can give their youngsters. Children usually detect phoniness, and the adult who states a belief in humanistic values and then denigrates others never deceives the young.

There is no guarantee, of course, that our children will always adopt our beliefs or ideals; at times they delight in acting in opposition to them. But as the long process of growing into social competence continues, most children do act on the values they absorb at home, even though they may interpret them in original ways. For parents and other caring adults, their own actions are the most valid philosophies they can give their children.

Peter Pan Was Wrong

ALICE MILLER and SEYMOUR V. REIT

One of the abiding myths of our society has to ao with "the golden years of childhood." And in truth, a great many of us do recall those years as happy and joyful, free of the cares and responsibilities that plague adults living in a very complex, frequently baffling modern world.

Certainly those early growing years are a time of magic and wonder; children are learning energetically, discovering new pleasures every day. But childhood is also a time of struggle and anxiety, of fear and frustration. Many a grandparent of today's children could tell hair-raising stories about how cruelly millions of American children were exploited—in factories, canneries, farms, and coal mines—for a good many years after the beginning of this century. Today's children, by comparison, seem to be pampered. But all children, even those who enjoy a great many advantages that their parents and grandparents lacked, suffer at times in trying to cope with a world over which they have little control.

The "Growing" Years

The chapters in this book have covered a wide variety of subjects, largely from a "majority" point of view—that of parents and other adults. But all of us, regardless of roots and backgrounds, were once members of at least one minority group. During the first dozen or so years of our lives, all of us belonged to the minority of the very young —and when we were members of that group, our grievances were often similar to those of other minorities. We, too, may have been subject to ridicule, name calling, disrespect, indifference, scorn, even physical abuse. Few youngsters would want to emulate Peter Pan and cling stubbornly to the "bliss" of early childhood. Rather, we're all familiar with that poignant childhood declaration, heavy with hope and expectation: "When I grow up—"

George Bernard Shaw once said that youth is such a wonderful thing it's a pity to waste it on the young. He was fairly long in the tooth when he made the statement; surely he wouldn't have wanted to relive everything in his youth, any more than the rest of us would. Conversely, the very young may sometimes think that age is such a wonderful thing it's a pity to waste it on the likes of parents and teachers.

To be young means a great deal more than school and carefree play. To be young means to be functionally illiterate for about half of your preteen years. It means to be only a third or half as big physically as those who have power over you (and who may at times abuse that power). It means suffering this powerload without effective redress: kids can't call attention to their plight by marching up Capitol Hill, chanting slogans and waving eye-catching banners.

A study by Russel Hamilton and Stephanie Greene, "What Bothers Us about Grownups" surveyed some twelve hundred children between the ages of eight and twelve, giving them a chance to speak up anonymously. Although some of those questioned had no complaints and expressed strong positive feelings toward parents and caregivers, a great many others voiced a long litany of grievances. Perhaps their strongest feeling was a general sense that adults weren't "fair" and that the opinions and attitudes of children simply didn't count.*

Another survey, conducted among eight- and nine-year-olds in the Bank Street Children's School asked students to discuss the shortcomings, if any, of the adults with whom they lived. Three main factors emerged. The children were consistently upset and troubled when their parents "yelled" at them. "Yelling" encompassed a wide span of behavior, ranging from parental tantrums to mild bickering and nagging. But the youngsters felt hurt; the "yelling" demeaned them and signaled some degree of indifference to their needs and feelings.

---

* Russel Hamilton and Stephanie Green, "What Bothers Us about Grownups" (Brattleboro, Vt.: The Stephen Green Press, 1971).

The children in this survey also reacted with anxiety when parents quarreled with each other. Children need to understand and accept that disagreements, including outbursts of temper, are a part of close relationships, but continued arguments can disturb a child tremendously, in part because such hostile encounters threaten his or her own security.

The other paramount element in the survey was most of the kids' desire to have their parents "spend more time" with them. This reflects the children's desire for involvement—a strong need to interact and interrelate not only with their peers but with those powerful adults who serve as their nurturers and their role models.

In contrast to the "yelling" habit is what psychologists call "sympathetic listening." Parents need to simply listen to what their children are trying to say and read "between the words" as youngsters sort out their rush of thoughts and feelings. Listening to the words and understanding the body language of kids is a basic, vital force of communication.

The Rights of Children

During the recent International Year of the Child, a United Nations conference developed a Declaration of Rights that is applicable to children everywhere. The points developed by the U.N. are:

> The right to affection, love, and understanding.
> The right to adequate nutrition and medical care.
> The right to free education.
> The right to full opportunity for play and recreation.
> The right to a name and nationality.
> The right to special care, if handicapped.
> The right to be among the first to receive relief in times of disaster.
> The right to learn to be a useful member of society and to develop individual abilities.
> The right to be brought up in a spirit of peace and universal brotherhood.
> The right to enjoy these rights, regardless of race, color, sex, religion, national or social origin.

Of all these valuable rights, this book is concerned chiefly with the first, since affection, love, and understanding are classically rooted in our family units and patterns. And it is well within the capacities of parents and caregivers to supply this right directly.

The inevitable comparison between child and plant is an apt one. With the loving help of a nurturer—an "enabler"—the plant grows and flowers; without it, the plant withers. So, too, with our children, each of whom is a splendid living potentiality. Peter Pan notwithstanding, the growth process goes on inevitably, and whether the growth is healthy or distorted depends to a great extent on the adults involved. As the poet Wallace Stevens wrote, "In the service of love and imagination nothing can be too lavish, too sublime or too festive."

Contributors

NANCY BALABAN

Parent, author of many articles on early childhood education, instructor and adviser in the Graduate School of Education, Bank Street College.

BETTY D. BOEGEHOLD

Parent, grandparent, teacher, author specializing in books for young children, senior associate editor of Bank Street Publications.

BARBARA BRENNER

Parent, teacher, award-winning author of more than forty books for children, specializing in natural sciences, associate editor of Bank Street Publications.

CAROL DUNHAM

Parent, teacher, author of magazine articles for parents. A Bank Street alumna with graduate degrees in child development.

ELLEN GALINSKY

Parent, teacher, author of several books for adults on child care and parenting and author of books for children, associate editor of Bank Street Publications.

MONA GOLDEMBERG

Parent, teacher, guidance counselor, member of the Bank Street Program Development Institute.

DR. DOROTHY GROSS
Parent, grandparent, author of many articles on parenting and early childhood development, member of the Bank Street Graduate School of Education faculty.

WILLIAM H. HOOKS
Director of Bank Street Publications, television consultant for ABC and PBS, author of many books for children in the middle years.

ELEANOR KULLESEID
Parent, author of articles on children and library science, director of the Bank Street College Library.

DR. CLAUDIA LEWIS
Recipient of Distinguished Specialist in Children's Literature award from Bank Street College. Author of many books of poetry and fiction for children and books on writing for children.

SUSAN J. LEWIS
Teacher, author of articles for parents on child-related subjects. A Bank Street alumna with graduate degrees in early childhood development.

LOIS LORD
Author of many articles on children and the arts, author of a book on collage, instructor at the Museum of Modern Art, faculty member of the Bank Street Graduate School of Education.

ELLEN PRESS MENDELSOHN
Music editor for the American Book Company, teacher in the Bank Street Children's Demonstration School, author of many articles for children and parents in the field of music and music appreciation.

ALICE MILLER
Parent, author of books for children in the middle years and for adults, member of the Bank Street Writers' Laboratory.

MARK LUNDEEN
Parent, teacher, hospital administrator, program analyst on the Bank Street College faculty.

JOANNE OPPENHEIM
Parent, teacher, author of numerous concept and picture books for young children, associate editor of Bank Street Publications.

PAUL SCHWARZ
Parent, teacher, member of the Bank Street Children's Demonstration School faculty.

DR. EDNA SHAPIRO
Parent, teacher, researcher, psychologist, author of numerous books and articles on children's development in the preschool and elementary years, member of the Bank Street College Research Division.

SEYMOUR V. REIT
Author of more than thirty books for children and a number of nonfiction books for adults, associate editor of Bank Street Publications.

DR. FRANCIS ROBERTS
Parent, school administrator, author of many articles on child development, former president of Bank Street College.

DORIS B. WALLACE
Parent, researcher, author of numerous articles on parent/child development, member of the Bank Street College Research Division.

PEARL ZEITZ
Parent, grandparent, author of many articles on children and school settings, adviser to the Bank Street Children's Demonstration School.

CAROLINE ZINSSER
Parent, teacher, researcher, author of articles on children and school settings, director of the Bank Street Children's Demonstration School.

Bibliography

A Child Goes to School, Sara B. Stein. Doubleday, New York, 1978.

As the Twig Is Bent: Reading in Early Childhood Education, R. H. Anderson and H. G. Shane. Houghton Mifflin, Boston, 1971.

A Working Mother's Guide to Child Development, F. Philip Rice. Prentice-Hall, New Jersey, 1979.

Between Generations: The Six Stages of Parenthood, Ellen Galinsky. Times Books, New York, 1980.

Between Parent and Child, Dr. Haim G. Ginott. Avon, New York, 1965.

Child Development for Day Care Workers, Ruth Highberger and Carol Schramm. Houghton Mifflin, Boston, 1976.

Children's Secrets, Thomas J. Cottle. Anchor Press, New York, 1980.

Every Child's Everyday: Learning about Learning, Cindy Herbert and Susan Russell. Anchor Press, New York, 1980.

Guiding Your Child from Two to Five, Molly M. Jones. Harcourt Brace, New York, 1967.

Joy in Parenting, Jo Schlehofer. Paulist Press, New York, 1978.

Kids: Day In and Day Out: A Parents' Manual, Elizabeth L. Scharlatt, editor. Simon and Schuster, New York, 1979.

Language in Thought and Action, Samuel L. Hayakawa. Harcourt Brace, New York, 1972 (3rd ed.).

Partners in Play, Dorothy and Jerome Singer. Harper & Row, New York, 1977.

Recipes for a Small Planet, Ellen Ewald. Ballantine, New York, 1973.

The Father's Almanac, S. Adams Sullivan. Doubleday, New York, 1980.

The Incredible Television Machine, Lee Polk and Eda Le Shan. Macmillan, New York, 1977.

The Incredible Year-Round Playbook, Elin McCoy. Random House, New York, 1979.

The Learning Child, Dorothy Cohen. Vintage edition, Random House, New York, 1973.

The Parents' Encyclopedia of Infancy, Childhood and Adolescence, Milton I. Levine and Jean H. Seligmann. Crowell, New York, 1973.

The Show and Tell Machine, Rose K. Goldsen. Dell, New York, 1978.

The Uses of Enchantment: The Meaning and Importance of Fairy Tales, Bruno Bettelheim. Knopf, New York, 1977.

Toddlers and Parents, T. Barry Brazelton. Delacort, New York, 1974.

Total Learning for the Whole Child, Joanne Hendrick. C. V. Mosby Co., St. Louis, 1980.

Toys and Playthings: A Practical Guide for Parents and Teachers, John and Elizabeth Newson. Pantheon Books, New York, 1979.

Understanding Your Child from Birth to Three, Joseph Church. Pocket Books, New York, 1977.

Your Child's Sensory World, Lise Liepmann. Penguin Books, Maryland, 1974.

Index

Nibble, Nibble (Brown), 60
Nightmares, from TV shows, 94
Nobody Asked Me If I Wanted a Baby Sister (Alexander), 64
Noisy Book, The (Brown), 59

Objectivity, in child's thinking, 10
Our Animal Friends at Maple Hill Farm (Provensen), 66
Outings. *See also* Trips, day
  with other people's children, 291–96
Owl at Home (Lobel), 62

Packaging, of toys, 31
Packing, for long-distance trip, 283
Paddington Bear (Bond), 66
Painting, as creative activity, 185
Panda (Bonners), 67
Parachute, made from newspaper, 203
Parakeets, as pets, 153
Parent(s). *See also* Adults; Parent(s), single; Parent(s), working
  children visiting workplace of, 118, 315
  death of, 239
  as interpreter, 6–7
  as partisan, 7–8
  as play partner, 5–6
  as role models, 8–9, 122
  as support, 10–11
Parent(s), single, 312–26
  emotional adjustments of, 313–19
  non-custodial, 327–31
  priorities of, 321–22
  relationships with children, 322–24
  special events with, 319–21
Parent(s), working, 337–38, 341–50
  needs of, 345–47
  private time for, 347–48
  resentment about, 343–44
  sick children and, 341–42
Parent's Guide to Children's Reading, A (Larrick), 47
Parents Without Partners, 326
Partisan, parent as, 7–8
Party, birthday, 251–68
  big, 251–57
  decorations for, 268
  entertainment for, 253

Party, birthday, *cont'd.*
  games for, 254–55, 256–57, 263, 266–67
  for middle-years children, 261–66
  small, 258–68
  for small children, 258–61
Payment, for household chores, 124
Peanut hunt, as party game, 263
Peek-a-boo, playing with infants, 234
Pencil games, for waiting times, 220–29
Personal space, need for, 112–15
Pets, 149–58
  choosing of, 151–57
  exotic, 157
  need for, 149–50
Physical laws, children's grasp of, 10
Picnic
  indoor, 109
  while traveling, 284
Picture gallery, for each child, 113
Pinkerton, Behave! (Kellogg), 67
Pin the Tail on the Donkey party game, 256
Pippa Mouse series (Boegehold), 64
Placemat, made from newspaper, 204
Planetarium, taking children to, 211
Plants, studying on nature walks, 209–10
Play. *See also* Dramatic play; Games
  adult-child, 12–21, 139–40
  board games, 18–20
  outdoor sports, 138–48
  as work, 119–20
Play (Garvey), 12
Play areas, near home, 138–41
Play dough, homemade, 192, 201
Play partners, parents as, 5–6, 12–21
Playthings. *See also* Toys
  for physical skills, 39–41
Play with Me (Ets), 61
Poetry, books of, 60–61
Praise, helpful, 25–26
Preschoolers
  day trips with, 271
  developmental needs of, 6–9
  divorce and, 315
  make-believe by, 36–37
  toys for, 40

Privacy, in living arrangments, 112–15
Puberty, passage rituals for, 240
Public Action Coalition on Toys, 33
Puddles and Ponds: Living Things in Watery Places (Busch), 212
Punchinello party game, 267
Puppets, for make-believe, 168
Push Pull Empty Full (Hoban), 60
Puzzles, benefits from, 21

Quiet Noisy Book (Brown), 59

Rats, white, as pets, 155
Reading, by child, 71–75. *See also* Books
Reading aloud, 55–67. *See also* Storytelling
books for, 58–67
Red Light game, 234, 266–67
Reflecting back, for effective communication, 23
Relationships, special
fathers, 332–40
friends, 351–56
grandparents, 299–311
non-custodial parent, 327–31
single parent, 312–26
working parents, 341–50
Repetition, children's love of, 57
Resentment, about working parents, 343–44
Respect
for living things, 214–15
treating children with, 25
Restaurants, taking children to, 132
Rest rooms, public, 285
Ring Around the Rosy game, 234
Rituals, 233–41
birth, 237–38
changing seasons, 241
daily, 233–36, 328–29
death, 238–39
holidays, 236–37
passage, 240–41
Robots, child-made, 200
Role models. *See also* Sex roles
parents as, 8–9, 355–56
on TV, 81–82

Room, of child
cleaning up of, 120–21
personal space in, 113–14
Routine, day-to-day
making more interesting, 107–11
of single-parent household, 313
Rubbings, child-made, 199
Rules, of games, importance of, 38–39, 234
Runaway Bunny, The (Brown), 62

Safety, of toys, 33–35
Sam (Scott), 62
Sam, Bangs, and Moonshine (Ness), 64
Santa, store, fear of, 16
Scarry, Richard, books by, 48, 66
Scavenger hunt, as party game, 253
School work, child's responsibility for, 123
Seashore, exploring with children, 212–13
Seashore Noisy Book (Brown), 59
Seasons, rituals for, 241
Self-confidence, toys and, 31
Separateness, as emotional need, 3–4
17 Gerbils of Class 4A, The (Hooks), 155
Sex roles, 8, 18, 333–34
housework and, 122
in make-believe play, 164
toys and, 31
on TV, 81
Shapes of Things (Hoban), 60
Shopping trips, taking children on, 270, 274–75
Simon Says party game, 256–57
Singing, 171–75
while doing chores, 108
Skywatching, as nature study, 211–12
Sleep-overs, readiness for, 351–52
Snacks, for children, 103–4
on trips, 272
Snakes, as pets, 157
Social values, presented in books, 48
Some Swell Pup (Margolis), 156
Special occasions, 231–96
birthday party, big, 251–57
birthday party, small, 258–68
holidays, 242–50
rituals for, 233–41